BECOMING MORE CIVILIZED

A Psychological Exploration

BECOMING MORE CIVILIZED

A Psychological Exploration

LEONARD W. DOOB

New Haven and London, Yale University Press

©1960 by Yale University Press, Inc.

Set in Caledonia type.

Printed in the United States of America by
Vail-Ballou Press, Inc., Binghamton, N.Y.
and reprinted by The Murray Printing Company,
Forge Village, Massachusetts.

First published November 1960
Second printing November 1961
Library of Congress catalog card number: 60-14577

To sub-Saharan places from Durban to Zaria
And to times like 1954–55 and Tuesday
Which transformed certain Africans and Europeans into the friends
Whom this book would fondly salute

CONTENTS

PREFACE

A BOOK which has the word "civilized" in its title and which purports to explain what happens to people as they become more civilized requires an unperfunctory preface. I would immediately explain, therefore, that of course I am not using the word "civilization" either in a snobbish or a derogatory sense. We need some kind of concept to call attention to the differences between people who unwittingly live next to one another in the bush and those who wittingly live on top of one another in modern apartment houses. If "civilization" suggests the possibility of a variation not only in the dwelling places but also in the values of the two groups, then the term is satisfactorily discharging its function. Whether one set of values is better or worse than the other is not proclaimed. In addition the title of the book proposes a continuum rather than a sharp distinction: not civilized and uncivilized but more and less civilized people are compared.

Without a blush—or at least without a conspicuous one—it is admitted that the scope of the book is much too broad and cosmic. There can in truth be no definitive account of what happens to people when they become more civilized because, as is repeatedly shown throughout the book, adequate data are lacking. The theme, however, remains hopelessly intriguing: the focus is not upon whether less civilized men learn to smoke cigarettes or to put on pants but upon what changes occur in their way of thinking, in their systems of self-guiding rewards, in their beliefs, and in their personalities. Perhaps the subtitle of the volume should be in larger print than its title: this is a psychological exploration, not a handbook or an apocalypse.

I hesitated for a long while to write the manuscript and then to suffer the trauma of allowing an editor and a publisher, however kindly, to turn it into a book and eventually to offer it to readers who can always make a writer feel uncomfortable about as effectively as his own conscience. Without being overly masochistic or modest, I am quite aware of my own limitations which thus become the book's. As a person it is my right to become attached to Africa, to carry on research in a limited number of African societies, and then concisely to report my findings in scholarly journals. I have made the reports. But then, ununiquely, I wondered about the generality of the findings: To what extent are all less civilized people like the Africans I have interviewed? And so I have read the analyses of other investigators; my search for comparable materials has been persistent, necessarily not exhaustive, and unquestionably biased in favor of African accounts. Maybe, I told myself at first, maybe it is possible to formulate a first approximation of what happens psychologically anywhere during acculturation.

Three experiences have given me courage, or at least have made me feel that I might not be committing too vast a blunder by publishing the book. The editor and the managing editor of a reputable periodical—the *Journal of Nervous and Mental Diseases*—accepted an article for whose blatant title, "On the Nature of Uncivilized and Civilized People," I am responsible. It appeared, I was not excommunicated from academic life, and wisps of praise were visible. I next risked "unofficially" and "informally" submitting a semipolished draft to the Director of this Press. In the cautious manner of an entrepreneur functioning without a signed contract but in the hospitable role of a friend he conceded that he had not been completely unstimulated, that now he knew why Africa attracts me intellectually, and that it would be helpful and useful to have a clean copy typed. During the typing I spent a summer doing research in Ghana, Togo, and Nigeria. There, as a result of the relative anonymity foreign countries offer and of the feelings of excitement and release they engender, I discussed reasonably freely the ideas in this book with social scientists, government officials, and other friendly Africans and Europeans. Most of them were not shocked, and I think I observed through my inverted bias that sometimes a few appeared more than politely intrigued. And so I decided to plunge.

The writing of this Preface, it should now be evident, provokes the old uncertainties and conflicts. No matter—let's get on with it. Here is an attempt to formulate a set of hypotheses which claim little originality; to use the hypotheses as principles to sharpen our perception and to organize samples of existing research; to explore problems whose importance, at a time when "underdeveloped" areas are at the tip of political, economic, and philanthropic tongues, can scarcely be questioned; and hence, at the very minimum, to provide a target—or many targets—which better marksmen and better ammunition in the future will hit more effectively. Brave, brave words, I must say unapprovingly. Stress is placed upon quantitative data, no matter how trivial or even statistically unconvincing, not because they lead rapidly to Wisdom but because they suggest the need for precision if better truths are to be discovered. The presentation, it will be seen, is tentative. In fact, nothing seems to please me more than to expose the weakness of the evidence which I present to support an idea of my own, especially if I myself have collected it. Almost every sentence is qualified. Cautiousness of this kind, although it produces neither breath-taking reading nor bold ideas, is offered without the trace of an apology, for surely it stems from the state of the art and the method of science.

At the risk of doing them a disservice by associating them with this reckless, timorous volume, but as an enthusiastic expression of deep gratitude which cannot be repressed even in their behalf, I would briefly express thanks to some people by citing their institutions and to a few others by naming them unabashedly:

The Carnegie Corporation of New York: for arousing my interest in Africa by means of a red-carpet trip in 1952; for enabling me to carry on research in East and South Africa in 1954–55; and for sagacious advice ever since, especially from Alan Pifer.

Yale University and its Department of Psychology: for providing the spiritual and material bases for trouble-free thought.

The United States Public Health Service, National Institutes of Health: for permitting me (Grant M-1940) to conduct research and assemble my thoughts during the summer of 1957 in Jamaica, B.W.I., a lovely land resembling Africa in many ways but for my purpose so much simpler.

Paul J. Bohannan and our committee functioning from the National Academy of Sciences, National Research Council, under Contract No. DA-19-129-Am-1309, with the Quartermaster Research and Engineering Command, U.S. Army: for persuading me permissively to go to West Africa during the summer of 1959. None of the material gathered during that expedition has penetrated the present volume, but the general stimulation therefrom has enabled me not only to scrub the manuscript which, beautifully typed by Patricia L. Cunningham, awaited me at home but also to renovate some of its more turgid thoughts.

Lloyd A. Fallers, Sydney A. Kark, Hilda and Leo Kuper, Hansi Pollak, and Gordon Wilson: for intellectual assistance and generous hospitality in Africa.

Sidney W. Mintz and also Archdeacon L. A. Lennon, Pat Levy, Olive Sharp, and Michael G. Smith: for advice and friendship in Jamaica.

Melville J. Herskovits, Carl I. Hovland, George P. Murdock, Seymour B. Sarason, and particularly Audrey I. Richards: for serving, symbolically and completely without their knowledge, as critical goads during many intellectually lonely moods.

Jane V. Olson: for her editorial labors performed with brilliant conscientiousness and forceful tact.

LEONARD W. DOOB

New Haven, Conn.
January 1960

Chapter 1.

PSYCHOLOGICAL EXPLORATION

THE KNOWLEDGE sought by men serves some function. In areas like medicine, agriculture, and transportation the function is self-evident. Elsewhere the gain is more difficult to detect, especially in comparison with other advances: new information about a writer in antiquity seems less essential than the discovery of a way to combat a virus, to improve the yield per acre of an established crop, or to lower the accident rate of airplanes. In perspective, it must be immediately added, judgments concerning the relative value of knowledge cannot be ultimate. The most abstract, remote fact at the very least brings internal fulfillment to its discoverer, it may produce a similar feeling among some of his peers, and conceivable it may eventually—alone or together with other facts—turn out to be imaginatively or mundanely useful.

The writer, while of course having faith in the enlightening or beneficial function of all knowledge, feels impelled to state at the outset the convictions motivating him to strive to understand some of the problems which recur when societies become civilized. Tritely but very truly it is apparent that people in an interdependent world must understand one another: you may not love your neighbor dearly when you are acquainted with the reasons for his peculiarities, but you may become more tolerant. In this century and especially in the next decade, moreover, the less civilized are growing more and more civilized, partially because civilization is forced upon them, partially because civilization is attractive to them, at least in some respects. Can their entrance into the civilized world be eased?

Knowledge about others, in addition, increases self-knowledge and can be acquired in different ways. Great men are observed,

1

and the solutions which they achieved or failed to achieve can timidly guide their descendants. Likewise characters in art, literature, drama, and poetry can be inspiring. But greatness in fact or fancy is not essential since insights can be gained from neurotics, who, like normal people, cannot cope adequately with all the problems which beset them, or even from detached psychotics. The most gentle, the most stubborn, parent learns something about himself from his own child. It would seem, too, that more ought to be discoverable about civilization from watching peoples becoming more civilized: if they would be like us, then perhaps we can discover what they imagine us to be, what in reality we are, and even what we ourselves might become.

Finally there are academic, scientific objectives. Can modern social science adequately embrace the problems of people who become more civilized? In assaying the embrace—in plainer words, in seeking to provide satisfactory methods for collecting data and theories for systematizing those data—can social science thereby improve itself?

Appropriately noble functions, then, are to be served by this book, its opening chapter not unexpectedly avers. After the display of such sentiment, it is well to turn to the business at hand. "Becoming more civilized"—what is meant by civilization? Fine and fancy distinctions and definitions suggest themselves, but a single denotative statement will suffice: Civilization refers to the culture, or the way of life, possessed by modern literate and industrial nations in Europe and America. The statement would not suggest that ancient Greece or modern India is not "civilized" according to many of the honorable connotations that word has acquired. For purely pragmatic reasons attention is focused upon countries like England, Russia, France, Argentina, Canada, and the United States because they are important per se and because they have affected, are affecting, and will affect other societies. One writer uses the term "modernization" to refer to the transition through which underdeveloped areas are now going, but he notes that the culture being sought is that of the West: "Western society still provides the most developed model of societal attributes (power, wealth, skill, rationality) which Middle East spokesmen continue to advocate as their own goal" (Lerner, 1958, p. 47).

Since the attitudes and practices of rural or peasant communities in civilized societies may be unique (cf. Redfield, 1956), urban areas are considered the prototype of "civilization." Other societies are not called "uncivilized," because the word sounds uncomplimentary or garish; rather they will be referred to as "less civilized." Anthropologists have been seeking euphemisms to replace adjectives such as "uncivilized," "primitive," and "savage"; but the ones they prefer—preliterate, nonliterate, underdeveloped, etc.—possess no special advantage. In any case, the difference between societies is a matter of degree, and throughout this book the process of becoming more civilized is neither praised nor condemned. By and large attention is confined to the modern world because, unlike their remote ancestors, less civilized peoples must "contend against almost insurmountable difficulties inherent in the vast contrast between their own condition of life and our civilization" (Boas, 1938, p. 13).

Two principal questions are being raised concerning people in less civilized societies: 1. Why do they become more civilized in certain respects? 2. What happens to them as they become more civilized?

Such questions, in terms commonly employed, pertain to the *acculturation* of noncivilized or less civilized people having *contact* with civilized societies; to quote from the most widely quoted and more general definition of acculturation, they concern themselves with at least some of "those phenomena which result when groups of individuals having different cultures come into continuous first-hand contact, with subsequent changes in the original cultural patterns of either or both groups" (Redfield, Linton, and Herskovits, 1936, p. 149).

It is perfectly true that the change from less to more civilization can be described without asking why people change and what happens to them. A society, let it be said, had been cultivating the soil without the use of the plow; it had had relatively few animals; its social structure had included polygyny; it had feared two of its neighboring tribes but not a third. Then contact was established with the West, and within a few decades there were changes: some men used tractors to help them raise the new crops which they now grew; herds of animals were introduced because there was a great external demand for milk, meat, and hides; almost no polygyny survived among the people who had been converted to Christianity; organized sport as practiced by civilized people was utterly rejected; peace if not friendliness existed with neighboring groups. In such a seemingly objective manner external changes might be catalogued without necessarily indicating why the changes occurred and whether the inhabitants became different people as they changed their customs and their way of life.

Fascinating and exasperating questions, however, are avoided by the cool, objective account of changes in a single society. Why did these hypothetical people allow themselves to be influenced by civilization? Why, of all the traits associated with modern civilization, did they accept the particular ones they did (the plow) and reject others (sports)? Closer examination of the society, moreover, is likely to reveal that not everyone adopted the changes either immediately or, in rare instances, ultimately; why, under the given conditions, were some of the inhabitants more eager to accept some of the traits of civilization than others?

The asking of such questions raises a number of dreadful, dampening problems. It is not easy or sometimes even possible, in the first place, to chart the changes in people as they become civilized over a period of time. One ought to be able to begin with stage A (the original, less civilized state), note a transitional stage B, and then end at stage C (the changed, the more civilized). The society at first had a crude hoe, its people learned from Westerners to use the ox-drawn plow, and now some of them drive tractors. Most unfortunately, similarly concrete information concerning people and their social relations is seldom at hand. Available records of stage A, for example, are not likely to be adequate; and even the oldest members of the society may not be able accurately to recall their youth. In fact, one anthropologist has contended that the pursuit of such a "zero point" is not only perilous because the inferences inevitably are so shaky, but also useless if the goal is insight into the present functioning of society (Malinowski, 1945, pp. 27–34).

Doubts must be raised, secondly, concerning the measuring instruments that are employed to detect the changes at all three stages. As will be repeatedly pointed out in these pages, the in-

struments—and how misleadingly dignified the word sounds—
are neither standardized nor extremely sensitive within our own
society. How, then, can they possibly be used in quite different
societies for which they have not been originally designed?

If adequate information were miraculously available for a particular society, in the third place, it would be necessary to select
the institutions or traits for which changes are to be plotted. Here
there need be no wavering, at least for the moment: changes
within people are of primary interest in this particular study of
acculturation. It has been persuasively argued—not by a psychol-
ogist but by a pair of anthropologists—that only such changes are
really significant. For changes in the material culture may be
very superficial; an object from another society (such as an iron
stove among the Ojibwa Indians) simply replaces a less efficient
piece of apparatus in the traditional society without affecting appreciably the people or their way of life. Likewise changes in the
nonmaterial culture may be only formally adopted; some of the
same Indians adhere to the religion of their ancestors but pay lip
service to Christianity (for example, by attending church occasionally in order to appear respectable or at least not discourteous)
(Gillin and Raimy, 1940). Two caveats, however, must be entered.
It seems reasonably certain, as will be indicated in subsequent
discussions, that new appliances like stoves and the formal acceptance of a doctrine like Christianity have repercussions beneath the surface of the people making the change. And the
selection of the psychological changes to be watched is by no
means a simple task: what aspects of personality should be analyzed?

Fourthly and finally, the results emerging from a particular
study are difficult to interpret grandly because of ignorance concerning the general attributes of less and more civilized peoples.
It is evident that noncivilized peoples are diverse. They live under
every conceivable climatic condition, from the equator virtually
to the Arctic and the Antarctic. They belong to tribes whose numbers range from several hundreds to many millions. They follow
customs corresponding to values at opposite ends of the spectrum
of judgments concerning good and beautiful or bad and ugly.
Some are now extinct as separate peoples, others linger on, and

still others flourish. Civilization also is no less elusive, since differences, for example, between national groups are staggeringly large: what have Swedes and Spaniards, Turks and Canadians, Poles and Brazilians in common? Unless the noncivilized beginning point and the civilized goal are fairly explicit, it becomes virtually impossible to locate a specific society whose people are changing. This is a discouraging state of affairs. In fact, the case for not writing the book has often appeared quite convincing as a result of these theoretical and methodological complexities.

The diversity of less and more civilized people seems baffling at first, second, or even tenth glance but eventually, like all diversity, can be forcibly led toward uniformity at some level of abstraction. Every event, every object, every person is clearly unique—common sense and science agree that the universe and its components are in a constant state of flux. Two pebbles differ from each other: the eye may not detect the differences but an instrument like a microscope eventually can. Is it important, however, to stress their differences? Sometimes it is, but sometimes it is not. Their slight difference in shape or weight is critical on a delicate balance but unimportant if they are to be mixed with cement as gravel. One of the two pebbles, moreover, is obviously different from Alexander the Great, it can be said if one wishes to indicate the cosmic importance or the biological significance of the pebble and the personage. But as objects in space, as objects heavier than air, the pebble and Alexander share a common characteristic and from that standpoint can be called identical. From that standpoint, let it be repeated. From others the differences are legion and can be admitted: the pebble never had a lung, Alexander while alive could never remain so motionless, etc. Diversity need not preclude uniformity, but on some level of abstraction there is only identity.

Admit, then, that each noncivilized society is unique, that each society becomes civilized for a unique reason and in a unique way, and that each civilized society is unique. But simultaneously the search for uniformities can go on. You may, if you wish, stress that differences between Eskimos and Bushmen are as great as those between Danes and Italians; but you may also seek similarities between the first pair, similarities between the second pair, and differences between those two sets of similarities (Doob, 1958b).

Logically no revolutionary position is being maintained. In fact most anthropologists, concerned as they must be during an actual investigation with the particulars and hence the uniqueness of each society, force themselves—usually in the less formal atmosphere of a classroom or a textbook, but sometimes in a formal work of scholarship—to produce some kind of abstract generalization. A not necessarily typical illustration will suffice. In the next to last paragraph of a book which presents data concerning acculturation in seven American Indian societies, one anthropologist writes: "In conclusion, it may be said that the only constant phenomenon in . . . acculturation . . . is the establishment, in the two cultures involved, of mutual modifications and adaptations which will enable the two groups to live together." In the very next sentence he withdraws the conclusion: "Even this is not absolutely constant, for one of the groups may not succeed in making such adaptations and become extinct in consequence." But the succeeding sentence rescues the conclusion by indicating the condition which must be fulfilled if it is to be tested: "However, if both groups survive, the adaptations will be made" (Linton, 1940, p. 519). Only a single, conditional generalization emerges, it can be said, because the writer has seen fit in this context to observe the concrete particulars of each social contact. Elsewhere in the same chapters, when he has pulled himself onto a more abstract plane and has thus reduced the particular historical contacts to instances of a more general process, he has in fact unhesitatingly found resemblances everywhere; for example, only 37 pages before the passage quoted above, he has noted that the "basic stimulus" for all social changes is "discomfort or discontent of a society's members."

The level of abstraction being sought in a book with the subtitle of "a psychological exploration" is of course a psychological one. It is felt that on this level relations between diverse phenomena can be demonstrated and thus a contribution to the unity of knowledge concerning behavior may emerge. The link between acculturation or the contact of less and more civilized peoples on the one hand and migration within civilized areas on the other hand has been clearly recognized in anthropological or sociological terms (e.g., Beals, 1951). On the surface the situation seems vastly different. Less civilized people come in contact with aspects of civilization while their culture is still intact and while they continue to live in their own territory. In contrast, immigrants who move from one civilized country to another, farmers who drift into cities, and ambitious families who rise in the social hierarchy are engulfed by outsiders. Beneath the surface identical psychological questions lurk: in each situation, some people are attracted to change and others are not; and each person who changes must unlearn old habits and acquire new ones. The same point is theoretically true whenever there is contact between two cultures, even though in practice a competent historical account of how people have absorbed some traits and customs from their neighbors (e.g., Schultes, 1954) does not or cannot provide data which enable the specific carriers or recipients of change to come into focus.

Still greater generality is achieved when social change is viewed in terms of learning. Whether the small child is becoming an adult; whether the adult would improve his swimming stroke; whether the neurotic would become less miserable, with or without the help of a professional teacher, the psychiatrist; whether the radio or television audience, however unwittingly, is influenced by the commercial message that interrupts the entertainment; or whether an Indian or an African is becoming more civilized—in all these instances something new is learned on the basis of previous learning. Identical or similar principles, consequently, ought to be discernible.

Limitations

By asking why men become more civilized and what happens to them when they do, the analysis of acculturation or social contact is being deliberately curtailed. It is well to recognize most explicitly the self-imposed limitations, for it is never possible to give a complete account of a phenomenon. All relevant data cannot be assembled, and there will be new data in the future. Everything, especially in the affairs of men, can be related to everything else. Any event springs out of the past and hence rests upon innumerable causes ranging from the geological to the ideological. For purposes of explanation arbitrary boundaries must be established (Korzybski, 1945).

One common way to limit an investigation, which will be generally adopted in this psychological exploration, is to overlook historical roots. Only a moment's reflection is necessary to remind oneself that every event in the present has some relation to a series of events in the immediate past and eventually to a much larger series still farther back. Ultimately the backward glance must end with the beginning of life on the earth, with the beginning of the earth, or with the beginning of the universe. How far back should or must one go? To explain the outcome of a municipal election seems to require no reference to the ice age, but the immediate causes of that outcome in turn demand explanation in terms of other, earlier causes, and those too must be explained, until, in brief, the story could really be pushed back into geologic time. Obviously what must be done is to call a halt at a point that seems arbitrarily satisfying.

Abandoning in large part the historical approach becomes a trifle less painful when it is realized that such an approach in its own right also suffers from the limitation of incompleteness. Every single detail concerning an event will never be known and in fact need not be known since some details are bound to be trivial and unimportant. Many nonhistorical problems, moreover, are left unsolved even after the historian has functioned professionally and effectively. In the present day, for example, it can be observed that two Hopi communities have absorbed different amounts of white civilization. Why? The basic historical fact has been uncovered: in the early seventeenth century a Franciscan mission was established in one village and not in the other. Ever since that one event there has been "a significant difference" between the white pressures upon the two groups (Thompson, 1950, p. 30). To halt the explanation at this point, however, is just as arbitrary as it is to ignore completely the past event. For surely one could ask why the mission made the decision to settle in one place rather than another; and just as surely, if the data were available, the decision would have to be attributed not to chance but to a host of factors which might include certain qualities of the communities and the personal preferences of the missionaries. But why stop here? Ought not an explanation be given too for the preferences of the missionaries? No matter how far back the inquiry is pushed, however, no insight has been obtained into the nature of the differences between the Indians of the two villages at present, and the establishment of such differences happens to be the subject being investigated in this book.

In different words, historical factors can be neglected, no matter how interesting and fascinating they are in their own right, if and when a significant phase of the problem can be understood through a nonhistorical analysis. It is possible, for example, to understand an instance of behavior without delving into the society's past. If an African whose wife has deserted him uses black magic in order to get back the cattle he presented to her father before their marriage, his behavior can be viewed as an effort to ease his frustration in a manner prevalent within that society. Once again, it is freely admitted, such an account is incomplete. For it would be important to know that formerly a native court would have awarded him the cattle under these circumstances, but now, since European law does not recognize such a function, people resort to sorcery as a substitute for legal action (Mair, 1934). The historical account provides an explanation of the context in which the man behaves, but it throws no light on details of the behavior such as the degree to which he feels frustrated by his wife's desertion and by his failure to recoup the dowry.

Now if the poor frustrated husband is acquainted with the history of his society and if he deliberately uses sorcery rather than the native courts whose absence he deplores, the historical background reenters the psychological picture. Note, however, that his longing for the good old days of the native courts could be ascertained by investigating him at the moment and not necessarily by also probing into the history of his society. In more general terms, historical circumstances can be ignored if there are adequate measures of the present pattern. The ahistorical approach is usually superb in the case of machines. For here the problem to be investigated—why the engine fails to run, for example—can be approached with adequate instruments and techniques which produce a diagnosis; how a flaw has come into existence is not relevant, if the goal is only its elimination (Hilgard, 1948, pp. 15–16). For human beings and events involving human beings, however, the instruments are less perfect. If you are interested in knowing whether a person's happiness will continue, you have no psychic ray to measure him, and so in all probability you must make more than a perfunctory effort to account for his present state historically. The historical information provides a preliminary estimate of how a factor functions at the moment, and then it can be investigated in its own right.

Three kinds of historical information, it can now be stated, ordinarily will not be sought in the present exploration of becoming more civilized:

1. The history of the two societies (one less, the other more, civilized) prior to contact with each other, especially the historical reasons for their cultures and institutions.

2. The historical reasons which account for the initial contact and for the subsequent relations between the two societies.

3. The complete history of the contact.

Immediately after stating these three limitations, the writer must explicity express the regrets which he has been not very subtly suppressing while trying to justify a nonhistorical approach. The regrets are of three kinds. In the first place, the description of each contact is enriched when an historical account is given, however frugal that account may be. Consider, for example, one of the three societies that will be frequently mentioned in this book, the Zulu in South Africa. As the tribe migrated southward in the eighteenth century, it possessed a culture of a distinctive kind: a strongly organized warrior group, polygyny, a passionate interest in cattle, etc. The Boers who began trekking north at the same time carried with them a distinctive blend of cultural elements derived from the Netherlands, from France, from Germany, and from their own experiences in the Cape Province. Clearly the background for the first bloody contact and for the subsequent relations between these Africans and Europeans must be traced to their original cultures. Then a complete explanation must include a description not only of the factors which caused the two societies to migrate and thus establish contact with each other but also of the original leaders on both sides who played so important a role in the early battles. It would be desirable, too, to have a complete history of the relations between the two societies, to trace in detail the practices and the policies which have led eventually and perhaps inevitably to the present-day policy of apartheid. In brief: the attitudes of modern Afrikaners and Zulu toward each other and toward themselves spring out of a complicated past, and it is good to know how that past has produced the present.

Then, besides excluding historical accounts of specific cultural contacts, an ahistorical approach has the further disadvantage of eliminating certain historical or quasi-historical problems which have a humanistic or even a scientific fascination in their own right. It is important to know, for example, the kinds of factors which encourage or discourage contact between groups. In the past, certainly the physical location of a society was often crucial; the tribes on the coasts of Africa have had much longer contact with the West than those in the interior. Now new modes of transportation necessarily have changed the importance of geographical forces. By confining the psychological analysis to the present, furthermore, another exciting problem is regretfully circumvented: How have societies evolved from simpler to more complicated forms?

In the third place, the absence of historical data often prevents the preliminary discovery of a cause-and-effect sequence between two sets of factors. A casual connection between the advocacy of a belief by missionaries and the subsequent appearance of the belief among the people of a society can be suggested only if it is known that the belief did not exist in the society prior to contact with the missionaries and that it made its appearance after contact. Such reasoning, though suggestive, is not conclusive because historical events lack adequate controls; hence the belief could have developed in the absence of the missionaries, though the historical evidence may make this seem unlikely. Eventually, it must be said in passing, the causal sequences indicated by historical analyses may be more subtly expressed through the use of ahistorical principles in historical contexts. In one society in the northern Philippines, for example, head-hunting ceased after contact with the Spaniards. Did the Spaniards therefore "cause" the change? In one sense, yes, since their action immediately preceded, and hence must have been connected with, the change. In another sense, the answer must be negative, since the people themselves already had "an effective mechanism" to achieve the same end, viz., peace pacts with other villages that were patterned after their own marriage agreements. Spanish authorities succeeded easily with them but not in two neighboring societies which had not developed the mechanism (Eggan, 1941, p. 17). Two forces interacted, an external and an internal one; the event resulted from "causes," not a single cause.

One aspect of history cannot be excluded from an analysis of acculturation because it affects the behavior of people in the present: the knowledge of history which they themselves possess. "As each Dakota man or woman now looks back to the past either from experience or through the stories which have been told him," it has been reported, "he senses the self-assurance and the ability of his ancestors to cope with life" (MacGregor, 1946, p. 121). Such a view of history makes the Indian of Dakota society perceive the modern world in a particular way, contributes to his misery, and hence is highly relevant to the moment. Whether that view is historically correct, however, is another question which needs to be investigated in its own right. Both approaches could converge; for example, if the historian were to show that the present view of the past is distorted, the social scientist might then seek to account for the distortion.

Ironically, a psychological approach which must be limited historically also suffers from restrictions on its own nonhistorical level. After changing institutions are identified and examined, it becomes necessary to find and analyze the specific people who are learning or not learning to change. Historians and anthropologists who have their own important problems to study either cannot or do not necessarily provide such psychological data. A series of droughts, for example, leads to change in a society, as a result of which certain institutions become "dislocated." It is quite legitimate to note the temporal connection between the disasters and the change without ever knowing whose hunger pangs led to the acceptance of the innovation. It is important to know that a mob stormed a prison without being able to locate the particular men who shouted at the sensitive moment. In general it is useful to analyze any "dislocation" in a society without discovering how it is reflected in particular people and without inquiring whether there can be social dislocation without individual dislocation. Since the accounts of the events do not mention specific people, it must be concluded, they are not within the scope of this volume. Alas, it must be added, such purity is perhaps pointless, inasmuch as the relevant psychological data may be neither procurable nor recoverable: it is usually impossible to swoop down upon the leading or even the minor actors in an historical event and have them pause long enough to be analyzed. Under these circumstances, risky inferences from social materials must often be made. It may be easy to infer that people are hungry when the crops fail, but what can one say about the probable reaction of people in a jungle to the sight and sound of a jet plane? Unless they can in fact be directly observed or interviewed, again only inferences are possible—but let the inferences be as sagacious, as theoretically oriented, and as empirical as possible!

Finally, it is well to acknowledge that, when applying a psychological approach to a large group of people, almost always all members of the group cannot be embraced by any single generalization. Like events, people are more or less unique. If a change occurs or does not occur in a society, it may be presumed that some or many (but not all) people have or have not changed. One can only discuss modal tendencies. For a society as a whole, it is sometimes convenient to suggest not one modal tendency but many, each of which corresponds to subgroups based upon meaningful categories such as sex, age, and prestige. This limitation causes no particular difficulty until a particular person, such as an outstanding leader who is not included in the postulated tendency, turns out to be the critical factor in the situation.

The weaknesses of a general psychological approach to acculturation have now been exposed. It seems that a thorough historical or even momentary analysis of a single situation cannot and hence here will not be assayed. "The essential questions" to be raised in studying the contact of two cultural systems, one anthropologist has noted, "are the specific conditions under which individuals of either group gain an opportunity to learn about the ways of the other group, how far such learning is promoted or discouraged, what is learned and the various incentives to learning, the kind of people who have taken the initiative in learning, and the results of the process with respect to the subsequent relations of both groups and their cultural systems" (Hallowell, 1955, p. 318). Such a statement may be unrealistic but at least it suggests the kind of analysis that is needed when the aim is either to write a complete historical account of an instance of contact or to predict what will happen in a given situation. Many instances of acculturation are thus appraised, so that eventually general hypotheses emerge which relate somewhat to all of them and by means of which predictions hopefully become possible.

Concepts

For purposes of economy and precision certain terms must be introduced at this point. Without them too many words would have to be expended to express simple thoughts, or else the thoughts when expressed might be confusing or ambiguous. There are relatively few, fortunately, and they are not very complicated.

Whatever existed in a less civilized society prior to contact with Europeans or Americans, whether or not it continues to exist thereafter, will be called *old;* and what has been or is being introduced from the outside will be called *new.* The point of reference is the people themselves. The corn some Indian tribes cultivated before the coming of Europeans thus represents an old food, the horses and the guns they acquired from the early Europeans, new traits. If this account were focused upon the Europeans—as it is not—then the position of the adjective would have to be reversed since corn was new to the early explorers, and horses and guns were old.

Whenever appropriate, the aspect of the old or the new under discussion will be termed a *form of behavior.* The phrase has no inherent virtue in comparison with others (e.g., custom, trait, habit) that could be used, except perhaps that it forcefully suggests the human beings involved in the contact between the two societies and the varied reactions which they display. The corn of the Indians cannot be labeled a form of behavior, but growing, harvesting, distributing, cooking, and eating corn obviously are. Behavior includes actions that are directly observable—roasting the ears of corn—as well as those that must be inferred by an outside observer—the taste of the maize.

Contact between the two societies always occurs over a period of time. At least three phases are distinguishable: first, the initial phase; then the continuing one; and a final outcome. Certainly only in retrospect can a contact be considered final, as for example that which once occurred between ancient Greece and Rome. For purposes of research in the modern world, most contact is of the continuing kind.

The distinctions between old and new and between the temporal phases of contact are related to each other. During the initial phase everyone in the society who demonstrates the new form of behavior has had to learn it after learning the old or after reaching some degree of maturity; those who have learned it can be called *changed,* those who are learning it *changing,* and those who have rejected it or have not been exposed to it *unchanged.* During the continuing phase and at the final stage, there are likely to be also a group of people in the second generation who have learned the new from the very outset of their lives and not in later life after having learned the old; they have in effect been socialized as Westerners or Europeans. When a new religion is introduced into the old society, those who are converted obviously are changed, those who are learning its tenets are changing, and those who resist it are unchanged. The children of the converted, being brought up in the new faith, are *socialized* in this respect.

One other set of distinctions involves the forms of behavior which are or are not changing. If that behavior is unimportant, it will be termed *segmental:* the person cares relatively little whether he conforms to the old or the new. If it is important, it will be viewed as *central* within him: the decision regarding change is likely to involve many aspects of the man's way of life or many of his values. Shoes from Western civilization, for example, are for sale in almost all less civilized areas. For some people the wearing of shoes is segmental: they consider them an interesting novelty or they use them to protect their feet under some circumstances. For others the same form is central, for thereby they gain prestige among their own people and indicate to others that they aspire to be civilized.

Finally, the activity embodied in the form of behavior may be specific or general. If *specific,* the learner grasps more or less exactly what he must do or accomplish; if *general,* he is acquainted with numerous specific goals to be attained but does not know their relative importance nor can he be certain that additional ones may not appear. Wearing shoes, whether segmental or central, is quite specific: the feet must be enclosed in a prescribed manner. Becoming a clerk, on the other hand, demands more than the specific skills of the particular position since some kind of general code must guide conduct in innumerable situations (including perhaps the man's behavior outside the office: he must appear respectable) which cannot be easily catalogued.

A not unexpected disclaimer must be made explicit concerning all the above distinctions: each pair represents a continuum on which the dividing lines are blurred. At what quantitative point a new form of behavior is to be called segmental or central, for example, depends upon the problem at hand; one cannot say in general that behavior is segmental when it occurs for five minutes on the last Tuesday of each month. Contrasting terms, relatively simple as they are, would only categorize some of the behavior of people becoming more civilized.

Hypotheses

The discussion of why historical considerations are to be largely neglected ought to have made it abundantly clear that this book aims to achieve some working principles concerning contact and acculturation. The principles will be presented in succeeding chapters; all of them are assembled in Appendix C (p. 324). Here there will be a brief discussion of their nature and scope.

The hypotheses—as well as the corollaries to which, rigorously or not, they give rise—must be thought of as first approximations which would transcend the level of the concrete society and ascend into the realm of abstraction. It seems evident that the precision varies inversely with the specificity of the generalization but that wider applicability is achieved as more and more concrete details are omitted. A series of propositions can be imagined:

1. After contact with Europeans, these people immediately modified their view of creation by ascribing genesis not to a coterie of gods but to a single divinity; yet they continued to pay homage to their traditional priests.

2. After contact with Europeans, these people immediately modified some religious beliefs but not others.

3. After contact with Europeans, these people modified some religious beliefs but not others.

4. After contact with Europeans, these people modified some beliefs but not others.

5. After contact with a more civilized society, less civilized people everywhere modify some beliefs but not others.

6. After contact with a more civilized society, less civilized people everywhere modify only those beliefs which are blinkety-blank.

The first generalization is purely descriptive and remains close to the facts: it reports concretely and vividly what these people did after contact with Europeans. Their religious changes are stated more generally in the second statement and are then separated from a specific time interval in the third. The fourth generalization by itself seems flabby, but its very looseness enables it to be cast in a form applicable to less civilized peoples in any society. At this stage it would be impossible to anticipate the kinds of religious practices which changed (No. 1) or whether and when some religious beliefs were modified (Nos. 2 and 3). The fifth version, however, virtually demands that consideration be given to the problem of why less civilized people modify some beliefs and not others, and thus it leads to a final revision (No. 6) which presents an hypothesis. In such a way would this volume transcend less general statements and emerge with hypotheses concerning why people become civilized in some respects and not in others, and indeed concerning what happens to them as they become more civilized.

The hypotheses to be presented are of three kinds. First there are *causal* hypotheses, of which the above discussion is an illustration. These would specify why people become more civilized in certain respects: What induces them to learn some new forms of behavior and not others? The second type will be called *consequential*. They would suggest the consequences of becoming more civilized: What happens to people as they come to resemble Europeans and Americans? Most of the hypotheses are mixtures of the first two and are termed *interactional*. In many situations cause and effect cannot be disentangled either because data are lacking and methodological tools are weak, or because indeed various factors, interacting in the manner of a Hegelian dialectic, produce the synthesis of a civilized man. So much space will be devoted to discussing interactions that here a hypothetical illustration is imagined for purposes of further clarification. Let omniscience be assumed; then these propositions emerge:

1. At the outset only the stronger members of the tribe were attracted to learn certain new forms of behavior.

2. By learning the new forms these particular people and their descendants became still stronger.

At a later point in the history of the tribe, the order of mean strength might then be: the socialized, the changed, the changing, and the unchanged. Strength has been thus one of the original causes which produced learning but it has become also a consequence. There has been interaction.

All the hypotheses except one and most of the corollaries contain the word "likely." That word reflects more than the timidity of their formulator. For knowledge is never certain, and knowledge about less civilized peoples is peculiarly uncertain, in part because it is so scant, in part also because its validity in many instances is, if a euphemism may be employed, disputable. Then the hypotheses and corollaries, although they would refer to specific people, can perforce signify only the modal reaction of people: like all generalizations on this level, it is only likely but not certain that they are applicable to a specific individual. Finally, each hypothesis and corollary would isolate a single factor or a relatively small number of factors; in real life other factors operate simultaneously; the "other things" which one must assume are equal for the generalization to be true are in fact not equal; once again, there is probability, not certainty. Probability, not certainty—a good goal and worthy of effort.

Chapter 2.

THE ATTRIBUTES OF
LESS CIVILIZED PEOPLE

BEFORE indicating why men seek to become more civilized in certain respects and what happens to them when they do, it is necessary to uncover some of the attributes which they probably possess before they change. Without a baseline changes cannot be sensibly observed. Unless that baseline is cautiously established, however, the outcome will be no better than that provided by the snob in modern society who with little encouragement can indicate the characteristics of people less civilized than himself by oblique references to taste, manner, niceties, or the best that has been thought or said or composed in the world. Into such a quagmire of values it is best not to dip. Instead let attention be paid directly to the less civilized peoples of this earth, whether they once lived or continue their existence at the moment in some relatively isolated area. What attributes do they share? Or, better, on a high level of abstraction in order to transcend their uniqueness, what attributes can be assigned to them?

Actually there is a strong tradition against making generalizations about less civilized peoples. On methodological and ethical grounds objections have been raised whenever less and more civilized peoples have been sharply separated. Methodologically many of the ways in which the less civilized have been characterized are now known to be premature and too sweeping. As more data from underdeveloped areas have been accumulated, some society has usually been located which does what the induced principle states no "primitive" people anywhere do; in fact, anthropologists are almost always able to find the exception

to any glib statement about human beings. Ethically the biological overtones provoked by an expression like "the mind of
primitive man" have produced opposition: the implicit or explicit assumption that "primitive man" is primitive because he has
a primitive mind and that he has a primitive mind for genetic or
innate reasons has been denied and refuted, as well it should
be. Comparisons between the behavior of less civilized peoples
and that of more civilized children have not added prestige to
this kind of investigation, inasmuch as it is perfectly clear that
in the most "backward" of societies the adults are on their own
standards not children but adults. Among laymen too—especially
among European settlers in colonial areas—aggressive assertions
concerning the "savage" or "primitive" character of the so-called
"native" have doubtless prevented some serious students from determining whether valid propositions can be induced.

Perhaps the greatest inhibition to research was provided by the
French sociologist Lévy-Bruhl. In a stimulating and provocative
manner he sought to characterize the "prelogical mentality" of
primitive men. His generalizations seemed too sweeping: "Primi-
tives perceive nothing in the same way as we do." Or they were
operationally unclear: "The collective representations of primi-
tives are not, like our concepts, the result of intellectual processes
properly so called" (Lévy-Bruhl, 1926, pp. 43, 79). In consequence a generation of non-French colleagues sought to avoid
similar blunders by neglecting the problem.

A very bland illustration can reveal the flavor of much modern
academic discussion. An anthropologist finds fault with another
anthropologist, the one to whom he has dedicated his book, for
using the concept "folk society." That concept, he says, "rides
slipshod over fundamental cultural differences" because it "would
group together food-gathering, hunting, pastoral, and agricultural
peoples, without distinction." One group of Indians, he asserts, re-
minds him more of "American urban value systems" than of another Indian society; hence "the two Indian societies should not
be grouped together as folk societies" (Lewis, 1951, pp. 433–4).

The anthropologist or the social scientist, however, cannot consistently avoid the problem of describing and contrasting less and
more civilized people. In fact, he is already operating at two

levels of abstraction, one more specific and the other more general than the problem under discussion here. In the first instance, no ethnologist collects and reports just the so-called facts about a society. If he states that fish caught in a particular way constitute the chief food in a patriarchal society which lives on an island in the Pacific and that American naval personnel stationed there are liked or disliked, he is referring in effect to modal tendencies from which there is virtually no deviation (eating fish, reckoning descent), some deviation (the fishing technique), or relatively great deviation (attitude toward Americans). Central tendencies are thus abstracted in order to locate uniformity amid diversity. In more recent times, moreover, attempts have been made to generalize not only about the specific details of a people's existence but also about their general personality or "national character"; and thus documentation is provided for those who have always guessed that the behavior of a new acquaintance is "typically" French or Chinese.

From a level of abstraction concerning an entire society, a leap has often been made, in the second instance, onto the much loftier one of seeking to discover attributes applicable not to all less civilized peoples but to mankind in general. "Students of cultures," a distinguished anthropologist once stated, "find that the same general outline will fit all of them; thus, we say the facts of culture may be comprehended under nine heads" which —in his own terminology—are speech, material traits (food habits, shelter, etc.), art, mythology and scientific knowledge, religious practices, family and social systems, property, government, and war (Wissler, 1923, pp. 74-5). The line of inquiry has been extended by postulating "constants" of human nature which account for the universality of such an outline (Murdock, 1945). All men, for example, grow hungry and hence every society without exception must make some provision for obtaining food. These constants are ascribed in part to a common biological inheritance which is modified by experience in growing up and in remaining respectable within each society and in part to the nature of social life, whose continued or stable or peaceful existence always requires the establishment and perpetuation of sanctions which curb basic impulses.

The kind of generalization being sought in this chapter falls between the two levels of abstraction just outlined: it must be more abstract than the one which pertains to a single society but not so abstract as the one which would specify universal constants. Actually the impression is gained that few anthropologists who have written more than an ethnographic report on a particular tribe, and especially those who have emitted textbooks, have been able to avoid generalizing precisely in such a manner. In a book called *The Mind of Primitive Man,* which, though written very early in his career, he must have always esteemed since he revised it shortly before his death, Boas disposed of the racial explanation for the behavior of less civilized peoples but also made statements like the following: "The primitive man views every action not only as adapted to its main object, every thought related to its main end, as we should perceive them, but . . . he associates them with other ideas, often of a religious or at least of a symbolic nature" (Boas, 1938, p. 226). These generalizations have been largely overlooked, it appears, the way people try to pass over quickly the minor blunders of their respected friends. In the United States, therefore, the name of Boas is associated instead with his careful ethnography in the Pacific Northwest and with his relativistic view that each society is adaptively unique.

"At first glance," a sociologist says of the "little people" who are the peasants on every continent, "it would seem ridiculous to lump together people of so many languages, of so many creeds and colors." Immediately he adds that "underneath their apparent divergencies are many ways in which they are much alike" (Sanders, 1945, p. 37). Then he proceeds to specify those ways in useful detail. Likewise abstract statements appear, however reluctantly, whenever any specific social process is discussed. Among less civilized peoples, the author of a book on innovation states at the outset, there are vast differences regarding the ability "to conceive of something beyond the limits of the conventional range of routine." Within forty pages, however, he avers that "our philosophy contrasts with that of many primitive peoples" in respect to change: we consider that change is "natural, inevitable, or morally good"; they do not (Barnett, 1953, pp. 20, 62).

The critics of those who generalize about less civilized people overlook the simple methodological point that has already been argued in Chapter 1: abstractions deliberately seek out similarities and ignore differences. The anthropologist who states that folk societies differ markedly from one another is making a correct statement but one that is irrelevant if the interest is in similarities. When the speed of a falling body is to be calculated, let the point be repeated, it matters not whether the body is a human being, a bomb, or a piece of cheese. Of course people are different from bombs and bombs different from cheese, but for purposes of the abstraction they have the attribute of weight in common. For that matter, no two people are alike but, by agreeing to accept the limitation of focusing upon modal tendencies, it is possible to generalize about an entire society. Similarly, from a logical standpoint there is nothing evil or wrong in seeking parallels between less civilized peoples and children, provided that the abstraction is acknowledged and provided no inference concerning a cause-and-effect sequence is made. It would be quite legitimate to point out similarities between less civilized people on the one hand and elephants, seaweed, or the twenty greatest geniuses of Latvia on the other hand if one had a serious purpose in mind and did not conclude that therefore less civilized people are elephants, seaweed, or Latvian geniuses. In this book parallels between less civilized people and children are not pointed out, not because the writer is afraid of the task—he herewith recommends one book containing an interesting attempt to do just that (Werner, 1948)—but because other problems seem more pressing.

If the inquiry is, then, legitimate, how does one proceed to establish some of the attributes of less civilized peoples? A clue has been provided, paradoxically, by the very relativists who abhor the search for uniformity among less civilized peoples. According to the modern doctrine of cultural relativity, each society is more or less unique and hence must be judged uniquely. A society has come to possess its unique attributes because it has developed and is now functioning in the midst of a pattern of rather unique geographical, economic, and historical circumstances. Food may be scarce because the people live in an inhospitable environment, one in which few plants grow, few crops can be cultivated, and few animals survive. But why, the question can be asked, do not the people move to a more hospitable environment? The question cannot be answered with dispatch or certainty: they like their present abode, they have lived there for centuries, they know that better land is not immediately available, they are surrounded by tribes who bar migration, etc. Clearly, however, the conditions under which they live—whether they wish to live thus or are forced to do so is irrelevant—make them develop talents to cope with the problems of their existence. Those talents exercise a determining effect upon important aspects of their behavior. The kind of adults to which such behavior eventually leads affects the way in which they subsequently socialize their children. In brief, people are formed by the conditions engulfing them; the diversity of which they as newborn infants were once capable has been severely limited by the force of circumstances; a modal or central tendency has had to emerge for them to survive.

Here, then, is a formula: environmental conditions, regardless of origin, produce central tendencies in behavior and hence reasonably similar people. The sequence is not inevitable but it is probable; it may not always be directly observable, and instead—and here is the admitted psychological limitation from which this volume suffers—it must be inferred. Reactions to similar adversity, it can be contended, may be quite diverse: some people are depressed, some feel challenged, or some become elated. True, but a common core involving, for example, the conviction that some solution to the adversity is necessary or at least desirable undoubtedly also exists. If it can be shown, therefore, that all less civilized people live under conditions that are different from those under which all civilized ones live, then it must follow that their "minds" or their personalities or their behavior or their actions differ too. The problem is thus reduced to two questions. First, is it possible to specify the environmental conditions that confront less civilized peoples everywhere? To narrow the scope of the inquiry, let the explicit assumption be made that the less civilized societies being considered cultivate the land and do not depend completely on food-gathering, hunting, or fishing. Secondly, if uniform conditions can be indicated, what general (rather than specific) effect do such conditions inevitably have upon the behavior of men? What follows should be interpreted as a series of working hypotheses derived from this writer's impression of the impressions of those scholars who have addressed themselves to the questions. In fact, he is struck by the apparently high degree of unanimity they reveal. Perhaps the agreement results from an unconsciously shared prejudice of the age, but hopefully their thoughts, occurring as they have within a scientific tradition, are based upon facts.

Security and Restriction

Less civilized societies tend to be small. Among American Indians it is estimated that in 1650 the Iroquois numbered about 25,000; in 1706 the Navaho, between 2,000 and 4,000; in 1833 the Crow, 3,500; in 1850 the Tubatulabal, between 200 and 3,000; and in 1905 the Ojibwa, 30,000. Elsewhere in the world other estimates are: in 1804 the Tasmanians, 8,000 or less; in 1866 the Aranda, around 2,000; in 1922 the Trobriand Islanders, 10,000; in 1929 the Tikopians, 1,300; in 1939 the Tiv, 530,000; and in 1945 the Samoans, 61,000. Such figures indicate the total number of people who share certain traditions, who think of themselves as belonging to the same society, but who do not ordinarily associate with certain out-groupers. Throughout their existence most of these people are confined to the community of their family or lineage, and that community, most competent authorities seem to agree, is extremely small. In modern English the community would be called a village. The urban developments in ancient Mexico, Peru, Nigeria, and the Sahara appear to be exceptional. In fact, according to one social scientist, "the primitive world" has been "transformed" into the modern world by the rise of cities (Redfield, 1953, p. 12).

In a small society or community it is highly likely that the individual has meaningful face-to-face contacts with almost everyone. If the tribe is relatively large—for example, a population of over a million, which is the situation in some modern African societies—direct contact is less likely, but significant bonds among members are promoted in at least two ways. The immediate subgroup to which the person is attached is generally larger than the nuclear family in more civilized societies and has a variety of functions besides procreation and child-rearing, such as economic activity and political jurisdiction. In addition, the social structure as determined by membership in a clan, a moiety, a sib, and the like relatively rigidly and extensively prescribes the relations of people. Again and again anthropologists report that two strangers from the same tribe quickly indicate the position they occupy in their lineages, not to satisfy their genealogical curiosity but to know how to behave toward each other.

In any society the behavior of people depends in large part upon the roles they are expected to perform in connection with the various statuses which they occupy, and those statuses in turn depend upon their sex, age, family affiliations, and so forth. In less civilized societies the roles seem to make greater demands than in more civilized lands, perhaps because in a relatively small group which may be living under somewhat precarious conditions freedom of choice can be disruptive. From birth to death the individual in the underdeveloped area is usually not called upon to make a vital decision concerning, for example, the career which he would follow. Certainly there are spheres in which the assignment of a role does not occur automatically. Craftsmen may compete for positions of honor, the title of chief or subchief is awarded to him who deliberately displays some unusual talent, for example, but by and large it appears that competitiveness of this kind is muted in less civilized groups.

Virtually all the significant activities of the individual in less civilized societies occur within a small, meaningful group which achieves therefore a high degree of self-sufficiency in many senses. Economically, for example, people grow or catch the food they eat. There may be some trading between groups within the society or even between different tribes, but apparently the quantity of goods so exchanged is seldom very great. Inevitably specialization and division of labor occur, if only to produce articles such as boats or idols which require unusual technical or artistic skill. The specialists, however, are members of the local community, and the division of labor (for example, on the basis of age or sex) is likely to be confined to a small group such as the family. In any case, most if not all of the economy functions literally within the purview of each person.

Another kind of stability results from the circumstance that changes in less civilized societies occur relatively slowly. The organization and ingredients of the society into which the individual is born are likely to remain very similar throughout his lifetime. What he himself has experienced his children will also experience, and indeed in a very similar context. The future he can assume will be like the past and hence equally comprehensible or incomprehensible. When anthropologists and others seek to reconstruct the state of affairs in a less civilized society prior to contact with the Western world, they usually suggest such a static picture (e.g., Gillin, 1942, p. 546).

The normal exigencies of life in uncivilized societies, in brief, tend to be provided for. Deviations from the accustomed code are handled by a formal or informal system of law. Otherwise, custom and social pressure induce conformity within a small group.

The impression must not be gained that less civilized peoples live in a sort of dull paradise in which expectations are accurately and monotonously fulfilled. The normal pattern in a given society may involve hostility or suspiciousness, which are certainly this side of both paradise and monotony, but these traits of one's peers —and this is the only point to be emphasized—can be anticipated. It is wise to state, too, that there are always social or personal emergencies for the less civilized man. A typhoon or a drought brings disaster to almost everyone; or the youth is rejected by the family of one of the relatively few girls whom he is allowed even to consider as a wife. Once again, however, the painful events in a sense are anticipated, and the appropriate conduct is likely to be prescribed and known. The prescription may not always be followed, and there is panic or neurosis; but modally or normally tradition suffices.

Finally, "the simpler cultures are more directly conditioned by the environment than the advanced ones" (Steward, 1955, p. 40). Like farmers and cultivators everywhere, they are dependent upon the vagaries of soil and climate. Almost always they are unwilling or, more importantly, unable to acquire a surplus in time of plenty to be used during famine or scarcity. The immediate causes of a period of prosperity or adversity, however, are clearly perceptible: the rainfall has been normal or abnormal, the beetles have or have not been absent, and so on. Against these catastrophes, moreover, the community or the small group mobilizes its forces and strengthens people's attachment to their in-group. The society as a whole may be leading a precarious existence, but each person knows that everyone shares a common fate. In fact, according to one observer, "all aboriginal peoples accept the theory that every human being has the inalienable right to an irreducible minimum, consisting of adequate food, shelter, and clothing"; for this reason, "the actual difference in the standard of living [between rulers and followers in virtually all such societies] is not very great" (Radin, 1953, pp. 106, 216).

In general, therefore, less civilized people operate with a set of expectations concerning themselves, their contemporaries, and their general environment which tends to be confirmed. Within the relatively small groups in which they spend their lives they know one another well. They participate in, or observe directly, the economic activities which enable them to survive. They have their parts to play and by and large they play them; they likewise know that others will be equally faithful to their expectations. They can and do anticipate with great accuracy the course of events which affect them.

Under these circumstances of stability and intimacy, people must come to believe that they comprehend the functioning of their society. They have little uncertainty concerning people's expectations and hence concerning the behavior which they themselves must exhibit. In their personal relations, it may be inferred, they feel secure: there are few surprises. Growing boys may not know the precise contents of the secrets which will be revealed to them during the rites of passage into manhood, but they do know that they will participate in those rites and that perhaps secrets will be divulged. At the same time people in less civilized societies must be aware of the restrictions which surround them since the penalty for nonconformity is likely to be serious and quickly imposed. Still they can feel relatively safe among their contemporaries, inasmuch as "primitive and pre-civilized communities are held together essentially by common understandings as to the ultimate nature and purpose of life" (Redfield, 1953, p. 12).

It must be strongly emphasized once more that these generalizations about less civilized peoples are abstractions from the standpoint of outside observers. It does not follow that every person in a less civilized society feels restricted by his conventional ties or that he has few alternate courses of action available to him. From his own subjective standpoint, the choice which he does have—involving minor matters in the day's or the year's routine—may seem to afford him virtually unlimited, subjectively real freedom. When after contact with some other society, and especially with the West, he obtains the perspective he now lacks, then and only then will the traditional existence appear to him to be or to have been restrictive. As ever, too, there is great variability from society to society, especially with regard to the quality of the contact members of small groups have with one another. The range seems to extend from real intimacy to the kind of distant relation that occurs when people (like some Indians in Mexico), "although living side by side . . . communicate little of their innermost thoughts, aspirations, fears, likes, and dislikes and, for the most part, remain strangers to one another" (Lewis, 1951, p. 289).

An interesting hypothesis has been proposed which, though unproved and perhaps unprovable, vividly points up the contrast between less and more civilized peoples that has been discussed in this section. It is suggested that everywhere "the total degree of dependence upon others" is the same; the number of people on whom one is dependent as well as the "intensity" of the relationship, however, varies considerably but the product of these two factors, as it were, tends to be constant. In the old societies in Central Africa, on which the hypothesis is based, "comparatively few people were in close relations." In contrast, as such societies become more civilized, the first factor increases and hence the second decreases: comparatively more people tend to be in distant contact (Wilson and Wilson, 1945, pp. 28, 40).

Faith and Absolutism

In any society men tend to sanctify traditional beliefs and values, for these guide their conduct and give meaning to their lives. They must always devise ways to obtain food, and the methods they come to adopt after centuries of trial and error are supported by experience and then by faith in their efficacy. Actual consumption thus vindicates the faith. In metaphysical realms the evidence for retaining faith is less tangible but no less compelling, since subjective convictions can suggest that a belief has been helpful in practical or spiritual ways.

Faith in the absoluteness of beliefs and values wavers whenever evidence at hand suggests that they lack validity or goodness. If the crops fail again and again, then people may begin to question their agricultural techniques or the devices they employ to induce the gods to act propitiously toward growing plants. They may question them, but are they eager to abandon them? Probably not, if they have found them satisfactory in the past. The present failure can be ascribed to other causes. The crops are failing, yes, but perhaps the customary method of cultivation has not been correctly executed: the seeds have been planted too deep or too shallow, the rows are too close or too far apart. It may be difficult to gainsay the empirical facts, and so defects can be found not in the powers of the relevant deities but in the execution of the prayers and rituals which bring divine cooperation: somebody has been showing internal disrespect. The ancient faith, consequently, can be retained; the culprits must be discovered and punished.

The hypothesis is advanced that less civilized people have less of a tendency than those more civilized to question the efficacy of their beliefs and values. The empirical, experimental spirit of Western science as well as the tendency to adopt fads, fashions, and changes seem to be relatively weak in less civilized societies. The reasons for their weakness are so numerous and complicated that only two can be mentioned in passing. Certainly the close attachment of cultivators to the soil must play a role: when once the techniques of producing crops or of herding animals are mastered, there need be little change, and so one uses "the crude experience of generations" as the best available, conservative guide (Boas, 1938, p. 221).

Travel between less civilized societies, moreover, is often difficult or dangerous and hence is likely to be considered undesirable. As a result the stimulation and challenge which can come from contact with outsiders is usually lacking. In fact it may be said that less civilized peoples tend to be thoroughly encased in their own language and dialect because they do not travel, and in part they do not travel because they are so linguistically confined. Prior to contact with the West, the ability to communicate in Central Africa was "sometimes confined to a few thousand people, and nowhere, we think, exceeded half a million"; in this area "though the languages were nearly all related, it appears that a very small proportion of the population spoke any but their own" (Wilson and Wilson, 1945, pp. 7–8).

In a less civilized society, consequently, the customary way of thinking, feeling, and acting is not challenged by outsiders. Nor is it in fact likely to be challenged by insiders. The last point can be easily dramatized by referring to those institutions in the West—such as academic universities or the manufacturers of fashionable clothing for females—whose principal function is to challenge beliefs and practices. Nobody outside civilization is likely to raise questions "too difficult to answer" (Mead, 1956, p. 85); or at least traditional replies are procurable. In a Mexican community having accelerated contact with urban civilization a man once said:

> In the city people are always talking about their problems, wondering how to solve them. Out here, even if we do not use books, we have some way to solve every difficulty. In the old days, there could have been no books, and yet people knew what to do in every situation [Redfield, 1950, p. 145].

Almost wherever one turns, some symptom of absolutism seems discernible in less civilized societies. The great religions of the East and the West, for example, are sufficiently abstract to be universal and thus, potentially at least, to embrace all mankind;

"in the primitive societies," in contrast, "the gods were the ancestors or other spirits whose influence was limited in range" to the group harboring the beliefs (Wilson and Wilson, 1945, p. 11). It has been said that "aboriginal peoples" assume that the order of the world has existed "from the beginning of time" or else that it was established "at some particular time in the dim past"; in either case "its characteristics are fixed" (Radin, 1953, p. 72). With such a belief, and especially in the absence of an experimental approach, it has been suggested, less civilized people seek only to placate or live in harmony with, rather than to control or master, nature in general (Redfield, 1953, pp. 105–6).

In concluding this section, again the polite but unperfunctory disclaimer must be expressed: no absolute distinction between less and more civilized peoples has been asserted. Certainly the beginnings of science exist everywhere; and fads, fashions, and changes are discoverable too. Likewise, relatively few people in highly civilized societies are acquainted with science or exhibit its spirit, and not all of them are victims of petty changes propelled at the moment. The difference here delineated is not absolute but it is quantitatively important.

Unity of Behavior

To some extent no human activity occurs in isolation. Even the simplest and most segmental reaction of all, the patellar reflex or knee jerk, depends not only on the correct application of the adequate stimulus upon the nerve endings in the area of the knee cap but also on the general state of the organism; thus the leg of a tense person is likely to respond with greater amplitude than that of one who is relaxed. More complex phenomena such as beliefs are seldom completely isolated from one another, for they tend to be general rather than specific in scope. If a modern American subscribes to the view that certain races are inferior, he is also likely to believe that such seemingly diverse groups as labor unions, children, and communists should be treated authoritatively and firmly.

Not all behavior of course is closely or immediately unified.

At one extreme is the somnambulist, one phase of whose existence is dissociated from the normal waking state. In less dramatic form every human being has dreams which cannot be immediately or easily related to his ordinary conscious state. Still there is a certain amount of consistency in everyone. Even those who separate values into logic-tight compartments react relatively consistently within each of the separate compartments.

The roles assigned to each person in a less civilized society, it has been indicated, tend to be relatively rigid. People performing such roles must demonstrate a high degree of consistency and generality in their behavior. Under these circumstances, they must have a strong tendency to see a relationship among all or most forms of behavior, or at least not to feel a lack of harmony among the goals they seek. The evidence is much less clear, but they may also find no boundary or virtually none between their internal feelings, attitudes, and beliefs on the one hand and their overt action and conduct on the other. The reality which dreams are said in some societies to possess; the stress which is often placed upon the correct emotional attitude of the cultivator or the pastoralist in growing crops or raising cattle; or in general the great emphasis upon ritual and ceremony—phenomena like these cannot be dismissed simply as evidence of magic unless it is immediately recognized that magic is employed to make experience seem more inclusive and its elements more interrelated.

A contrast between less and more civilized peoples with respect to the unity of behavior can be hazarded. Inhabitants in the West tend to make sharp distinctions among their various institutions. The most naive layman and the most practical extrovert use words like *politics, religion, family, neighborhood, nation, public service,* and *economics* to refer to the varied phases of their own existence. They can also debate the question of the relation of these practices or institutions; for example, should religion be concerned with politics or politics with religion? Such a question, though vaguely and platitudinously phrased, is nevertheless meaningful and can provoke discussion: Are politicians guided by the ethical precepts they hear on Sundays in church? Less civilized men, on the other hand, are not so likely to compartmentalize their various activities. It has been frequently noted that for them there is a "religious" or "moral" element in all activity, including that which is realistically oriented. The words *religious* and *moral* must be placed in quotation marks in order to suggest that the distinction between the religious or moral element and the remainder of the activity is one which is made by a Western or outside observer and not necessarily or at least not spontaneously by the persons so engaged. Empirically, for example, within an isolated Mexican community—a criticism of the city and books by one of its inhabitants has been quoted above— "the idea of religion, as a body of faith and practice pursued by one member of the community and not by others" did not exist, so far as the visiting anthropologist can remember, until Protestant missionaries entered and converted some of the people and until continuous contact with the outside world had been established (Redfield, 1950, p. 88). Occasionally, though perhaps exceptionally, less civilized peoples also draw sharp lines. The "minds" of Indians in Guatemala, for example, are said to be "clouded with animism," but these beliefs do not intrude upon their "economic relations" and many of their "social relations" which follow matter-of-fact procedures (Tax, 1941, pp. 38–9).

The views of some less civilized groups may be faulty from the empirical standpoint of a Westerner, but often—perhaps always?—they may be internally consistent or even more insistently deterministic than some scientific doctrines. In a civilized society the idea of bad luck is frequently invoked to explain "an accident," for example, when a falling brick hits someone who happens to be passing the building. Bantu peoples, it is claimed in contrast, virtually never acknowledge such an element of capriciousness: whatever happens they attribute to "the working out of forces in Nature, often regarded as personal or semi-personal, which intend just that effect, or of powers in the possession of certain private individuals, or of official persons, like chiefs, or of specialists in strange powers, like magicians—powers enabling their owners by the use of appropriate methods to ward off evil and to procure differential advantages" (Hoernlé, 1937, p. 222). Thus a general hypothesis is employed to explain not only the isolated instance of "bad luck" but also a variety of events.

It is not assumed that less civilized men are consciously aware of the apparent fact that their behavior is relatively consistent and their actions unified. They are not necessarily behaving like the truly devout Christian in modern society who relates, or tries to relate, all his discrete actions to an overpowering ethical ideal. When questioned, they may be unaware of the principle which guides them, or the questioning itself may draw their attention to the unity and the possibility of disunity. No doubt, too, an uncivilized man can specify when he is functioning as a husband, as a parent, as a cultivator, as a fisherman, as a warrior, etc. In fact, anthropologists have long noted that in some societies fairly rigid roles are played by the same person at different times, depending on the situational context; while fishing, for example, he may be the leader, but while dancing in a ceremonial rite he will be following the lead of some of the men he directs on a fishing expedition. Certainly, under these conditions, he must detect differences in his social relations, or he can be made to note them. In general, it is being suggested, whether he is serving as leader or follower, he is more likely to be conscious not of his different roles but of his unified role as a functioning member of the society.

Simplicity

Let there be no trite misunderstanding: the simple life is not being called idyllic and desirable, rather it is asserted that factually the life of less civilized people appears to be relatively simple. Their culture in a fairly stable state is likely to have evolved a series of customs and adjustments that provide for bodily needs, procreation, education, recreation, and metaphysical yearnings. One set of practices and beliefs exists, not conflicting sets, largely because limited contacts with the outside prevent conflicting versions from penetrating.

In less civilized societies the standard of living, on a Western norm, is usually low. In many but not all of these societies survival for the person tends to be precarious. Rarely can cultivators be certain of their harvest, for usually droughts and pests appear or threaten to appear—and virtually all less civilized peoples are cultivators. In addition, effective ways to cope with disease, though not entirely lacking, are not highly developed, so that infant mortality and the incidence of disease tend to be high. Under these circumstances people must be dedicated fairly one-sidedly to survival, and not to the pursuit of an ideal like the good life. Here too is another reason for following ancestral ways: unless there is a crisis or an emergency, why question the efficacious, why risk trial and error, why try an experiment?

When the history of Western man is quickly viewed, moreover, it would appear that diversity breeds diversity: the more complicated a society, the greater the number of innovations which pour forth as more cultural elements can be combined into novel arrangements (DeGrange, 1953). Internal changes in less civilized societies tend to be relatively few and to occur relatively slowly. People living close to a subsistence level do not have the leisure to be creative. With rare exceptions, furthermore, the differences between the ruling elite and other people in less civilized societies are not great, or not great enough for the former to enjoy real leisure as a result of the labors of the latter. The discussion here would not imply that less civilized people do not speculate and that they are not disturbed by cosmic questions; rather they are less likely either to be tempted or to be able to escape momentary, mundane pressures.

When less and more civilized cultivators are compared, it can be seen that civilization produces complications. In less civilized societies crops are grown to satisfy the needs of the family or the local group, whereas the more civilized farmer produces goods primarily to sell in a distant market. The more civilized man is thus part of a larger economy, and with the cash from his crop or crops he purchases, instead of producing, what he needs. For economic and other reasons, furthermore, the more civilized cultivator is likely to judge himself and his accomplishments by referring to urban values as well as to those of his local group. The double set of values usually does not appear in less civilized groups until contact with apparently superior or more powerful outsiders has been established. At the same time, as suggested by the same sociologist who has indicated the above differences between rural life in Europe and America and in "folk and preliterate society," the civilized orientation toward the city can simplify some aspects of life. Land and cattle in less developed areas, for example, are often viewed as sacred, or at least attached to them is some mystical connotation; whereas the modern farmer more probably considers them simply as capital investments which provide a livelihood (Zimmermann, 1945, pp. 138–45).

"What is the essential difference between the primitive and the higher societies?" A popular historian answers his question by suggesting that "in static primitive societies" prestige is directed "towards the older generation of the living members and towards the dead," whereas in societies being civilized "the creative personalities who have broken new ground" tend to be imitated (Toynbee, 1946, vol. 1, p. 48). If the distinction is valid, then clearly less civilized people are more conservative than more civilized ones, and conservatives everywhere can encompass life more easily by traversing old roads rather than following new and hence less certain and more tortuous trails.

In this chapter, then, some of the possible attributes of less civilized people have been tentatively suggested. Certainly the list is pitifully incomplete. But this book claims only to be a "psychological exploration," and on a single expedition no more than a limited number of possibilities can be investigated. If the reader has become convinced that the goal is sensible and therefore that other investigations are desirable, enough has been achieved.

Chapter 3.

EVIDENCE AND METHOD

BOLDLY but perhaps foolishly it has been said that hypotheses will be formulated throughout this book in order to indicate why men become more civilized and what may happen when they do. Hypotheses require evidence if they are to be tested and then appraised. For the first time let the stark fact be proclaimed which will be repeated again and again: the evidence at hand is insufficient to test the general hypotheses being presented here.

The evidence is insufficient for good reasons. Traders, missionaries, settlers, colonial officials, anthropologists, and all those concerned with less civilized peoples have been faced with problems more pressing than those suggested by the questions at hand. They have had to guide or observe changing institutions, and perforce they have concentrated upon externalities. Will people in the tribe buy these goods or work for Western companies? Will they join the church and quit their pagan rites? Will they be friendly and cooperative and allow themselves to be hired as servants and laborers? Which parts of their political system should be preserved? How can "natives" be prevented from wanting independence or aided in achieving it? Which aspects of their old culture have they retained, which have they modified? These have been the types of questions that have been asked, and the answers do not necessarily provide insight into our present concerns.

Some systematic attempts have been made, however, to obtain data that are relevant. Almost all studies of this kind have been understandably, commendably, and scientifically cautious: their hard-won conclusions, the author asserts, are valid only for the society being studied and indeed for the particular time period, the particular informants, and the particular techniques of the inquiry. A principal feature of the present "psychological exploration" is to try to determine whether such discrete studies reveal a degree of consistency which can justify a general hypothesis. The results of the research have been squeezed and squeezed until only the most general finding remains, hopefully not seriously distorted by the pressure being applied. A final disclaimer: like most other people, this writer is not omniscient and hence does not pretend that he has explored every relevant scrap of information. He has tried, has tried hard, to find the most varied and provocative of the studies.

The plan of presentation to be followed in succeeding chapters can be briefly described. Before stating each hypothesis there is an introduction in which the need for the formulation is explained and clarified. After the statement, relevant evidence is outlined, and often additional problems or difficulties are stressed. That relevant evidence will be of two kinds: that from the writer's own research in Africa and Jamaica, and data from other studies elsewhere in Africa or the world.

Why is so much attention being paid to the writer's own research? Truly not because it is better than other studies—quite the contrary in some, perhaps most, instances—but only because it is his and therefore he knows its imperfections better than anyone else possibly can. To point out imperfections so that others can improve their techniques, moreover, is a significant consequence of exploration, psychological or otherwise. Almost all the hypotheses, in addition, were formulated in connection with this research, that is, before or during the field trips and in some instances after examining the sorted data. Unshamefacedly—because abstraction is the goal—it is admitted that other evidence has been fitted into their mold. Is this such a terrible thing to do? The writer thinks not. For he would only modestly seek to show that the hypotheses, formulated with very imperfect African and Jamaican data in mind, have at least the possibility of being a first approximation of theories that reflect the facts gathered elsewhere in the world.

Other investigations, like the writer's own work, are cited so frequently throughout the book that once and for all their method is also explained in this chapter. Thereafter they will be referred to by means of the tag which has been arbitrarily plastered upon them. The technique of the Rorschach test figures so prominently in so many studies that a number of critical strictures concerning that instrument will be entered. What will be flamboyantly christened the Spiraled Explanation is mentioned in a final section.

Most people are not enthralled by descriptions of the methods that are employed in specific pieces of research. The remainder of this chapter follows the grand tradition: it is dull, so dull that succeeding chapters doubtless will benefit in contrast and appear more lively than they are. The forewarned reader, therefore, may wish to skip ahead and return later to swallow the pill when he comes to appreciate, as appreciate he will, the need for knowledge of these sources from which the subsequent ideas and hypotheses spring.

Africa-Jamaica Studies

The themes being investigated demand a psychological approach: specific human beings must be studied. A selected sample of informants in three African societies and in Jamaica were interviewed, with few exceptions, only once. During the interview the informant was asked a long series of varied questions and given a short series of tests. The African societies, each containing about a million people, were the following: the Ganda, a Bantu group in the British protectorate of Uganda; the Luo, a Nilotic group in the British colony and protectorate of Kenya; and the Zulu, another Bantu group in the province of Natal in the Union of South Africa. These Africans were surveyed in 1954 and 1955. The British island of Jamaica has a population of about one million and a half; the study was conducted during the summer of 1957.

The psychological approach can be appraised only by considering three problems in sampling: the choice of the particular societies; the choice of particular people within each society; and the choice of observable and inferred forms of behavior as obtained during the interview. Choice of the societies affects the

degree to which generalizations about other societies can be
made. Choice of particular people limits the extent to which
generalizations about the society in question are justified. And
choice of behavior determines the aspects of the person assessed
and hence does or does not provide adequate measures of his
specific and general tendencies or valid indexes of his personality
as a whole.

The choice of the three African societies was most arbitrary.
The writer, for reasons not relevant to the present discussion,
wished to carry on research among Africans. After arriving in
Africa, he chose the societies either because they were accessible
to him, because anthropologists and others helped both to establish contact with the proper African and European authorities
and also to understand their cultures, and because these peoples
are politically important within their particular areas. They
definitely are not a representative sample even of African societies, and hence fail dismally to meet any sampling criterion for
the world at large. At least they differ from one another not
only with respect to their old and traditional ways but also in
terms of the European context in which they find themselves. The
Ganda were progressing toward greater political freedom and
eventual independence in a land almost without European settlers. The Luo mixed freely with other Africans and with Europeans but were part of a territory in which Europeans firmly
held political power and in which the Mau Mau rebellion was
then active. And the Zulu, a proud people, were acutely experiencing the effects of the apartheid policy promulgated by
the firmly entrenched Afrikaner government.

Jamaica resembles the African societies in many ways but
differs from them in one important respect. Like them, it is a
tropical area under British influence, and the British stamp upon
political and economical life is unmistakable in every land England has controlled. The descent of most Jamaicans from African
stock is, from the viewpoint of their modern culture, almost
completely irrelevant, although a number of the problems produced in part by the color of their skin resemble those confronting some Africans—or, for that matter, Negroes in the United
States. In Africa, however, African and European forms of be-

havior remain in direct contact with each other, whereas in Jamaica, since so little from the African heritage survives, the contact is between what might be called a less and more complicated form of European civilization. It is, therefore, no exaggeration to say that the Africans are either unchanged or changing but that the Jamaicans are either changing or socialized Westerners.

The four societies can be very roughly ranked in terms of the degree to which most of their members have learned European forms of behavior; the order is from least to most:

1. Luo
2. Ganda
3. Zulu
4. Jamaica

The position of the Luo and Ganda is controversial. On the whole it seems clear that the Zulu have had longer, more frequent, and more influential contact with European society than the other two African groups. *The above ranking will be subsequently employed in all tables and discussions pertaining to the societies.*

A single investigator feels staggered when he seeks to solve the next methodological problem, the selection of a representative sample of informants from among a population numbering more than a million people. In more civilized terms, the magnitude of this problem can be appreciated by imagining what a pollster would do if he entered a large European city in order to determine how people feel about a question involving the United Nations. Should he start surveying in the middle of the city? Should he go to the wrong side of the railroad tracks as well as to the right side? If both sides are to be approached, how many people should be seen in each area? In this research modern sampling techniques could be only approximated, largely for mechanical reasons: adequate data concerning the population universe were usually lacking; not enough time was available to locate randomly selected informants; and only a relatively small number of people could be interviewed during the field trips and with the investigator's own quota of patience. Sampling procedures were adapted to local conditions but, in general, sampling areas in each society were found which satisfied three criteria. The area could be placed along a continuum of acculturation so that, for the society as a whole, those having many, fewer, and fewest contacts with Europeans or with European civilization were represented. The investigator, secondly, could be quickly and cordially introduced to the community (or its leaders) either by a respected European (an anthropologist, a physician, an official) or by a respectable African or Jamaican; otherwise the investigation would have been long delayed until an equivalent amount of rapport could be won. Then, finally, an effort was made—seldom successfully—to select at random particular people within the area. With few exceptions, each sample came from a separate, distinct community.

A brief description of each sample follows:

1. *Luo:* 47 interviews. The informants were scattered throughout the province of Nyanza, Kenya, in which this society now lives: 33 were relatively outstanding leaders who were carefully selected by competent African and European authorities under the guidance of an anthropologist; the remaining 14 were followers haphazardly selected from the same communities.

2. *Ganda:* 139 interviews. The most highly acculturated group was composed of men who had attended Makerere College, the University College of East Africa affiliated with the University of London, at least five years ago; some who lived in the immediate vicinity of Kampala, the principal city of Uganda, were interviewed ($n = 28$). The others came from four communities within and at varying distances from Kampala:

a. A community within the city limits of Kampala. Names of males were randomly selected from a list previously prepared by a sociologist, but this perfect method of sampling was imperfectly executed: the list, though recently compiled, was often out-of-date since turnover of the inhabitants tends to be rapid; and some men refused to be interviewed since at the time the Protectorate Government had sent the King of Ganda into exile ($n = 38$).

b. A community within commuting distance of Kampala by bicycle, the favored and practical mode of mechanical transportation for Africans. Informants were haphazardly selected, but an effort was made to have all occupational strata represented ($n = 19$).

c. A community slightly more distant than the preceeding one. Here all informants were supplied by a powerful informal leader to whom the idea of a representative sample was carefully explained; he may have grasped the idea but, unless corrected, he tended to summon only his friends ($n = 30$).

d. A community almost as remote from Kampala as can be found; commuting by bicycle is absolutely impossible. An effort was made to interview all males as determined by a census conducted by an anthropologist, but only 24 could be located or agreed to be interviewed.

3. *Zulu:* 106 interviews.

a. A highly organized urban area for Africans (called a "Location") on the outskirts of the metropolitan section of Durban, most of whose inhabitants are permanent urban dwellers and some of whom in effect have been socialized in the Western tradition. Names were randomly selected from a list prepared by social workers attached to a public health clinic, and 86 per cent of those so selected were in fact interviewed ($n = 57$).

b. A municipal Location in the center of Durban designed for males who, coming from the rural areas or "Reserves" where Africans must live, work in the city for a relatively short time before returning home; many of them repeatedly appear, work for a while, and eventually leave the city permanently. Informants were selected haphazardly from this homogeneous group ($n = 24$).

c. A Reserve quite detached from urban areas. Two educated informal leaders recruited all available men from their respective clans; these informants were either old men who no longer could work in the cities or on the farms of Europeans, or they were younger men who were home on vacation ($n = 25$).

4. *Jamaicans:* 112 interviews.

a. A relatively prosperous small town (population slightly

under 3,000) detached from the tourist belt. Attention was concentrated upon the important people: the two most prominent lawyers, most of the owners of the big shops, and a scattering of government officials and clerks ($n = 13$). From the standpoint of Jamaican society, and by almost any other criterion, these men may be considered socialized Westerners.

　　b. Accessible female social workers in the city of Kingston ($n = 8$).

　　c. A very depressed housing project on the outskirts of Kingston. Names of husbands and wives were randomly selected from a list compiled of all families with children who were living in the development; cooperation was excellent, with the result that 94 per cent of those selected were interviewed ($n = 30$).

　　d. A relatively prosperous village on the sea having contact with American tourists. Workers, mostly fishermen, were haphazardly selected ($n = 19$).

　　e. An extremely depressed rural section, quite remote from urban areas. Again husbands and wives were randomly selected from a list similar to the one used in the Kingston slum; almost all of these people were cultivators ($n = 30$).

　　f. A plantation growing citrus fruits and bananas, in an isolated rural area. Almost all available hired hands were interviewed ($n = 12$).

　　All the interviewing was done by the writer, with the exception of that in the second Ganda community, where the work was carried on by a competent, well-trained African interpreter-assistant. In this phase of the study no females were interviewed in any of the African societies. In Jamaica, on the other hand, 43 of the 112 informants were women.

　　The third and final sampling problem involves the actual interview of each informant in the four societies: did the questions and the tests elicit a representative sample of his feelings, thoughts, attitudes—in short, his inferred and observable behavior? The magnitude of this problem can be appreciated by recalling the varied kinds of behavior every person anywhere displays; how can one ever assay or assess it in good measure? In theory it would be necessary to make thousands of observations to be certain of a representative sample, since at the outset the kinds of behavior which a person exhibits and of which he is capable remain unknown. In fact, especially when only an interview and not a series of observations is employed, a risky but necessary assumption must be made: people are sufficiently unified and consistent so that rather fortuitously selected samples are likely to reflect their central tendencies.

To diminish the risk it is sensible to sample each person heterogeneously, and that was the procedure adopted in the interviews. Each session with an informant lasted about two hours. The items in the schedule were selected because they seemed to be related to problems of acculturation, because they had been used in previous studies, because they were not too complicated to administer, and/or because they appeared to be utilizable in different cultures. At this point only a quick summary is necessary; the details of the schedule appear in Appendix B and will be mentioned in passing in the tabulated results. The items range from relatively straightforward questions ("What is your occupation, what do you do for a living?") to so-called projective situations, in which the individual, hopefully caught off guard, reveals his feelings when he describes the stimulus pattern in front of him ("Here you see a European and an African," the investigator says as he places a vaguely drawn sketch of two human beings in front of the informant. "Tell me, please, what you think they are doing"). Three or four plates from the Rorschach test were included as well as a more specific test which seeks to measure visual retention of simple geometrical figures ("I am going to show you some simple drawings; you will look at each one carefully; I will then take it away and show you four drawings, one and only one of which is exactly like the one you have just seen; you find that one which is exactly like the one you have just seen and point to it"). All phases of the interview were carefully pretested in each society, and necessary modifications were introduced.

The validity of the behavioral sample can be questioned on another ground: even if the questions and tests of the schedule may under some circumstances adequately reflect the person, do they in fact perform this function during a particular interview?

In blunter words, what assurance can be given that each informant was telling or revealing the truth about himself? Complete assurance cannot be given (cf. Ombredane, 1951). Usually
more than one item on the schedule pertained to the same realm
of behavior; hence the informant would have to lie consistently
if he sought to be deceptive. Many items, especially the projective ones, disguise their purpose. Aside from a slight mone-
tary or other reward provided in many instances, the person
being interviewed had nothing to gain from the interview and
hence from being deceitful; in all situations the investigator
made no promises and specified his role correctly, viz., as an
American educator seeking to become better acquainted with
people in different parts of the world. Still the possibility cannot
be denied that many people wish to make a good impression
upon a stranger—by telling him, for example, what they imagine, correctly or incorrectly, that he wishes to know. Without
exception, all interviews were conducted with no one present besides the informant, the investigator, and—in the African societies—an interpreter. An interpreter—did he introduce a bias?
Each one was carefully selected so that he would be acceptable
to the informants. Among the Luo, for example, an older man
acted as interpreter because it was known that people do not
talk frankly in front of those younger than themselves. The interpreter was patiently trained to ask questions only when asked to
do so by the investigator and to keep quiet when silence would
elicit information; he was indoctrinated with the idea that literal,
not polished, translations were desirable. By and large it is felt
that the interpreter probably introduced no distortion beyond
that produced by the presence of the investigator himself, a
statement of faint praise to be sure.

All the data collected from the various samples in the four
societies are quantitative and hence can be thrown into statistical form. The number of comparisons or tests which can then be
made turns out to be staggering. One way to reduce the number
and thus to make the presentations less burdensome is to single
out an index of acculturation, which thus becomes the dependent
variable. What shall that measure be?

A direct measure of contact is difficult to validate or make meaningful. One cannot easily count how frequently an African sees a European, nor can one easily determine for what reasons a Jamaican cultivator visits a sophisticated religious or political leader. Even if these facts were available, moreover, they would have to be assessed in terms of their influence. Infrequent contacts between an African and a European missionary might have profound spiritual effects upon him; whereas contacts between an African and a European foreman can involve only the orders the latter transmits to the worker and have no other repercussions.

On a priori and practical grounds it has been decided to use *formal education in Western schools* as an index of acculturation. In the African societies, formal education clearly differentiates less from more acculturated persons because relatively few Africans attend school and because the schools are run by European mission groups, European officials, or Africans who have been trained by Europeans; at the higher levels the teaching in the three areas is in English. Competent observers, moreover, agree that education produces or is accompanied by significant changes; for example, "any schooled Zulu is in general much readier to accept European innovations than are the pagans" (Gluckman, 1940, p. 51). Likewise in Jamaica only the elite, with few exceptions, can progress as far as secondary school since the tuition (and often the board and room) of each student must be paid for by the student or his parents.

Actual analysis of the data, furthermore, reveals that formal education is a useful variable. It produces more significant differences than a variable such as leadership (Doob, 1957b). According to Table 1 (p. 282), it is related in Africa to such other criteria of acculturation as knowledge of English (row 1), occupation (row 2), place of residence (row 3), religious affiliation (row 4), the claim of having a European as a friend (row 6), and the ability to smoke a Western-type cigarette (row 7). And it is also related to the general acculturation rating given each informant by an anthropologist among the Luo and by the writer's interpreter among the Zulu; but no significant difference emerges for the ratings by a sociologist of the Ganda informants from the one urbanized community (row 9).

The procedure illustrated in Table 1 will be employed throughout the succeeding nine tables derived from the Africa-Jamaica studies. The informants from each of the three African societies are divided into two groups, one with a *low* and the other with a *high* degree of education from a Western standpoint. In fact, the division in each society has been made at a socially meaningful point that also, when possible, produces roughly equal numbers in the low and high groups. The low group always begins with no formal schooling whatsoever, and the high group always includes some who have been to college or university. For the African societies the modal amount of education in the low group is zero, but a few informants attended school for as long as four years; in Jamaica, the mode in the low group is five years. In all the tables based upon this study, the figures are percentages unless otherwise noted. An asterisk after a figure indicates that the difference between it and the figure to its right is statistically significant, viz., it is likely to be a "true" or "real" difference and not due to the chance factors inherent in sampling. Significance has been ascertained for percentages by means of chi-square, always with a correction for continuity, and differences between means have been appraised by *t*-tests; *p* must be .05 or less, with a two-tail test, for the difference to be called significant. Nonsignificant differences are often mentioned in the text either because they are provocative or encouraging or because they are part of a trend which itself is significant (as determined, for example, by a sign test).

The "maximum number of informants" in a low or high group is indicated in the first row of each table. Sometimes the number falls below the maximum because a section of the schedule could not be given to everyone in the sample—the reasons therefor under field conditions range from the very dull to the very exciting—or because a special breakdown is being considered. Similarly blanks on any of the tables signify absence of data; the item, for example, may not have been included on the schedule for the society, or the subgroups are too small to permit a meaningful comparison.

Tables designated by arabic numbers are all derived from the same schedule; tables from other schedules have roman numerals when they come from the writer, capital letters when from others. The particular item of the schedule from which each row is derived is indicated in parentheses after a number sign (#), except for a few items derived from ratings or observations. The wording of each item, even when quotation marks are present or implied, is of course a paraphrase. If the foregoing explanation sounds too simple, the reader is referred for additional complications to the paragraphs introducing the schedule in Appendix B.

Other samples of Africans and Jamaicans were also investigated during the same field trips but often for a different reason and always with a different schedule. Among the Ganda and Zulu further studies were made of adults:

Ganda: a schedule containing a few questions from the long schedule and also new questions pertaining to leadership and personality traits was administered by two Ganda, a male and a female student at Makerere College who were trained and supervised by L. A. Fallers, an anthropologist, and the writer (Doob, 1961). They attempted to secure a random sample by interviewing at various homes according to a prearranged plan; but in fact the informants were usually haphazardly selected. The male student interviewed men within the limits of Kampala, included among whom were nine graduates of Makerere College ($n = 50$); the female student interviewed women living within one of the areas mentioned above, viz., the same community in which the writer's own interpreter worked ($n = 38$).

Zulu: in the city of Durban a Zulu woman, trained and employed by the writer, interviewed three haphazardly selected samples of Zulu women to ascertain some of their beliefs and attitudes. One sample consisted of women living in the same suburban Location in which the writer carried on his investigation ($n = 70$); another, of unmarried women living in a different Location and seeking to earn their own way; ($n = 56$) and the third, of wives, sweethearts, or sisters temporarily visiting the men of the urban Location where this writer also interviewed ($n = 36$). The first group was highly urbanized, and included many women who spoke excellent English; the third was quite unacculturated, a symptom of which was the "native" clothing all the women wore; and the second represented a rather mixed parcel of both types. Salient results appear in Table III (p. 302).

Other work in Africa and Jamaica employed a written questionnaire administered during regular class sessions in secondary schools. One problem involved the relation between the language in which a statement was phrased and the expression of attitude: do children agree more readily with a viewpoint when it is expressed in their native language than when it is expressed in English? In the same study the children were asked to recall the statements, half of which they had originally seen in their native language, the other half in English: which statements do they more readily recall, and is their performance affected by the language in which they are instructed to write? An experiment was designed in which some children received and recalled half of the 20 statements in one language and the remaining in the other (Doob, 1957a). In Jamaica, the presentation was made not in written form but orally, since the two languages being tested —the patois and standard English—differ significantly with respect to pronunciation (Doob, 1958a). Among the Luo, 101 boys in a Protestant mission school and in a technical or vocational school were tested; among the Ganda, 113 boys in a Catholic mission school; among the Zulu, 101 boys in a public high school for Africans; and in Jamaica, 72 girls in a private high school. Another questionnaire, containing 24 items, was given to 215 boys in a junior secondary school in Uganda; here the purpose was to determine whether ascribing beliefs to various sources affected the expression of attitude. The results of the investigations among children are utilized in this book and especially in Tables I and II as another form of survey only when they have not been appreciably affected by the experimental variables which the writer manipulated to investigate the problem at hand.

Indian-White Study

The principal part of this investigation was carried on for a year beginning in July 1942 under the auspices of the Committee on Human Development in the University of Chicago and of the United States Office of Indian Affairs. A skilled group of social scientists, psychiatrists, teachers, and officials surveyed children between the ages of 6 and 18 in six different Indian societies and in a Midwestern community which had a population of around 6,000. Their findings have been competently and copiously summarized in a single volume (Havighurst and Neugarten, 1955). Around the same time, moreover, anthropologists worked within the Indian societies, so that through their published works the survey of the children can always be viewed and interpreted in perspective.

In two of the Indian societies the work was carried on in a single community; in three, in two communities; and in one, in three communities. Within each community an effort was made to include every child falling within the selected age range. When more than 150 children were available, which was the case in a few instances, a representative sample was selected. The modal number examined in each community was around 100, except that in the Midwestern town 733 children in grades 5 to 12 were surveyed. A bias admittedly appeared only in the case of children in very isolated communities since there it was often difficult to establish contact with those not at school (ibid., p. 131).

The six Indian societies studied are the Navaho, Zia, Hopi, Zuni, Papago, and Sioux. The first five are located in the Southwest; the Sioux belong to the Plains Indians group. According to the ratings of some anthropologists "who knew American cultures" (ibid., p. 173), the societies are arranged in the above list in increasing order of acculturation. An exception, however, must be noted: one of the Navaho communities (Shiprock) is considered to rank highest in acculturation among the Southwest tribes and just below the Sioux.

The following paper-and-pencil tests were administered to a varying number of children in each community:

1. *Emotional Response Test:* direct questions concerning the circumstances under which the child reports that he has experienced happiness, sadness, fear, and shame.

2. *Moral Ideology Test:* direct questions concerning "what boys and girls of your age think are good things to do and bad things to do."

3. *Moral Judgment Test:* direct questions concerning the rules of children's games, especially their origin and the possibility of changing them.

4. *Belief in Immanent Justice and Animism:* direct questions concerning events in a six-sentence story (e.g., Paul, who has stolen a melon, cuts his foot with an ax. Did the ax know that he stole the melon?).

5. *Free Drawings:* production of eight drawings whose content the child selected and one drawing of a human being.

6. *Intelligence Tests:* The Grace Arthur Point Performance Scale and the Goodenough Draw-a-Man Test, which were administered in the standardized way.

In addition, the Rorschach test in its entirety and a form of the Thematic Apperception Test were used among the Hopi and the Navaho (Henry, 1947).

Among the Indian children the tests were conscientiously and patiently given individually in order to overcome the shyness which many displayed in front of white examiners, to win their confidence, and thus to diminish the culturally imposed handicap. The American children were tested in groups. Whenever possible the reliability of the instruments was ascertained either by repeating the test on the same group after a period of time or on different but comparable groups; in general, the reliabilities are encouragingly high. Studies were also made of the significance of the factor of language, which seems in this instance to have played a very important role.

The monograph by Havighurst and Neugarten (1955) summarizes the data in statistical breakdowns which include not only the societies, the separate communities, boys vs. girls, and the various age groups but also the specific items composing each test. Throughout this book references will be made to these specific findings as well as to the anthropological studies; but the most relevant facts are embodied here in Table A (p. 304), which represents a radical rearrangement of two summary tables in the monograph (Nos. 38 and 39), provided by the investigators themselves in order to draw "from the several tests a number of variables that seemed to us significant" (ibid., p. 156). The rationale of Table A will now be explained so that hereafter only brief references to it can suffice. First, the number in parentheses after each item in a row indicates the particular test from which the measure has been derived; the numbers correspond to those used above in describing the tests. Then, whenever possible, four kinds of information are provided concerning each measure:

Column 1: Association between the rank order of the societies arranged according to their mean scores on the measure heading the row and their degree of acculturation. In computing each figure, the writer has considered as separate groups two of the Navaho communities, each of the five remaining Indian societies, and the Midwestern whites. The statistical measure is a so-called rank-order correlation or *rho* ranging from +1.00 to −1.00, the former signifying a perfect association of a positive nature (the higher the society's rank with respect to the measure, the higher its rank with respect to acculturation) and the latter a perfection association of the reverse kind. The figures in this column must be at least .50 to be considered significantly above one that could be obtained by chance. That magnitude is difficult to attain since, with only eight groups to be ranked, a single exception can appreciably lower the entire correlation; it may be noted that only about one-third of the *rho's* reach this level of significance.

Column 2: A comparison between the five Southwest Indian tribes and the white children with respect to the measure heading the row. The authors themselves recognize great differences among the tribes, but for some purposes they feel that the grouping is justified. Here the question is asked: Do the children from the Southwest Indian societies differ significantly from the American children? No significant difference is indicated by a zero; when significantly more of the Indian children possess the trait or the attitude in question, the letters "SW" (Southwest) appear; when more of the Americans, the letters "MW" (Midwest) appear; if no data are available, an interrogation mark appears. To determine whether differences are significant, the writer whenever possible has followed the investigators' own rules; otherwise he has utilized their tables, usually after combining the separate scores for boys and girls, and he has made his own calculations.

Column 3: A comparison, executed in the same way as in column 2, between the Sioux children (SX) and the Midwestern Americans (MW).

Column 4: A comparison, executed in the same way as in column 2, between two Navaho communities: the less acculturated Navaho Mountain (NM) and the more acculturated Shiprock (S).

One investigator, associated with the same study, concentrated not upon children but upon adults, to whom only the Rorschach test was given. He selected samples of males from the Navaho ($n = 27$) and the Zuni ($n = 53$) and included for purposes of comparison two non-Indian samples from the same area, Spanish-Americans ($n = 23$), who can be considered more acculturated than the Indians, and finally Mormons ($n = 20$). Each of the four samples contained an unspecified number of veterans of World War II and nonveterans. Such a variable, it could be anticipated, would be related to acculturation for the two Indian groups and the Spanish-Americans since participation in the American Army necessarily increased the number of contacts with Americans and their forms of behavior. Some of the principal data have been summarized in Table B (p. 306). Hereafter this investigation will be referred to as the Adult Section of the Indian-white study (Kaplan, 1954).

Menomini Indians

In the late forties and early fifties 68 male Menomini Indians were interviewed and given a Rorschach test (Spindler, 1955). They represent 20 per cent of the adult males who were living on the Menomini Reservation in Wisconsin at the time and who also were at least one-half Menomini in racial origin. The important feature of this study for present purposes is the continuum of acculturation established by the investigator in selecting his informants. He used five groups which are listed and described below in order of increasing acculturation:

A. Native-oriented ($n = 17$).
B. Members of the peyote cult; for them this form of religion

is said to represent "a special solution to the strains created by the adaptive process" of living in two cultures ($n = 13$).

C. Transitionals: men who have experienced both cultures without subscribing wholeheartedly to either ($n = 15$).

D. Acculturated men of the lower or poorer class ($n = 10$); these and the next group have been socialized in the Catholic Church.

E. Acculturated men of middle-class or elite status ($n = 13$).

In Table C (p. 307) many of the data have been summarized by converting into percentages the raw figures supplied by Spindler himself on two of his tables (ibid., pp. 213–24); the letters A through E which head the columns correspond to the five groups as just defined. In addition, 12 white men who live and work on the reservation were similarly interviewed and tested; comparable results from them, when available, appear in the column headed W. Since the percentages in Table C are based upon so few cases within each group, relatively few of the differences are statistically significant. For all the items except those listed under "Rorschach test" Spindler has made a comparison between the two least acculturated groups (A and B) and the most acculturated groups (C, D, and E) by means of a measure (tetrachoric correlation) which shows the relation between acculturation so measured and the item heading the row (ibid., p. 111); for the Rorschach results, his statistical tests to determine whether group A significantly differs from groups D and E are also represented on the table (ibid., p. 123).

Spindler has established the validity of his continuum of acculturation through the use of 23 sociocultural indexes, 19 of which are listed in rows 1–19 of Table C. All the correlations that are shown in the last column are positive and all of them, with a single exception (row 13, pertaining to alcoholic beverages), are significantly above chance. Clearly, then, there is a decided tendency for the two least acculturated groups to differ from the three most acculturated ones in 18 respects which involve such diverse phenomena as family background, contacts with American culture, beliefs, and detailed habits and modes of living. Two of these significant indexes refer to education—the educational status of the informant's father (row 1) and of the man himself (row 4). It is noteworthy that, in spite of the fact that almost all the men had some formal schooling in the Western sense, the factor of education proves discriminating here as it does in the Africa-Jamaica studies.

Ojibwa Study

The Ojibwa Indians of North America have split into different groups and have migrated to different areas of the continent since contact was established with white men. An anthropologist and his assistants have taken advantage of this situation by carrying on field work in three widely scattered communities of the tribe, and have given selected samples in each community the Rorschach test. Relevant results are presented in Table D (p. 309). The "Inland" sample of the Berens River group lives in the north of Canada and has had relatively little contact with white civilization ($n = 44$). Close by but on or near Lake Winnipeg are the "Lakeside" people, whose contacts have been much more numerous ($n = 58$). Across the border in Wisconsin is the most acculturated branch of the tribe, the Lac du Flambeau people ($n = 115$). The selection of the three communities has an important methodological advantage: it can be presumed that all three groups originally had the same culture and that they are of course descended from the same racial stock; whatever differences appear must be attributed to the different experiences they have had in the interim. Unfortunately, however, the experiences vary not only with respect to degree of contact but also in terms of the physical environment in which each segment lives (Hallowell, 1955, pp. 333–46).

Middle East Study

Beginning in the fall of 1951 approximately 1,600 interviews were conducted for the Bureau of Applied Social Research at Columbia University in six countries of the Middle East: Turkey, Lebanon, Jordan, Egypt, Syria, and Iran. The interviewers were "native scholars" in each country who were trained and then supervised by American technicians. No attempt was made to obtain a representative sample of an entire country; instead interviewing was deliberately confined to three provinces in each of the six countries, and therein samples were selected which were stratified with respect to sex, residence (rural vs. urban), age, income, and radio-listening habits. The interview covered a long schedule which had been pretested in Greece and which, in addition to certain background and psychological information, devoted itself largely to determining people's practices concerning, and their reactions to, the mass media of communication. The data have been ably analyzed and interpreted by Daniel Lerner (1958); he revisited the areas in 1954 in order informally to assess changes which had occurred since the original surveys.

In each country the sample has been divided into three groups to which colorfully descriptive labels have been attached: the Traditional, the Transitional, and the Modern; they correspond roughly to the less exciting ones here adopted, viz., unchanged, changing, and changed. Lerner's terms have varying operational definitions throughout his book. Sometimes they refer to behavior as specific as exposure to mass media (e.g., p. 136); at other times the division is based upon the number of opinions people have concerning public questions, since having an opinion is thought to be "a distinctive mark of modernity" (p. 71). Or each person is categorized on the basis of the following five attributes: the size of the community in which he lives, his education, his occupation, the degree to which he exposes himself to the mass media of communication, and the amount of empathy he reveals. Empathy, "the capacity to see oneself in the other fellow's situation," is measured by noting the replies to nine projective questions which ask what the person would do if he occupied certain positions (for example, that of an editor or head of the government) or were confronted with certain contingencies like having to choose another country in which to live; people with empathy are defined as those who can reply to the questions. All five attributes have been shown to be positively related—indeed the three "types" emerge empirically from a statistical analysis (ibid., pp. 438–46)—and result in a division of people not too dissimilar from that achieved by the other definitions. The weighting of the attributes for the two extreme types must be self-evident. The Traditional, for example, lives in a small community, usually rural; he has had an elementary education or less; he has a low-status occupation; he pays relatively little attention to the modern mass media like the newspaper and the radio; and he cannot imagine what he would say or do under circumstances different from his present ones. There is evidence indicating that "empathy" is the first attribute with respect to which the Transitional becomes Modern and that education is the last.

Interpretation of Rorschach Findings

Without question the Rorschach test is the formal instrument currently most popular among anthropologists, psychologists, and others who would obtain systematic insight into the traits or personalities of people in less civilized societies. The studies cited above, including the writer's own, and others which will be mentioned throughout these pages use some or all of the ingenious ink blots originally designed by the Swiss psychiatrist. The test has indeed two tremendous advantages.

In the first place, it is efficient. The technique of administration can be learned relatively quickly and painlessly by researchers whose primary interest is not in testing, clinical psychology, or psychiatry. The administration itself, moreover, is also no great chore, although repeated testing can become quite boring. An anthropologist can go about his principal occupation, that of collecting ethnographic data, and in his spare time or as a welcome variation administer the Rorschach. Then, secondly, the task of the test—reporting what one sees or what the blots remind one of, and then later indicating the portion of the blot producing the report and the reasons therefor—is one which people everywhere apparently can grasp. The culture of the person taking the test neither assists nor handicaps him, at least in comparison with other cultures.

The first advantage, efficiency, is freely and gratefully admitted. The second claim requires closer examination. Certainly diverse peoples are able to cooperate by responding to the blots, and in this sense the test does transcend the Swiss culture for which it was designed. The instrument, however, is not culture-free. Experience in the society, for example, affects the content of the responses. A number of this writer's Luo informants reported that the white space in the middle of Plate II reminded them of Lake Victoria next or near to which they reside; obviously this particular reaction is culture-bound. For present purposes, however, the fact that culture plays some role in eliciting the responses is in truth an asset, since the aim is to discover the effects upon people of varying degrees of civilization, and "varying degrees of civilization" is another way of saying "different cultures."

Intrinsically the scoring of Rorschach responses presents no particular problems when a quantitative approach is employed. A system of categories is selected from among those supplied by Rorschach experts; the number of times each category appears in the set of protocols obtained from each informant is counted; ratios between categories can be computed; and there emerges for the individual a profile of responses. The first difficulty arises when the scores from one person are compared with some standard in order to determine, for example, how "normal" he is or in what respects (i.e., Rorschach categories) he differs from his contemporaries or from any group. The quantitative norms of Rorschach scores, when they are made available, turn out to be like most norms, viz., they are central tendencies from which there are marked deviations even for a very restricted group. One Rorschach expert, for example, offers scores for "the population groups of various sections of Switzerland" (Oberholzer, 1944, p. 631). He does not specify the nature of those groups but his figures indicate marked variability; thus the "average" number of whole responses (W) is given as 8.27 and that of movement responses (M) as 2.68, but the standard deviation of these two figures is, respectively, 3.12 and 2.07. In the United States a group of investigators administered the Rorschach test to a random sample of 157 men and women chosen from the 4,650 employees of a Chicago mail-order house. They ranged in age from 17 to 69, with a mean around 30. From the principal findings which have been summarized in their Table 22 (Beck et al., 1950, p. 280), it seems evident that once again in almost all instances the standard deviation of a score either exceeds or approximates the mean. In different words, significant departures from the mean Rorschach scores are so numerous that the central tendency becomes a rather unimportant figure. The variability can be more easily grasped by noting how any one of the ten Rorschach cards were conceptualized in the study. On No. II, for example, the modal reaction was to report seeing dogs: 41 per cent of the sample did so. But the remaining 59 per cent produced a variety of impressions: bears (18 per cent); dancers, clowns, jitterbugs, or human beings (16 per cent); butterfly or moth (14 per cent); etc. (ibid., p. 280).

Since unknown and known groups within more civilized societies vary so greatly with respect to discrete Rorschach scores, it becomes difficult if not impossible to use such scores as a standard with which less civilized groups are to be compared. On an absolute basis, therefore, the precise position of a group on an alleged Rorschach continuum of civilization cannot with present knowledge be established. Even if civilized norms were known and represented more of a central tendency than they do, the scores within less civilized societies also vary considerably. In the Adult Section of the Indian-white study, described above, the investigator made a highly sophisticated analysis of the two Indian samples and the Spanish-American and Mormon groups; then he states:

> A very high degree of overlap among the groups is present, and this, coupled with the small size of the differences that do appear, indicates that the variability of individuals in any one culture is greater than the variability between cultures. . . . One of the conclusions we feel most confident about is that very great heterogeneity of personality occurs in all the groups studied [Kaplan, 1954, pp. 18, 32].

Often, however, differences between less and more civilized appear and, in spite of the great variability within the groups being compared, are of such magnitude that they cannot be attributed to chance. The differences may be based upon the quantitative scoring categories which have so far been discussed; or they may refer to qualitative patterns derived, for example, not from counting the various kinds of responses in each person's protocol but from a "sequential analysis" of the ways in which he tended to respond throughout. What then? It is of course possible merely to establish the fact of the differences, but any investigator wants to know more than that. What interpretation can be placed upon the differences?

The difficulty in providing an interpretation springs from the circumstance that even within the relatively restricted areas of Europe and America, there is no standarized way to interpret a protocol from a single person, much less from a group of persons. The disagreement occurs with reference to the interpretation to be placed upon quantitative scores as well as qualitative patterns. This is not to say that the Rorschach is valueless as a clinical tool to assist in the diagnosis of a particular person. In the hands of a skillful and experienced analyst the instrument is most valuable, but the artistry is most impressively demonstrated in relation to a specific person or problem at hand. On the basis of Rorschach protocols alone, for example, two Rorschach experts once clearly indicated—far, far above chance expectancy—which children in a large group were delinquent and which nondelinquent (Schachtel, 1951). Their success, however, resulted not from applying standardized interpretations to a group of Rorschach categories—as a matter of fact, few quantitative differences of any significance emerged—but by hypothesizing how delinquent and nondelinquent would react to being given the Rorschach test and by using what must be vaguely called clinical experience from the past. The Rorschach is such a promising instrument because of the fruitful assumption on which it is based: almost any response of a person, and certainly one which depends more upon him than upon blots which are such ambiguous stimuli, is likely to reflect some enduring disposition within him.

Even if there were Rorschach norms in a more civilized society such as the United States and even if the norms were found to be symptomatic of certain kinds of traits or personality among most people in particular groups in this country, nevertheless, it would not follow that results from Rorschach protocols in other cultures could be similarly interpreted. Perhaps they can be, but in each instance evidence must be adduced to justify the procedure. Fail-

ure to do so in the studies to be cited will occasionally be referred
to as the *Jumping Fallacy:* the investigator jumps from one society into another without saying why and how he does so. In
the anthropological literature which uses Rorschach data this
fallacy assumes two forms: in one, the jump is made without
documentation even from our own society; in the other, such
documentation is provided.

The first form seems more common. For 3 of 25 Indians in a
Guatemalan community who were given the Rorschach test, the
number of movement responses (M) exceeded the number of
color responses (sum C); for 14, the two numbers were equal;
and for 8, movement responses were fewer than color responses.
From this single finding, the investigators conclude in part:

> In their ultimate adjustment . . . most members of our
> Indian community try to establish an anxious and restricted
> balance in their responsiveness to inner experiences and en-
> vironmental stimulation. . . . They are not capable of re-
> sponding comfortably to any form of stimulus, and their
> marked rigidity causes them to constrict their inter- and in-
> tra-personal relationships, not permitting adequate spon-
> taneity [Billig, Gillin, and Davidson, 1947–48, pp. 328–329].

Without documentation two extravagant assumptions are thus
being made concerning this ratio of movement and color responses: it has the indicated significance in our society and it
has the same significance among the Indians.

The investigator in the Ojibwa study referred to above com-
mits the Jumping Fallacy when he seeks to shed light on a truly
fascinating problem, viz., which of the three groups—the least,
the most acculturated, or the one in the middle—is best "adjusted" to its environment and to the problems of the society. A
similar question pertaining to a disease could be answered with
dispatch by some objective measure like a blood count or chest
X ray. Indeed, he used the same approach for adjustment. He
compares the Indians' scores with some American norms and then
reaches his conclusion (Hallowell, 1955, pp. 353–6). Most unfortunately, with few exceptions, the norms have been obtained
from a single monograph which reports research on 102 superior

children in New York City and which also summarizes the interpretations given by three sets of Rorschach authorities in the
United States to various Rorschach categories, ratios, and combinations (Davidson, 1943, pp. 89–90). These measures have not
been adequately validated as "signs of adjustment"—or at least
relevant data are not supplied in the original source—but they
are utilized, apparently without modification, to interpret the responses of the Indian samples.

Other sins and fallacies committed by Rorschach testers among
less civilized people cannot be attributed to the test itself but
result from the difficulties confronting anyone armed with any
kind of psychological test. A very sophisticated study, for example, has been conducted among the Tuscarora Indians, a
small and highly acculturated group living on a reservation
within four miles of the city of Niagara Falls, New York. The
sampling problem ought to have been easily solved since the
author sought to select randomly only 70 informants out of a
total of 352 available adults. His sample, nevertheless, "does not
strictly follow the form of the population distribution," apparently because he could not use a random method of selection but
instead had to be recommended to new informants by those who
had already been given the test (Wallace, 1952, pp. 40–3). This
defect, however, cannot be ascribed to the Rorschach; if anything, the test usually wins cooperation more readily than an interview containing a series of personal questions.

In another study the investigator raises the intriguing question
as to why some North American Indian societies resisted white
men and others did not. Some of his answers will be suggested
elsewhere in this book (pp. 124, 185). For the moment consider
one tribe which cooperated, the Ojibwa, and another which resisted, the Dakota. Rorschach tests were given to small samples
of both groups. Protocols from adults among the former reveal
traits which are believed to be compatible with life both before
the white man and now on the reservation; whereas protocols
from children belonging to the latter tribe "reveal a personality
picture quite incompatible with what we know of the old society"
(Barnouw, 1950, pp. 64–5). From this difference the conclusion
is drawn that the personality of the Ojibwa did not have to

change but that of the Dakota did; hence compatibility between previous personality and that demanded by the white man's reservation accounts in part for cooperation or resistance. In order to support such a conclusion it is necessary to assume a relationship between a mode of living and personality traits, for otherwise there can be no assertion concerning traits that were compatible or incompatible with what is known concerning the old societies and concerning reservations. No doubt the assumption is justified, but its rationale—and the accompanying details and evidence—the investigator in question and no one else so far has made explicit. It is conceivable, for example, that the personality of the modern Dakota as revealed by a few children might have been quite suited to the old way of life. Certainly the nature of the Rorschach test as such does not demand that assumptions be recklessly made. Good anthropologists, when they are reckless, must be presuming that the Rorschach is as valid and reliable as Rorschach experts assert it to be or as their own instruments in fact often are; or else they do not apply their usual high standards to evaluate the borrowed technique.

The Spiraled Explanation

Virtually without exception all the evidence in this book is based upon a simple, straightforward procedure. Two groups are compared, one of which is known to be less and the other more acculturated. Both are measured or observed in a specified respect. Some figure is then made to represent each group because it reflects the average reaction of the people being measured or observed (as does a mean or a mode) or because it reveals how many people display the characteristic in question (as does a percentage). By means of a standardized statistical method, finally, it is determined whether the difference between the two figures could have arisen by chance or, if not, whether it can be called a "real" difference.

This cool, statistical approach has the decided virtue of being objective. In order to use a statistical formula at the very end of the analysis, it is necessary to have an apparent difference between two sets of figures which in turn reflect one or more attributes of the groups being compared. To obtain the figures, some kind of fairly precise measurement has been necessary. The investigator, consequently, is compelled to provide not just an impression of the two groups but a fairly precise estimate of the extent to which each one possesses the attribute that is the subject of the inquiry. "When we are told 'the rule is' for bride-wealth to be transferred at the time of marriage," one anthropologist declares, "it is a useful corrective to find that out of 60 married men questioned only 19 had actually followed the rule" (Schapera, 1935, p. 320).

The rub comes when a statistically significant difference is interpreted. It is literally true that the difference may be noted without comment, and so the conclusion is drawn only that the less acculturated group differs from the most acculturated one in the indicated respect. But why is there such a difference? The answer cannot come from statistics.

Consider briefly three kinds of differences:

1. Fewer people in the less acculturated group speak a European language (row 1, Table 1).

2. In two of the three African societies that were studied, the tendency for the less acculturated males to be older than the more acculturated is significant (row 8, Table 1).

3. A larger number of people in the more acculturated group are brighter as measured by a particular intelligence test (row 2, Table 9).

The statements indicate differences between less and more acculturated groups but they do not, and by themselves they cannot, reveal whether the differences have appeared *because* of acculturation. In each instance further analysis is needed.

In the first case, it ought to be easy to determine whether there is a connection between acculturation and speaking English. Those called more acculturated, for example, may have attended schools in which the language is taught, whereas the less acculturated have virtually no opportunity to learn another language. A *consequential* hypothesis seems called for, but the possibility of interaction cannot be excluded: those attending school do learn the language but those who learn the language, it might also be shown, are likely to attend school longer and hence become still more acculturated.

In the second illustration, the more acculturated African males in two of the societies tend to be younger. Here the definition of acculturation is explicitly based upon education. It is known that within recent years educational facilities for Africans have improved; hence more younger people are likely to have attended school and to have been included by definition in the more acculturated group. Other differences between the two groups, however, may be difficult to interpret. If the more acculturated solve certain intellectual problems more readily, for example, their superior ability in this respect may be related to their greater education or to their youth—or to both. Indeed the problem can be made more staggering by indicating that among the Ganda there is a significantly higher proportion of Roman Catholics among the less acculturated (46 vs. 19 per cent). The form of Christian religion, consequently, may have affected the ability in question either directly, because the less able may have been attracted to one religion rather than another; or indirectly, because one religion may encourage formal education to a greater degree. Obviously factors like age and religion could be equalized by selecting a less and a more acculturated group matched in these two respects. Among young Catholic Ganda, do those with little education differ from those with a great deal of schooling? Unfortunately, such a desirable procedure is seldom possible. For practical reasons, after the research is over, sub-subgroups of this type are likely to be too small to permit conclusions to be drawn. The locating of such people, moreover, may interfere with the sampling method. Most important of all, there may be no such people because in fact attributes like age, religion, and education are interrelated within the society itself.

The third kind of difference being discussed involves brightness. As Chapter 7 will argue at greater length, this factor cannot be conclusively considered a cause or an effect. If the items on which the score is based are ones which could have been learned only in a Western school, then it might seem that the superior performance of the better educated group results from the fact that they went to school. Still they may have gone to school originally because they were brighter; or if the less acculturated had gone to school, they might not have learned the items so readily. Again the possibility, doubtless the fact, of interaction appears.

In most instances of interaction it seems highly likely that the significant difference with respect to an attribute is the culmination of a process that extends either over generations or over a specific time period in the life of the particular groups being compared. For this reason most of the explanations must be called *spiraled*—as Ralph Linton once pointed out to the writer, this mathematical metaphor is better than *circular*, which suggests only movement without change. Originally a group changes for reasons that are known or unknown; while changing, it socializes the next generation differently; their acculturation is accelerated by the advantages they have had from the outside; and the spiral continues.

There ought to be at least two ways to escape from spiraled explanations and instead to provide truly causal ones. In the field of behavior, if there were measures not affected by cultural factors, a conclusion could be drawn concerning the role of such factors in aiding or preventing people from becoming civilized —but so far instruments of such a type simply do not exist. Then experimentation is the method par excellence of discovering cause-and-effect sequences. In less civilized societies, however, people cannot be randomly assigned to experimental and control groups; they select themselves in part and thus determine whether or not they will follow the spiraled path to increased civilization.

With imperfect instruments, it would appear that cross-cultural comparisons are especially risky and that comparisons of different groups within the same society are likely to be slightly more fruitful. Shortly after World War II, for example, two investigators administered a series of tests to 100 children in each of two societies on the island of Saipan. Children from the society they consider to be more acculturated were found to be "less reckless in their mental approach" to the Rorschach (Joseph and Murray, 1951, p. 195). Can this greater self-control be attributed to the greater degree of acculturation? Perhaps, but on a priori grounds it is just as likely that the trait may have been present in the society before contact with the West. If less acculturated children within the same society are more reckless than more acculturated ones, a spiraled explanation, to be sure, is not excluded, but at least it is not confounded with an additional cultural factor.

Remaining within a single society, moreover, has a closely related methodological advantage: imperfect measuring tools at least are likely to have similar significance to people sharing the same traditions. People react to questions and tests in different ways; hence one question or test may produce sharp differences between two societies but another which on the surface seems similar may not (Doob, 1957–58). There are literally thousands of forms of behavior that people in less civilized societies can learn from the more civilized: the objects range in size from a needle to a skyscraper, and the values range from the economic to the religious. In order to formulate consequential hypotheses, the forms of behavior must be central to the people concerned, and these forms vary more extensively from society to society than they do within a single society.

After having had its destination and mode of travel indicated in the first chapter, its point of departure in the second, and the anticipated scenery and trouble spots in the third, the safari is now finally ready to set out.

Chapter 4.

MOTIVES AND GOALS

WHY DO MEN become civilized? The psychological answer must immediately be: They become civilized because they are motivated to do so. They would or they may no longer seek some of the old goals; new goals appeal to them. What happens to them when they become civilized? Their goals change; instead of being motivated to engage in old forms of behavior, they engage in new ones. These rather banal statements are not quite so redundant as they sound, for the answers to the two questions are thereby reduced to motives and goals, which are postulated components of all behavior.

Discontent

Discontent almost always precedes learning. The perfectly satisfied person, it may be presumed, has no reason to exert himself and therefore remains unchanged. Normally, however, everyone faces a series of crises before and after maturation. The discipline distributed during socialization to encourage growth and produce conformity is far from pleasant. The adolescent must begin to assume greater responsibilities that require him to learn new forms of economic, social, and political behavior. Then the crop which the adult plans is ruined, the leader whom he reveres snubs him, the wife to whom he is devoted dies—tragedy or the possibility of tragedy faces him at every turn.

Ordinarily institutions are at hand to help frustrated people solve their problems, resolve their dilemmas, or attain different goals. In less civilized societies, it has been suggested, there is a measure of security for all people, or at least insecurity seems to be somewhat equitably shared. Sometimes, however, the crisis persists, and the institutions at hand are inadequate or seem to be. Then those who are truly and miserably discontent may be ready to depart from the usual routine and to change. Acculturation occurs during such a persisting crisis and must be viewed first as a response to, and then as a producer of, discontent.

Although the self-imposed historical limitations of the present book block an effort to glance at less civilized societies prior to contact and to account for the establishment of the contacts themselves, it is tempting to suggest that for most societies the original discontent has come in large part from outside forces. Less civilized people have tended to be weak either because they lacked numbers or the weapons with which to defend themselves. Or else the advent of more civilized men has had serious repercussions even though the old society has not been overrun; game becomes scarce, for example, because settlers from the West occupy the land or because native hunters learn to hunt more efficiently with civilized guns. In either case there is misery which can be alleviated only by modifying old forms of behavior or adopting new ones. The Indians of North America may have tried to reject white ways as they were pushed back into reservations, but some of them had to learn the customs of the invaders in order to carry on negotiations. Throughout most of sub-Saharan Africa, African males must contribute to government usually through a head tax; to earn the necessary money, they must often work in a European mine or factory or on a European farm; to be and to remain employable, they must acquire the necessary European skills. For better or worse, Pandora's box is thus opened either for society even when only a few people adopt the change or for the individual even when he appears to change only most segmentally.

The discontent within the less civilized person may be specific or general. When in fact he has the choice, he may seek to learn a new form either because the old one appears unsatisfactory to him or because he anticipates greater satisfaction from the new. Tools and machines very often have such a specific appeal. Or he may be generally discontent with his society either because too many of its institutions fail to satisfy his needs or because one specific frustration, being severe, colors his entire outlook. This latter kind of discontent may be facilitated by catching a glimpse of the new, since radical rejection of the old is more likely to occur after the individual has been convinced that life as a whole conceivably can be sweeter.

Whether the motivation to learn the new springs from specific or general sources—or from both—the ensuing learning itself is likely to prove disturbing for a variety of reasons: acculturation produces misery. In the first place, learning per se is seldom pleasant. Concentration and expenditure of energy are required, especially when old ways are unlearned. Many aspects of civilization are obviously complicated and intricate—think of the details that must be mastered for a less civilized person to become a clerk or a mechanic, and contrast that learning process with the older one in which traditional techniques could be almost unwittingly and hence relatively painlessly absorbed during socialization. The simplicity of the old may be unsatisfactory, but the complexity of the new is frustrating too.

The alterations in the old way of life, desirable though they may appear, can be viewed as a threat to the restricted security that less civilized societies usually provide. The crumbling of an absolute faith in the order of things is not pleasant. Uncertainty concerning one's role, one's responsibilities, one's group, in fact one's entire future, appears. Acknowledging that some old forms of behavior are imperfect suggests that the entire pattern may have its flaws. General criticism of this sort seems probable in view of the unified nature of less civilized categories that has been previously postulated.

Divine discontent can turn to bitterness and despair when the individual, fired to change himself, discovers that for reasons he cannot control the way to change is obstructed. He cannot obtain the money needed to carry on his education. He is the victim of prejudice and hence certain jobs are automatically barred to him. He would mingle socially with people already civilized, and he finds that he is either discouraged or prevented from doing so. He may conclude that the color of his skin, which he can never change, will always be a handicap to him. In fact, if the modern critics of colonialism and imperialism are correct, the frustrations have been both numerous and deep. One sensitive writer, for example, refers to "the cruelties, the crippling injury of spirit and the fundamental dishonor that African societies and other less advanced peoples in the world have to endure from being forced into contact with us" (Van Der Post, 1955, p. 130).

Opposition to change is also likely to come from vested interests within the old society. Their resistance appears both compelling and impressive when they have prestige because of age or position, and their hostility, flowing through the traditional channels of the group, is apt to be perceived by almost everyone. The proponents of change themselves may feel chagrined when they later discover that what may have seemed at first to be a few additions to the old society have later begun to alter its basic pattern and the traditional way of life. Even without such a discovery the attainment of new goals may mean the further recession of ultimate content. Needs may multiply: when one aspect of civilization is obtained, others may be sought. New responsibilities can create stress and strain. Guilt concerning the rejection of the old can remain, and the individual may regret that he has learned what he is now committed to retain.

Let an anthropologist provide the summary of the argument being advanced: "Because a culture is made up of interdependent parts, the acceptance of something new *always* entails stresses and dislocations" (Barnett, 1953, p. 373). The present writer has placed the adverb in italics in order to celebrate the rare occasion on which a universal proposition emerges from anthropology. Clearly, then, since people in pain are ready to change and since changing is painful, an interactional hypothesis is called for:

> HYPOTHESIS 1 (*interactional*): *In comparison with those who remain unchanged or who have changed, people changing from old to new ways are likely to be more discontent.*

After this, the first of many hypotheses, it may be well to pause and recall the psychological limitations from which generalizations in the area of acculturation inevitably suffer. Here the hypothesis merely asserts that the amount of discontent among the changing is greater than that among the unchanged. It does not suggest that increased civilization brings no satisfaction or that those clinging to traditional forms are perfectly content. In fact, it is highly likely that the modal reaction of various groups in a society varies, unless everyone is suffering from some common misery such as famine. Children in all probability respond differently from adults. They may be unacquainted with some or many of the problems their elders must face. Or they may be in a state of conflict their parents can avoid, for example, when in a Western-type school they are taught a set of beliefs at variance with those being promulgated at home.

Evidence from the Africa-Jamaica studies appears in the first five rows of Table 2 under the heading "Discontent" (p. 284). In the three African societies the trend consistently supports the hypothesis, but relatively few of the differences are statistically significant. In Jamaica, on the other hand, the better educated, although projecting misery to a greater degree (row 1), are otherwise significantly less discontent. From birth on they have been taught highly civilized forms of behavior and their frustrations, consequently, tend to be only those associated with leadership and responsibility; in contrast, the less well educated are changing and discontent.

An increase in discontent during acculturation seems evident in other studies too. In the South African cities of Johannesburg and Pretoria, 283 middle-class clerks and professionally trained personnel, coming principally from two African societies, responded in the midst of a long schedule to the following item: "Tell all the things you dislike about your job." To the two factors of education and urbanization which the investigator herself used as indexes of acculturation may be added that of occupation by assuming that professional people are better acquainted with European culture than clerks. Not all the differences are significant, but the data of the study reveal an unmistakable tendency for all the sources of frustration to be mentioned more frequently by the Africans having greater contact with European society. Differences are most marked with respect to occupation, least in the case of urbanization (Sherwood, 1959). The results reflect no doubt not only the misery as each person perceives it but also his ability to keep an inventory of his troubles and then to verbalize them.

American Indians in particular have experienced frustrations while becoming civilized or resisting civilization. Direct evidence on the point is not provided for the children who were the subjects in the Indian-white study. This writer, therefore, has taken data for each of the eight samples from tables 4 and 6 of the monograph by Havighurst and Neugarten (1955, pp. 36, 38) and, on the working assumption that discontent people are more likely to mention sad rather than happy incidents, has calculated the ratio of sad to all other incidents. The association between these ratios and acculturation ranks (*rho*) is found to be +.14—in the expected direction but not statistically significant. In Table A (p. 304) a relation between acculturation and the tendency to think in terms of individual rather than group goals is evident (rows 1 and 2)—perhaps discontent is less intense when the person thinks of others rather than himself.

The anthropological analysis of the Navaho as a whole, moreover, indicates profound discontent. Their culture has remained relatively intact in spite of prolonged contact with Americans. At one extreme are those who speak no English and have otherwise insulated themselves as much as possible from white society: "at the very least," according to an anthropologist and psychiatrist who have studied them intensively, they are "disturbed to see their children adopting non-Navaho ways, and indeed they see their whole world dissolving around them." At the other extreme are those who know English, especially those who have been to school: their "frustration and conflict" are said to be much more intense. School itself is a disturbing experience. The child must leave home in order to attend. He is taught not by Indians but by white Americans. Two values in the school particularly embarrass or distress him because they differ so markedly from what he has learned from his own family: "the great stress upon competition between individuals" and "the lack of definite status for the child at each age grade." By remaining at school he inevitably acquires new forms of behavior which then are at variance with those in Navaho society. He has become, for example, "accustomed to white food, white clothing, white standards of cleanliness." He feels himself a stranger because, having been away, he has not learned the myths and religious procedures of his own people. Although he is likely to retain deep affection for his parents, he may be disturbed by their older ways, and they in turn may be disturbed by his disturbance and by his new forms. Under these painful circumstances, he may decide to shift away from his Navaho home and move toward the white civilization whose ways he has been taught. At this point he experiences the most ironic frustration: members of the same society which has educated him do not bid him welcome, rather most of them are ready to block his progress through discrimination and prejudice. The very skills and values which brought him reward at school now produce only misery since they might enable him to compete successfully with white people (Kluckhohn and Leighton, 1946, pp. 112, 113; Leighton and Kluckhohn, 1948, pp. 68, 69, 74).

Any shift in culture, it would appear, requires some kind of "adjustment," which means that difficulty and pain are the lot of people anywhere either when they receive new ways from an outside society or when they themselves migrate from one country to another (Ruesch et al., 1948). The difficulty and the pain, however, need not be intense. In fact it has been contended that, when two societies have contact with each other, "radical modifications in the culture of either group" need not be precipitated and that the new learning may not be disruptive (Hallowell, 1955, p. 316). In the instances cited, however, peculiar conditions seem to have prevailed. The people were well satisfied with their own society. They carefully regulated the manner and the degree of contact. They accepted relatively little from the outside society. Neither society in contact sought to dominate the other.

Not only may the discontent accompanying acculturation be minimal but it may also be accompanied by gratification of a basic or superficial sort. The proportion of discontent and gratification, moreover, may vary over a period of time. During the first fifteen years of contact with Americans, the White Knife Shoshoni Indians of Nevada, for example, endured minor frustrations: they met only a small number of trappers, who in turn induced few changes in their society. Grief came later when the discovery of gold and silver brought streams of people into the area. Even then, although the transition from a food-gathering economy to agriculture and then to herding engendered some hostility toward white people, these Indians are reported to have been "comparatively free of maladjustments" for a unique combination of reasons. They did not have to associate intimately with white people. They had been living in a society sufficiently simple and also sufficiently similar to white society at crucial points so that there was virtually no conflict in values. They were pleased, finally, by the increase in material goods which the expanding economy brought (Harris, 1940). Such a relatively easy transition from a less to a more civilized state is not unique in the history of acculturation, even among American Indians (e.g., Honigmann, 1941). Both on a theoretical and a practical level, corollaries are needed to indicate the conditions promoting an excess of content over discontent. For example: *Acculturation can proceed more pleasantly and less painfully when during the transition people's basic needs (food, shelter, etc.) are satisfied and when their central values can remain intact.*

Hypothesis 1 suggests that the changing are likely to be *more* discontent than the unchanging. It is possible, however, that the latter may also feel discontent, though less. They may not like to see some of their contemporaries moving in nontraditional directions. They may feel that their entire way of life is threatened and that any shift to the new forms of behavior would be unsatisfying and undesirable. They may in fact—because the superior power from the West has seized land or laid down regulations—be unable to pursue the old ways. In contrast, those who are changing, although they must endure some difficulties, may derive satisfaction from the fact that they are changing. A case in point seems to be the Middle East at the present time. "In general, how do you feel about your life; are you happy with the way things have turned out for you, or not?" When that question was placed before the samples of the six countries, the highest proportion reporting discontent was—except for Egypt—not among the Transitionals but among the Traditionals. (Lerner, 1958, p. 100). These countries are seeking to modernize many of their ways as rapidly as possible. Traditional people, therefore, are frustrated either by the changes they must witness or by their own inability to change or to change sufficiently rapidly. Only in Turkey and Lebanon, the two countries which have "progressed" most, are the Transitionals and Moderns scarcely distinguishable from each other with respect to expressed satisfaction; in the other countries, evidently, *not* to be Modern is frustrating.

Aggressiveness

When people are discontent, they seek to mitigate their misery and to improve the state of affairs which surround them or which they are experiencing within themselves. The discontent accompanying social contact can lead to various forms of behavior. Those remaining unchanged, for example, may cling more fiercely than heretofore to the old ways and join so-called nativistic movements which emphasize, in slightly different form, the old glories of the tribe and its ancient ceremonies and beliefs. People in the process of changing may seek just as vigorously to accelerate the learning of more civilized ways by going to school, changing occupation, associating with Europeans, etc. Not an absolutely certain but a highly probable component of the reaction to adversity is aggressiveness: people would destroy their real or imagined tormentors either literally or symbolically. They seek, respectively, to hurt or harm them or else to imagine or dream of the damage which they would heap upon them (Dollard et al., 1939). Such aggressiveness is the present concern.

Every society contains potential targets for the aggression people inevitably experience as a result of living together and of scarcities that are naturally or artificially created. Presumably, when less civilized societies are enjoying stability, these targets by and large are traditional ones, like enemies from outside or people close at hand with whom a joking relationship, containing aggressive components, is countenanced. During social contact there is, it has been suggested, a differential increase in discontent, and simultaneously those bringing changes from the outside and those accepting or resisting change within the society can become new targets for aggression. In fact, the inability to know precisely against whom it is permissible and respectable

to express aggression is in itself frustrating, and can add to diffuse
aggressiveness. It must follow that:

> HYPOTHESIS 2 (*interactional*): *In comparison with those who
> remain unchanged or who have changed, people changing
> from old to new ways are likely to feel more aggressive.*

More often than not the above hypothesis is consequential: the
aggression results from the increased discontent arising from the
changes and frustrations characteristic of acculturation. It is
termed interactional, however, because in some situations aggression can play a causative role; for example, new forms of behavior
are learned in order to express hostility toward old associates or
toward outsiders.

In the Africa-Jamaica studies (see Table 2, p. 284, under "Aggressiveness"), there is a very slight tendency for more Africans
with a high than with a low degree of education to express hostility toward vaguely drawn characters in TAT-type sketches
(rows 6–11); to respond to the question concerning what "you
like and dislike" about other ethnic groups and leaders by mentioning only or by mentioning first what they dislike (rows
12–16); and to say in effect that hostility surrounds them (rows
17, 18). Few of the differences, however, are statistically significant and a very few are even opposed to the hypothesis. On a
single question, fewer of the relatively well educated African
adolescents than the adults project aggressiveness upon the external world (see p. 299, Table I, row 1), which is perhaps only a
tribute to the sweet hopefulness of youth.

The results from Jamaica are slightly complicated. On the one
hand, all the significant differences, with one exception, indicate
a higher proportion of aggressive responses among the better
educated; these differences have been obtained by means of
projective or semiprojective questions (Table 2, rows 6, 8–11).
On the other hand, the exception supports the hypothesis: more
of the higher-status informants find hostility surrounding them
(row 18).

It seems useful to pause for a moment and inquire why one
set of questions produces responses in Jamaica that are contrary
to the hypothesis and another question supports it. In theory what

is needed is a validating criterion. Informally the writer observed that in real life poorly educated Jamaicans often expressed hostility in brawls, jokes, complaints, etc., and that the better educated ones were externally much more placid and pleasant. Perhaps, then, the aggressiveness of the latter could be tapped only when they were taken unawares by the projective questions. Or the poorly educated may have deliberately controlled their aggression while being questioned by an American with whom they doubtless wished to curry favor. It may be that the presence or absence of aggression has not been correctly inferred from observed or verbal behavior—the investigator may be guilty of the Jumping Fallacy, i.e., applying his own standards to people for whom such behavior has a different meaning. In addition, it is also possible that in fact the aggressiveness of the two groups is expressed differently, i.e., in different situations or against different targets. It would seem, consequently, that measuring discontent and aggressiveness in a single interview is a hazardous undertaking: the search for general traits of behavior can be conducted only by ascertaining verbal replies concerning rather specific conduct. The failure to obtain more striking differences, consequently, may be due to faulty questions or to the fact that probably deeper levels of the personality cannot be reached within a period of two hours; or the hypotheses themselves may be incorrect.

Other data from Africa provide another illustration of the same point. Appended to the questionnaire which was used in the Ganda junior secondary school was a series of personal questions which were addressed to the 215 boys in a very crude, straightforward manner (Table II, p. 301). A comparison of the lower and higher forms or grades reveals no significant differences with respect to the percentage claiming that they tend to have unpleasant dreams, and that they tend to remember happy rather than unhappy events (rows 12 and 14). It could be assumed the older children had had more contact with European culture as a result of being in a greater state of conflict, for example, concerning Ganda and European values; hence greater degrees of frustration and aggressiveness ought to be reflected in the items just mentioned. Such is not the case. But two of the items did produce significant differences, and in the expected direction: more of the older than the younger boys claim that they "often feel afraid without reason" and that they "worry" about their health (rows 9 and 13). Evidently, then, this school population was identical in some but certainly not in all respects. The two hypotheses receive some vindication, which bringeth slight consolation.

Still more consolation comes from other studies which indicate a positive relationship between acculturation and aggressiveness. Within the same Guatemalan community, for example, live two quite culturally distinct groups, Indians and Ladinos. The Indians have "a heavily acculturated, but stabilized, version of native culture"; whereas the Ladinos are people of Spanish ancestry whose orientation is toward urban civilization. The Rorschach test was administered to samples of 25 males drawn from each group. The point-by-point statistical analysis of the protocols reveals, in the view of this writer, no startling differences, but the investigators themselves have noted—in large part, to be sure, by committing the Jumping Fallacy—that "aggressive signs appear about five times as often in Ladinos as in Indians." Both cultures, they add, are "restricted in scale." That of the Indians tends to be "homogeneous, integrated, relatively self-sufficient." In contrast, Ladino culture is "less closely integrated" and creates "wants and desires which cannot be fully satisfied by the cultural resources" of the community (Billig, Gillin, and Davidson, 1947–48, pp. 364–5).

One reason why it is difficult methodologically to ascertain aggressiveness stems from the fact that hostility can assume a variety of forms. Here the most pressing question must be: Will people become overtly aggressive or will they simply feel aggressive without expressing those feelings in action? In 1952, for example, it might have been difficult to find important differences between the Luo and the Kikuyu, two societies living in adjoining areas in Kenya. Both certainly felt frustrated by the European settlers especially with reference to the ownership of land. The latter, however, constituted the main stream of those who formed the overtly hostile Mau Mau, whereas almost none of the former were attracted to the movement. The Luo of course are not unique. Again and again Ganda told this writer that they disliked Europeans and that therefore they refused to be interviewed because the British had sent their king into exile. Aside from a certain coolness in personal relations and sporadic and unsuccessful boycotts of European shops, virtually none of the aggression spilled over into overt activity; instead the people maintained traditional discipline and restraint. The Ojibwa Indians felt hostile toward white men, as other Indian tribes did, but—for reasons which are ascribed to their social organization, their personalities, and various historical circumstances—they almost never openly attacked the invaders (Barnouw, 1950, pp. 30–48). In the same society, finally, people may be overtly aggressive at one time, covertly at another. Hawaii is a case in point, although usually different forms of behavior have been exhibited by different ethnic groups (Burrows, 1947).

The need for a corollary which specifies the conditions promoting one form of aggressiveness rather than another, therefore, seems evident. A beginning is suggested by a study based upon American college students: *The tendency for aggressiveness to be overt rather than covert is positively related to the seriousness of the discontent and negatively to the anticipated punishment from being overtly aggressive* (Doob and Sears, 1939). Whether or not such a corollary is applicable to, or can be tested adequately within, a particular society as a whole is not known. Certainly it is extremely difficult to try to estimate the strength of the two reactions—the seriousness of the discontent and the anticipated punishment—and then, when they point in opposite directions, to compare them. If the domination of the ruling group from the outside is fiercely resented, for example, overt aggression should be anticipated; but if a tradition against unseemly behavior is enforced by social punishment, then covert aggression should be anticipated. Which impulse will prove stronger?

One final note of warning must be struck concerning aggressiveness: while some forms of aggressiveness in a society are more important than others and while one form may characterize the behavior of more people or of all people more frequently than another, it is well to observe that reactions to the discontent of acculturation are usually varied. In the previous section the reasons why Navaho Indians feel frustrated and disturbed have been indicated. Their reactions to such misery have been catalogued as follows (Kluckhohn and Leighton, 1946, pp. 113–14):

> Focus their energies upon trying to be as like whites as possible
>
> Becoming followers of vocal leaders [within their own society]
>
> Factional quarrels
>
> Family fights
>
> Phantasies about witchcraft or [attacks upon] "witches"
>
> Verbal and other indirect hostilities toward whites
>
> Fits of depression
>
> Humor and . . . "joking relationships" with certain relatives
>
> Actual physical withdrawal
>
> The escape of narcotics, alcohol, and sex
>
> Intensified participation in rites of the native religion and [turning to] new cults (e.g., peyote)
>
> Rigid compartmentalization of their lives and feelings and . . . various rationalizations.

Each solution seems to contain an aggressive component. The effort to be as like white people as possible, for example, may be motivated in part by a desire to demonstrate the individual's own ability in spite of prejudice; or "fits of depression" could be a form of self-aggression. The existence of so many alternate forms suggests that neither the old nor the changing culture has provided solutions for the problem of how to cope with white civilization; the Navaho are still engaging in trial-and-error behavior.

Postponement and Renunciation

Some of the problems besetting people cannot be left unresolved for very long. These usually involve basic drives referring to food, drink, oxygen, the elimination of wastes, the reduction of physical pain, etc. Other problems need not be immediately solved but people are often reluctant to wait: the scratching of an itch, the lighting of the next cigarette, the appropriate response to an inviting smile, etc. Still others, like ambitions to be achieved at a later age, remain baffling or inspiring for long periods of time.

Perhaps one of the most outstanding human characteristics is the ability to tolerate delay. The child's period of dependence upon his parents, in comparison with that of animals, is so long that at some time during the period he must learn to anticipate instead of instantly realizing the goals which he seeks. It seems reasonable to suppose that a great change in the history of mankind was the invention or discovery of activities that bring future but not necessarily present gratification. A nomadic society lives in the present: its people wander until they find the plants or animals which, in the virtual absence of preservative techniques, are immediately consumed. In contrast, pastoral and agricultural people must tend their animals and crops before consumption can occur; they must work now so that they can benefit later.

There appears to be a fairly marked difference between less and more civilized peoples with respect to the amount of renunciation which is willingly endured. The contrast is especially evident in connection with educating children. In less civilized societies education almost always occurs in the context of the home and the immediate neighborhood. Again and again, for example, anthropologists have noted the important role older siblings play in the educational process. Only while learning a particular task, or perhaps while participating in an initiation ritual, is the child likely to be taken out of his normal milieu and then for a relatively brief period. Such education from most standpoints must be considered utilitarian: it seeks to teach the individual to solve the problems at hand or those which can be easily anticipated; it would indoctrinate him with the rules and values of his society so that forever after he will know how to behave and what to expect from his contemporaries under specified circumstances. In these ways, as it were, he is prepared for a relatively small society in which he will have face-to-face contact with the people of importance to him and in which the solutions for most problems are close at hand; he enjoys, as has been previously contended, a restricted and a momentary sense of security. Indeed a relatively absolute faith and a relatively absolute belief in the validity of one's values make it less necessary to find evidence for the faith and the belief in the future—the present suffices. It is possible that part of the simplicity which has been ascribed to less civilized people results from their partial confinement within the temporal dimensions of the present and the past.

Formal education in more civilized societies, on the other hand, is quite different. The knowledge and values required of good citizens are also taught, but after the first five years or so this teaching occurs in schools which are deliberately separated from the child's home and—during school hours—from the rest of society. Even at a primary level, moreover, the curriculum contains subjects whose connection with real problems is not always apparent either to pupil or teacher. Over and over again questions are raised which are supposed to "develop" the student; in fact, schooling through graduate and professional school in part prepares the student to solve problems whose content cannot be concretely anticipated. Such education is obviously geared to the future.

Without exaggeration it may be contended that life in general in more civilized countries is based upon the assumption that impulses can be curbed. Young people are urged to delay matrimony until they are ready to assume the financial and emotional responsibilities. People save money which they could easily spend now so that their children can be educated or so that they can provide for themselves in their old age. A modern state virtually depends upon the sacrifice and postponement inherent in its systems of currency, banking, and taxation. In the area of health, too, people forego the sweets and carbohydrates they crave because they have been taught that overweight taxes the heart— or some of them do. They are willing to endure the quick agony of the dentist's drill or the long trauma of the surgeon's operation for the sake of their future well-being. The future determines the present.

The theme of patient renunciation thus pervades the thinking of Western men. To his followers Jesus said, "In your patience possess ye your soul" (St. Luke). Rousseau would have Emile learn that "patience is bitter but its fruits are sweet" (Book 3). Freud (1930) emphasized the belief that basic impulses are curbed in childhood so that later they may be released in altered and acceptable form. Weber (1930) singled out Puritanical "asceticism" as part of "the spirit of capitalism" which the Reformation foreshadowed and encouraged before the coming of large-scale industry: if men had not believed it sinful to consume their earnings here and now, they would not have been ready to put aside large portions for capital investment.

A sociologist has specified that one of the "common human problems" men everywhere must face involves the question, "What is the significant time dimension?" "Obviously," she states, "all societies at all times must deal with all the three time problems . . . [but they differ] in their emphasis on past, present or future at a given period, and a very great deal can be told about the particular society or part of a society being studied, much about the direction of change within it can be predicted, with a knowledge of where that emphasis is." For middle-class America, which represents the dominant culture in the United States, she thinks the evidence points to a future orientation (F. R. Kluckhohn, 1950, pp. 378–80, 383). Empirical studies in fact support her view that such an emphasis upon the future—or on what others call "the deferred gratification pattern" or "impulse renunciation"—characterizes the more highly socialized and hence more highly civilized groups within the society. Both Negro and white middle-class children have been found to orient themselves toward the future more frequently than children from the lower class (Davis and Dollard, 1940). More children assigning themselves to the "working class" than those claiming "middle-class" membership replied to the question, "If you won a big prize, say two thousand dollars, what would you do?" by saying they would "spend most of it right away" rather than "save most of it" (Schneider and Lysgaard, 1953). When asked to compose stories, middle-class children selected plots extending over a longer period of time than those from the lower class (LeShan,

1952); and a similar difference emerged when stories of non-delinquent and delinquent boys were compared (Barndt and Johnson, 1955).

Out of such considerations emerges the following hypothesis:

HYPOTHESIS 3 (*consequential*): *People changing centrally from old to new ways are likely to become more tolerant of delay in the attainment of goals.*

Hypothesis 3 is thought to be consequential because the ability to tolerate delay, as suggested above, is emphasized in more civilized societies and, as indicated below, is less important in less civilized ones; hence those who are changing or have changed have acquired or improved their ability as a consequence of acculturation. It is possible that some members of the old society, for reasons to be found in their own peculiar experiences or perhaps even in the innate determinants of their temperaments, are prone to be patient before learning new ways and that they are singled out or choose to become more civilized for this very reason. Evidence for such a view, however, would be exceedingly difficult to collect. Attention is called to the word "centrally" in this and all other consequential hypotheses: unless people have been changed in central rather than segmental respects, the hypothecated consequence is not likely to occur.

Relevant evidence from the Africa-Jamaica studies appears in the last section of Table 2 under "Postponement" (p. 283). By and large the trend supports the hypothesis, although most of the differences by themselves are not statistically significant and in a few instances among the Ganda they are in the opposite direction. More of the highly than of the poorly educated Africans and Jamaicans feel favorably disposed toward planning for the future (row 19), although—except for the Ganda—they are not appreciably different with respect to the long-range plans they claim to have (row 20); they prefer money for investment, or prefer a larger sum in the future instead of a smaller one immediately (row 21); they know concretely and realistically how a windfall could be spent (row 22); and they can indicate what they think will happen to them within the next five years (row 24). Fewer of the better educated Jamaicans think of money as something to spend (row 23) or find it impossible to anticipate events in their country (row 25). In comparison with less well educated adults, fewer of the Luo and Ganda youth in European schools disapprove of planning, but more of them prefer to be punished rather than to endure a threat concerning the future; and in the one Ganda school taught by Africans disapproval of planning runs significantly higher, particularly in the lower grades (Table I, row 2).

In retrospect the writer feels that the questions upon which the above results are based are not sufficiently discriminating. The poorly educated Ganda, for example, with few exceptions were cultivators. At the time the Uganda government, through the Ganda's own chiefs, was carrying on an extensive campaign to spread scientific information about agriculture in order to increase the yield per acre and to counteract older methods that lead to the erosion of the land. Under these circumstances many cultivators had to have plans for the future and therefore replied affirmatively when asked whether "you make plans for a year or more in advance." In contrast, some of those in the more highly educated group worked for a government bureau and so, like civil servants perhaps everywhere, they did not at that time have to concern themselves with those aspects of their future which they knew would be ordained by official decree.

The only relevant evidence from the Indian-white study comes from a category the authors called "self-restraint" as they coded the spontaneous answers to the question concerning what the children considered "good things and bad things to do" (Table A, row 3). The quality was considered to be present when the child seemed to suggest that he was curbing "self-indulgence" not so much because of the effect of his behavior upon other people but "because of what we expect of *you* as an individual" (Havighurst and Neugarten, 1955, p. 99). In fact, "self-restraint" so defined distinguishes the more acculturated from the less acculturated Navaho, and it is correlated with degree of acculturation for the Indian societies as a group. The latter correlation is not significant, perhaps because only around 10 per cent of the children in each society reveal the trait. The fact that the measure fails to distinguish the Hopi from the Navaho is at odds with the anthropological finding that the former "stress foresight and preparatory activities" and the latter "take advantage of the moment, enjoying the excitement of sudden and intense activity for immediate gains" (Thompson, 1951, p. 42). More than one-quarter of the Midwestern American children, nevertheless, reveal admiration for such "self-restraint" and thus are significantly different from the Indians. The authors themselves offer the following explanation:

> It would seem that for white children the control of impulse life constitutes a real moral problem. Self-restraint and self-indulgence carry strong moral overtones; and the child is aware of a whole range of behaviors in this area that are condemned or rewarded, approved or disapproved. The white child, more than the Indian child, is concerned over what amusements he may or may not properly engage in; what people he should or should not associate with [ibid., p. 107].

Less systematic but dramatic evidence for the hypothesis is at hand in connection with the fiscal and banking forms from the West which in effect provide only symbols in the present for objects and services in the future. Almost any colonial official has a choice anecdote to recall on this score; a chief in Tanganyika, for example, is reported to have had no trouble in comprehending the depression of the thirties:

> I quite understand the situation. Do you remember about three years ago some white men came to Mwanza and started a shop they called "Banki"? Well, they started then to buy the shillings; now they've got them. That's all! [Mitchell, 1954, p. 135].

According to an old report, Africans in the city of Pretoria once evolved a system of saving which rendered the institution intelligible to them and also provided rewards not too distantly removed from the act of renunciation. A small number of friends each week or each month contributed a specified amount to a general fund which was then immediately handed to one contributor as a lump sum; the next time it would be another man's turn. The device was convenient: the participants did not have to deposit money in a bank during its regular hours, they did not have to have a bank book, and in general they did not have to follow usual banking procedures. It also seemed safer to them since only friendly Africans and not strange European tellers and guards were involved. Most important of all, according to the anthropologist who studied this informal institution, "The amount payable every week or month may not be greatly missed, or at any rate would never be saved at all without the aim of some binding force"; each person, consequently, periodically received "a large sum of money" which was exceedingly useful to him (Krige, 1934, pp. 101–2).

The last illustration suggests that some form of saving probably exists in most societies but that a reward in the present may have to be provided. Some modern Greeks, especially in rural areas, it is said, cannot be easily persuaded to invest money in industry since they "trust only a sure thing, the known present." Instead they derive satisfaction from continuing to perceive the money which they keep as a tangible "lump under the mattress" (Mead, 1955, p. 239). In Africa, according to one investigator, the cattle men prize so highly and also certain Western traits like clothes and sewing machines represent forms of "stored wealth" which, when the occasion arises, can be sold or exchanged. In the meantime the owner sees and enjoys the "living capital" or the useful objects; in contrast "European money is indirect and unreal in its more complicated symbolic valuation" (Thurnwald, 1935, pp. 285–6).

Similarly the Western method of taxation is not easily comprehended by people in less civilized societies. At some sad moment they must give to the tax collector money, goods, or services for which they will be rewarded in the future by governmental services whose existence or importance they may not appreciate. In fact, it seems that the symbolic value of money in general is learned only gradually and that at first the referents for which the money stands and which bring direct satisfaction are relatively close at hand. In the Guatemalan community previously referred to, both the Indians and the Ladinos seek money. The Indians, however, want money not to obtain the status, power, and prestige it eventually brings to the Ladinos, but "to buy food, shelter, and clothing, and to avoid the actual physical punishment which is involved in failure to pay taxes, rents, and other obligations" (Gillin, 1945, p. 10).

The extension of credit is another device whereby needs are first satisfied and then saving occurs; in contrast, paying cash usually means that people must save first and later satisfy their needs. Credit or installment buying exists throughout the modern world, but it is this writer's casual impression that virtually every shop in East and South Africa as well as in Jamaica extends credit and that very little is ever purchased for cash. Credit, it is said, is necessary because people becoming more civilized do not have enough money. The argument, though, is fallacious, for eventually people pay (or most of them do). Indeed, they pay more than they would under a cash economy since an elaborate system of bookkeeping must be instituted to keep track of their debts—clerks from the bush in Africa sometimes think that the essence of civilization is the form which must be executed in triplicate. Aside from reducing the feeling of sacrifice at the moment when the temptation to buy is strong, the credit system also provides a way to induce people to satisfy their needs by consuming new goods; and eventually they become more fully enmeshed in the Western economic system.

The shift in temporal orientation from the past or present to the future is frequently reported to be associated with acculturation. Such a change is clearly detectable in case histories of Navaho Indians who are in the process of acquiring American values and practices (Vogt, 1951, pp. 85–6). Officials from the West who work in so-called underdeveloped areas know that this change in orientation cannot occur immediately and hence at first the present cannot be completely neglected. "It takes months or even years," it has been stated, "to appreciate a change in nutrition, or to register the effect of a new way of planting seedlings in the increased yield of an orchard." Unless people are to lose interest as a result of the long delay in the appearance of the rewards, it is recommended that some "form of consistent praise, approval, privilege, improved social status, strengthened integration with one's group, or material reward" be provided (Mead, 1955, p. 276).

An excellent summary of the hypothesis on delay is provided by the inhabitants of the Palau Islands of New Guinea. Their society was markedly affected by events during and immediately after World War II. Their view of themselves and of their role in a more civilized status is reported to be: "It isn't our custom to worry about the future, but we know we are in a new day and must work for the future" (Mead, 1956, p. 27).

Old vs. New

The stranger who wanders among less civilized peoples directly observes not discontent, aggressiveness, or delay but a series of discrete events. In Africa, for example, it is immediately apparent either that Africans are using some, not all, of the material traits of Western civilization or that some of them and not others have adopted a particular trait. One workman wears a bright, shiny wristwatch but no shoes; another has shoes on his feet but no watch on his wrist. Women walking along the road may be dressed in Western-type clothes, or at least they have draped themselves in cloth manufactured in England, Belgium, or the Netherlands; but their hair is not distinctively feminine since, like men's, it is cut very close to the scalp. The roof of a chief or an affluent person is made of metal also obtained abroad, but its walls have been built from the surrounding dirt and clay to which a bit of cow dung has been added to strengthen the mixture. A cook employed by Europeans can prepare a five-course meal in the best English tradition, but he himself has a meal composed of plantain covered with a meat or peanut sauce or without benefit of any sauce. If the stranger could peer into African heads—this privilege will be extended in the next chapter—he would note the same mixture of old and new beliefs.

At any given moment, consequently, the less civilized person can be said to be learning not to become more civilized as such but to use certain forms of civilized behavior. For it is more usual, as will be suggested later (p. 236), for the tribesman in the bush not to come to a conscious decision in a cosmic manner to set out to get himself more civilized, but instead to consider whether he should grow enough extra vegetables or fruit in order to buy a pair of shoes or whether his son should try to become a clergyman. Why do people become civilized? The answer to this question must be found in large part in the new forms they accept and the old ones they reject. The question must now be rephrased until it can be faced directly in a later section (p. 243): Why do people become more civilized in some respects and not in others?

So far in this chapter only the causal aspect of Hypothesis 1 is relevant to the question: discontent drives people to learn new forms. If the forms are to be specified, additional factors must be taken into account. These factors will now be introduced, and in so doing the usual form of presenting a hypothesis must be altered for the first but not the last time. Relevant data have not been obtained by this writer in Africa or Jamaica. The factors, moreover, have been derived from general learning theory, not from the data of acculturation. Three have been singled out, and they are deliberately brought together into a very long hypothesis since they are related to one another:

> HYPOTHESIS 4 (*causal*): *People who are experiencing some discontent with a prevailing form of behavior are likely to accept rather than to reject an alternative form when that new form has one or more of the following attributes: (a) it is accessible; (b) it has advantages which are intelligibly demonstrable in the present and which can be anticipated to continue in the future; (c) it demands responses which people feel confident that they can learn.*

That a new form must be *accessible* before it can be learned is a truism requiring no more proof than the statement that an advertisement or any communication cannot possibly be successful unless it is perceived by its potential audience. In some, many, or perhaps most colonial areas the authorities make certain aspects of civilization more readily available than others. In the East Indies, for example, the Dutch tended to follow "a policy of nonassimilation," as a result of which they "sought to preserve, to revive where necessary, and to strengthen the native institutions and cultures." Inhabitants of the area had virtually no access to the Dutch language and Western science, and so they could not become acculturated in these crucial respects. On the other hand, in spite of the policy of noninterference, the same authorities permitted and encouraged certain kinds of contact, especially in the areas of religion, divorce, sanitation, and economic affairs (Vandenbosch, 1943).

People themselves as well as outside authorities affect the accessibility of a new form of behavior. The adult may lack the skill to learn to control a machine, or the child may not be "bright" enough to pass an examination; thereafter each is prevented from being exposed to innumerable acculturating influences. Only 26 per cent of a small sample of Ganda women claim that they have ever had a European friend; in contrast, 63 per cent of comparable males in the same village make the claim (Doob, 1961). The position of women in Ganda society accounts in large part for this statistically significant difference and for their relative isolation from intimate contacts with Europeans which the difference suggests. On the broadest level of all, some anthropologists refer to the "boundary-maintaining mechanisms" of societies, viz., "the techniques and ideologies by means of which a [cultural] system limits participation in the culture to a well-recognized in-group" (Barnett et al., 1954, pp. 975–6). The contrast drawn between the United States and the Southwestern pueblos—the former has "admitted diverse immigrants for many years," whereas the latter "admit few aliens and censure their own members who do not conform to the key values of the culture"—suggests that the extent to which people have access to outsiders is regulated by these "mechanisms." Also involved is the attitude of one's peers toward the new form, a problem that will be considered in the next chapter.

In fact, accessibility by itself, however necessary, does not guarantee the learning of the new form; other factors must operate simultaneously. It is reported, for example, that not until they were drafted during World War II and hence had the opportunity to observe other parts of the United States and the world did Navaho youths appreciate the complexity and technical superiority of white civilization. On the reservation and in school they had some opportunity to make such observations but they largely failed to do so for lack of appropriate motivation. Later through their experience in the army they discovered

the greater friendliness and respect Indians could anticipate outside the Southwest (Vogt, 1951, pp. 100–1). Money of course
is needed, as has been suggested, to gain access to the material
goods of civilization; yet money by itself may not be decisive.
In an Indian community in Mexico, wealth indeed is associated
with eating bread rather than the traditional tortillas; yet age and
not wealth is connected with wearing shoes and with sleeping
on a bed or cot rather than following traditional practices (Lewis,
1951, p. 176). Indians in Guatemala have numerous economic,
governmental, and ceremonial contacts with the more Westernized Ladinos who, as has been pointed out, often inhabit the
same communities; they still deliberately retain, nevertheless,
their own distinctive culture (Tax, 1941).

A second factor affecting whether or not the new form replaces the old, according to Hypothesis 4, is the *demonstrability*
of its present and future advantages. "Virtually all students" of
social change, according to one anthropologist, have stated that
"old elements are held to, or new elements accepted, when they
are *judged* to have greater usefulness than any new or old elements with which they may be respectively compared" (Keesing,
1953, p. 104). The word "judged" has been italicized here because it suggests the problem to which the factor of demonstrability is proposed as the solution: the judgment depends upon the
kind of demonstration and whether it is considered a success or
a failure. In the first place, there may be no discontent with the
old form, and so the advantages of the new form are unnoticed
or discounted. In many parts of the tropics, for example, a diet
that is rich in carbohydrates but very deficient in proteins seems
satisfactory to people because it satisfies their hunger. Even
though this imbalance often produces a painful, disagreeable
disease called kwashiorkor, it is not easy to persuade adults to
eat less of what they like and more of what they probably dislike: the connection between their present diet and a possible
illness in the future cannot be dramatically demonstrated. Many
if not most measures involving public health or the prevention
of disease encounter the same difficulty. People in less civilized
countries are much more likely to flock to dispensaries and swallow pills which reduce a single pain very quickly than they are

to dig the latrines that eventually help reduce the incidence of many pains. To a certain extent these new forms are not demonstrated intelligibly because, as suggested by Hypothesis 3, people in these societies are likely to be intolerant of delay.

Then, secondly, whatever pain is incurred in learning the new form can be interpreted as a demonstration that the old form is preferable. The digging of the latrine is patently laborious, especially to someone who is not completely convinced of its efficacy. On a subtler level, veterinarians in Africa know that a few cattle may die when herds are dipped into chemicals for prophylactic purposes but that the slight loss or risk is worth taking. A cattle-loving African, on the other hand, may interpret the dead animals, which he can easily perceive, as a demonstration that the procedure as a whole is dangerous or else conclude that Europeans have devised another method of reducing the size of his herd.

A demonstration of new forms is convincing, thirdly, when the advantages may be anticipated to continue into the future and when they do not appear to conflict with other aspects of people's lives. In different words, what is presented to the senses of people they interpret, and their interpretation springs from their predispositions and anticipations. In the field of agriculture, for example, demonstrations are said to be especially important. In introducing a series of reports on how scientific techniques can improve the lot of cultivators everywhere, the editors state that "the 'result demonstration' is a basic cornerstone in extension teaching, much of which has been by use of object lessons" (Ensminger and Sanders, 1945, p. 2); illustrations follow from areas as diverse as India (Hatch, 1945, p. 74), the Middle East (Tannous, 1945, p. 88), and Latin America (Loomis, 1945, pp. 133–5). In a definitive book on rural Mexico appears the generalization that "there is no substitute for concrete demonstration" as agricultural innovations are introduced (Whetten, 1948, p. 280). A careful examination of each demonstration, however, reveals the complexity of the process. A village in India enthusiastically accepted the principle of using green manure not only because the yield consequently increased by over 40 per cent but also because this demonstration occurred under conditions people could endorse: they had obtained the seed in a manner that conformed with their desires, they were given some responsibility in carrying on the experiment, and they had already had some conception of the benefits likely to result from "plowing under parts of leguminous plants" (Singh, 1952). Other cultivators, in Peru, desperately needing water for their crops, did not help dig a well which would relieve their plight, nor did they use the water after the well was finished. Clearly they were acquainted with the importance of water, and the well had demonstrated that it could produce water, but other values prevented them from accepting the innovation: they felt that they themselves or at least their real leaders should have been consulted before the project was begun; they were offended when the well was drilled on the land of a man they disliked; and they were convinced that the change itself would threaten their traditional way of life (Holmberg, 1952).

Finally, the anticipations of people can affect their reactions to a demonstration. They may acknowledge their present discontent but discount it: after the next rain or during a later phase of the moon, they convince themselves, their misery will disappear. The bases for such anticipations are of course varied. Some are likely to be actuarial: the future will differ from the present since there has always been that kind of change. There may be wishful thinking: everything will grow better because I pray that it will. Or influential people can be decisive: old or new leaders promise additional benefits.

This factor of anticipation explains in part why often the material aspects of more civilized societies appear more attractive than many of their nonmaterial values. When African informants were asked to comment upon the proposition, "Life in heaven will be better than life on earth," again and again they pleaded ignorance, because, they said most seriously, "no one who has ever been there has returned to tell us." In contrast, the goods offered by traders bring almost immediate rewards. Under some circumstances, nevertheless, ideas may be readily accepted. When people have been discontent for a long time, when they anticipate few changes, and when they believe that the continuation of their frustrations demonstrates the invalidity of their traditional beliefs, they are likely to be receptive toward the missionary from outside (Hallowell, 1955, pp. 323–5).

The utility of the new form must be demonstrated not only in advance but also after adoption. Unless there is such a demonstration, people may repudiate the newly learned form; but when the demonstration does occur, they may anticipate that satisfaction from the new form will continue in the future. The travails of American Indians after contact with white civilization have been numerous but clearly, since so many of the societies have survived, the frustrations must also have been accompanied by material and even spiritual benefits (e.g., Collins, 1950; Goldfrank, 1943). After adoption, however, new forms may have to be retained whether or not they demonstrate what has been anticipated. In the first place, there may be no turning back; when the man has left the tribe to move to the city, he may have cut his old ties or it may simply be too expensive to return. Then the new form, though unsatisfying, may become so entwined in the person's system of values that a slight to it may mean a slight to the values at the core of his existence: he cannot admit, even privately, that his choice was a poor one and so he rationalizes what he has. There are limits, of course: completely disillusioned people will push back or admit their mistakes if the new is too unbearable.

Both in passing and in conclusion the point must be made that it is often easier to demonstrate to children than to adults the superiority of new forms. They possess fewer preconceptions, or at least their preconceptions are likely to be weaker. A demonstration inside the school or classroom may be particularly impressive. Their teachers have prestige. Attention can be gained, and usually over a period of time. The schools may possess the materials to engineer the demonstration successfully.

Before a new form of behavior is learned, it has been indicated so far, that form must be accessible to people and its advantages must be demonstrable. Cultivators may be offered new seed or lessons in new techniques; indeed they may be convinced that the resulting grain grows taller than that produced by the older seeds or methods; but they may lack *confidence* in their own ability to duplicate the feat. The practical problem in spreading information to people in less civilized areas is to find a device which will give potential converts the feeling that they are capable of achieving the objective. Sometimes leaders or gifted individuals within the old society are taught first, and then their demonstrated ability to accomplish the deed gives others confidence in themselves: I may not be able to do what Europeans can do, they say in effect, but I can do whatever my own peers can be taught to achieve.

Confidence must also include the conviction that the problem at hand is solvable not only in terms of human capabilities but also as a general principle. Often people are sure that their misery is divinely ordained and hence they feel that alleviation is impossible. In an Arab village, for example, where the incidence of trachoma was very high, a medical officer and his colleagues were surprised that people did not respond to a simple program of treatment:

> They had had trachoma for generations and accepted it as normal. One day, in the course of a general meeting, the writer asked one of the leading elders what he thought of the health situation in the village. He felt it was fine. The medical officer pointed to the swollen eyelids of most of those who were present. The elder did not see anything wrong there. Finally, when a man who was completely blind in one eye was brought forward, the general remark of the audience was "This is from Allah" [Tannous, 1945, pp. 94–5].

People's self-confidence is undoubtedly affected by an interaction between the contentment the old form brings them and the central or segmental character of the form. As a corollary it may be suggested that *changes are made with greater confidence (a) when the form is central and there is discontent or (b) when the form is segmental and there is contentment*. If people are starving, they seek new solutions and in desperation will assay almost any new procedure; but if they have enough to eat, they will not be motivated to try other foods and may feel incapable of producing them. For segmental activities, like those involved in accepting or declining fashionably attractive clothing, on the other hand, the risks in changing are less perilous, and they are likely to seem more tolerable to someone not experiencing distress.

All three factors affecting the adoption or rejection of an innovation of course must be referred to specific people whose reaction in large part reflects their values in the society. Ultimately, for example, everybody in a society which grows its own food is affected by current or potentially feasible agricultural techniques. Proposals for agricultural change, however, may radically affect cultivators and distributors; whereas clerks, removed as they are from this part of production, appraise the change differently or may be indifferent to it. In a sense no change has restricted consequences, since people are interdependent; but the influential people who make or seem to make the critical decisions may be unable or unwilling to take the eventual repercussions into account.

Chapter 5.

ATTITUDES TOWARD PEOPLE
AND GROUPS

VIRTUALLY every form of behavior which a person changes or learns as he becomes more civilized involves other people. On and beneath the surface he may feel that he alone decides to modify his clothing or an old practice, but in fact his decision springs in part from, and is likely to affect, his relation to various groups. In all probability he has observed the innovation as part of another's behavior: his neighbor wears a Western hat, the outside official has indicated the advantages of contour plowing. When he puts the hat upon his head, he conspicuously suggests to his peers that he is rejecting an old form. When he plows differently, he wins praise and friendliness from the outsider. In most instances of acculturation, finally, those who change emerge not only with new habits but also with new associates.

The people who display or advocate the change or the learning involved in acculturation may be referred to as *instructors,* whose effects upon potential or actual learners in the old society can be appreciated by considering the attitudes and feelings they evoke. At least three factors can be distinguished. In the first place, some degree of *competence* is ascribed to the instructor. That competence may be demonstrated: the engineer obviously knows about machines because he can repair them. Or it may be suggested by some more general trait: the official is considered more or less omniscient because he appears confident in all observable situations or because any civilized man like him, according to the uninformed view of people in the old society, inevitably is sagacious and skillful.

Then, secondly, the learners have some kind of *affective rela-*

tion with the instructor. At one extreme their feelings toward him may be most positive, at the other most negative. In addition, they may view him narrowly as an instructor or broadly as a model for many kinds of behavior. If they think of him merely as an instructor, they seek to acquire the knowledge which he has and which they think will benefit them. But they may also seek the knowledge not necessarily because they consider it useful or enjoyable but because they would resemble him in as many respects as possible. In more concrete words: less civilized persons may learn to read when they are convinced either that reading will help them or that literacy is one of the attributes of the more civilized instructor.

Thirdly, the learners assume—correctly or incorrectly—that the instructor wishes or does not wish them to change, or is indifferent: what *attitude of the instructor* do learners postulate? Less civilized people may attempt to learn forms of behavior they know are being sponsored by outside instructors—the school teacher clearly wants his pupils to learn to add and subtract. They may also strive to acquire other forms which they realize are tabooed by outsiders—the teacher just as clearly does not want the children to acquire his taste for gin and bitters which they know he drinks.

The three factors interact in a very complex manner as they affect the learning process. The complexity can be indicated by assuming—to oversimplify—that the learners consider the instructor either competent or incompetent; that they either like him or dislike him and that they heed him either because they would learn what he teaches or because they would come to resemble him; and that they believe he encourages or discourages them. With gradations thus eliminated, sixteen different combinations appear: (competent-incompetent) x (like-dislike) x (learn-resemble) x (encourage-discourage). One radical possibility could be an adolescent who is studying in a theological school to become a minister of the gospel as promulgated by his missionary-teacher. He respects that teacher as the font of theological and ethical wisdom, for certainly no one in his tribe knows as much about Christianity and its doctrine. He has deep affection for him and hence he listens attentively and studies industriously. He prays that some day he will be like him in deed and word, and hence he seeks wherever possible to imitate his ways of behaving and thinking as well as his general manner of life. He is absolutely certain that the teacher also likes him and is supporting his ambition. With such a combination the outlook for learning is good: this man will master many new ways.

At the other extreme could be a tribesman who has complete confidence in his own traditional religion. He does not recognize the missionary as a potential teacher but considers him an interloper who would destroy some of the adolescent rites of his society in which he himself firmly believes. He dislikes him as a person, for he seems to behave differently and not as respectable people (from his standpoint) should. Obviously he feels no identification with the man who, he knows very well, opposes his beliefs. Such a person will not be converted by the missionary; the learning outlook for him is dismal.

Between the extremes are the other combinations. The Zulu factory worker may thoroughly detest his European foreman, he may have no desire whatsoever to adopt his philosophy, and he could not care less how the man feels about Zulu beliefs. His hostility, however, does not prevent him from appreciating the man's competence as a mechanic; hence the component of respect, however grudgingly bestowed, produces efficient learning. Or the same Zulu may follow the advice of his father who lives on a Reserve not because he considers him competent, not because he wishes occasionally or eventually to return to the Reserve, but because he knows that his father expects him to be obedient and also because he likes the old man and would not contradict him.

The bulky hypothesis which emerges merely specifies the attributes of the instructor that promote learning, without indicating the numerous and complicating effects of their interaction:

HYPOTHESIS 5 (*causal*): *People are likely to accept rather than reject a new form of behavior which is displayed by an outsider: (a) when they recognize his general or specific competence as an instructor; (b) when they are favorably disposed toward him, and more especially when they identify themselves with him; (c) when, provided they are favorably disposed toward him, they can assume that he would have them change.*

The validity of this hypotliesis is revealed in almost every anthropological treatise which presents the factual story of a particular social change in some detail. In fact, a prominent anthropologist, gifted though he was in finding somewhere an instance of behavior which could puncture any generalization, evidently was driven by the data of his craft to issue the following universal statement: "There is no group in the world where the general acceptance or rejection of a new thing will not be strongly influenced by the auspices under which it is introduced to the group and the associations which are attached to it in consequence" (Linton, 1940, p. 473). The writer would hastily turn the coin over lest the reader become smug in the face of such a sweeping conclusion: the very importance of the leader's role in any situation, it will be seen presently, makes it extremely difficult to formulate hypotheses relating to the general problem of social change.

Before the hypothesis can be effectively utilized, moreover, it is necessary in each situation to know who the outsiders are, how they function, and why they are or are not influential. Usually the agents of change are relatively easy to identify, but it is useful to note in passing the various guises in which they appear. Some are men who deliberately teach new forms of behavior: missionaries, teachers, traders, and public officials. Others from the outside may not conceive of themselves as instructors but unwittingly function as models: the wives and children of men from the West whose behavior necessarily is observed and evaluated by the people next to whom they temporarily or permanently live. Explorers, tourists, and soldiers are likewise appraised and then ignored, copied, or rejected. Within the society itself are formal or informal leaders who for varied reasons have been converted to the new and then function as its exponents. The original outside instructor in fact may be far removed in space and time but his teaching can diffuse through others or through printed words;

Islam, for example, reached parts of Nigeria through converts who, being literate, could consult the sacred texts in books (Greenberg, 1941). Influential insiders sometimes leave their own country temporarily to study or travel abroad; the men who influence them there may be utterly unaware of their influence or of the many repercussions which that teaching can have in the old society.

The kind of teaching situation in which the instructor functions can range from the informal to the very formal. In 1884, for example, Sir Harry Johnston led an expedition to Mt. Kilimanjaro and established his headquarters near its base. Without doubt he was genuinely interested only in providing a comfortable existence for himself; but simultaneously and unavoidably he provided stimulants to learning for many Africans in the area:

> Johnston himself was soon housed in a long three-roomed cottage comprising a laboratory, dining-room and bed-sitting-room to which was later added a wing of storesheds and a wing for his men, the whole forming three sides of a square. A poultry yard was quickly started and the kitchen garden sown with seeds brought from Europe, mustard and cress, radishes, potatoes, turnips, onions, tomatoes, borage, sage, cucumbers and melons. Within a week he was eating a home-grown salad; a month later his root crops were nearly ready and he was staking his young peas and beans. There was a daily market in the compound to which the Wachagga [the Africans of the area] brought sheep and goats, milk, honey and bananas, to be exchanged for exiguous strips of cotton cloth and strings of glass beads [Oliver, 1957, p. 63].

At the other extreme is the outside teacher who establishes a school and therein deliberately teaches boys and girls to read and write.

The efficiency with which outside teachers make known their attitudes toward those who would acquire their ways may have an effect on the learning process. It has been contended, for example, that immigrants in the United States have been able to learn "New England culture" more readily than that of the Western states because New England, being the older of the two areas, has evolved "clearly defined reward and punishment values," whereas "the West has not developed a regional culture of its own" (Ruesch et al., 1948, p. 22). African women beginning to use cosmetics in the Western manner are likely to be shocked when Europeans view them with disapproval: no one has told them that not all outside forms are suitable for them.

In more recent times, outside and inside proponents of change have functioned through surrogates, the mass media of communication. The hypothesis under discussion, therefore, can be applied without modification to the press, radio, books, magazines, posters, motion pictures, film strips, etc. In what fields, for example, are motion pictures considered to be competent sources of information? Two men who have had extensive experience showing documentary films in East and Central Africa suggest that a critical factor is the way in which the audience conceptualizes the function of the medium: "If Natives are to appreciate programs which are largely educational in a broad sense, they must be given such programs from the start before they have acquired from commercial cinemas a taste for programs consisting almost entirely of comics and thrillers" (Notcutt and Latham, 1937, pp. 123–4).

Why does the attitude toward the outside instructor or the medium of communication affect the learning of the new forms of behavior? The general answer, which stems from research on communications in American society (Hovland et al., 1953, pp. 36–9), can be formulated as another corollary: *The optimum conditions specified in Hypothesis 5* (an appreciation of the instructor's competence, a favorable attitude toward him, and—with a favorable attitude—the conviction that he approves of the learning) *facilitate learning since people who are so predisposed are likely to expose themselves to instruction, to evaluate favorably what they perceive and learn, and then to be both willing and able to behave appropriately.*

Very often it is not possible to determine from a report or observation precisely what has occurred during social contact. Writing of conditions in South Africa, for example, one anthropologist has stated: "Christianity may spread quickly in one district because the missionary is liked, and the chief well disposed towards his teaching, in another where the chief opposes the new teaching, and the missionary is personally unpopular, his preaching may have little influence" (Hunter, 1934, p. 349). Such a statement indicates only the outcome in each district; it does not suggest whether the first missionary attracted a large congregation and the second did not. It is conceivable, if not probable, that both had equally large audiences but that the words of the first man were listened to more attentively or considered more important than those of the second man. In other situations the role of the outsider is clear: "Indian boys and girls" in a Guatemalan community, an anthropologist states, "have not adopted basketball, because they are kicked off the court bodily when they venture to participate in a game" (Gillin, 1945, p. 11). Here it seems quite safe to infer that these children not only were prevented from learning the game but also that they became aware of how the dominant group, the Ladinos, felt toward Indians who would acquire the new knowledge and skill.

As ever, the usual historical limitations preclude any extended discussion of why people in the old society possess particular attitudes toward outsiders. In part the explanation must be sought in the behavior of the outsiders. "The Native's idea of Christianity," if reference may be made once again to the fate of this religion among the Africans in South Africa, "does not come so much from the Bible or from the official doctrine of the Church as from the missionary who preaches to him and who works in his area, and by the latter's conduct and treatment of his people he judges the life of a Christian" (Schapera, 1937, p. 363). But why, it must then be asked, do some missionaries demonstrate "conduct and treatment" which attract Africans and why do others repel Africans? The personality and training of the individual missionary must be decisive, but not completely so: the same missionary could be a success in one society and not in another or be successful within the same society for some people and not for others. Indeed the nasty Spiraled Explanation must be invoked. Hypothesis 5 has been stated in causal terms, but over time there can be interaction: the well-liked outsider attracts people, and the people then like him all the more when his teaching proves helpful to them. Some Tewan Indians, for example, originally sought refuge from Spanish domination and influence by moving into a residential area of the Hopi tribe in Arizona. In the new environment they continued to remain more or less "culturally aloof" for over two centuries. Later their kind of personality "proved congenial to Anglo-Americans," and, as a result of this new social contact, they began learning many American forms of behavior; since then the process has spiraled and they have adopted more and more of "the things which are symbols of success in American culture" (Dozier, 1951).

The Manus in the Admiralty Islands have had contact with European civilization for a long time but by and large had accepted relatively few traits from outside. Then suddenly the American army moved into their area during World War II. For various reasons they liked the Americans—"The Americans treated us like individuals, like brothers"—and soon they radically changed their entire way of life and attempted deliberately to live like civilized people on the outside. An important ingredient in this shift was not only the American instructors but also a particularly gifted leader of their own who appeared at the right moment and then skillfully guided them through the changes (Mead, 1956). Incidents like this suggest that attention must now be paid to groups and individuals within the old society who can affect the rate and the kind of learning during periods of change.

In passing it is possible to suggest the utility of the hypothesis in explaining an aspect of acculturation that is being deliberately neglected in this book, viz., the effect of less civilized people upon their more civilized teachers. Indeed contact between cultures, as all students of the subject emphasize, is always a reciprocal affair, no matter how one-sided the exchange is. At the very least the outsider, regardless of his sensitivity and receptivity, observes instances in which his teaching has not been successful and thus is compelled to modify his procedure. In colonial areas words, foods, art objects, and minor practical techniques diffuse from the indigenous to the newcomers. The evidence suggests, however, that *in recent times* only segmental forms of behavior have been influenced by the less civilized. After being in India for centuries, the British have learned to cook and enjoy curry and to use the word *chit,* but it would be difficult to show that the rich civilization of India and Pakistan have modified their values or philosophy. The colonial outsider, the hypothesis points out, is not likely to be in a learning mood. He considers the people whom he rules to be "inferior," "primitive," "underdeveloped," "inexperienced," or "uncivilized," or else he knows that they need, perhaps even ask for, civilization. In important matters, consequently, he does not even visualize them as potential instructors. Their "competence" in this respect he would rate low; clearly he does not "identify" himself with them; and he is not interested in whether or not they would have him change. In addition, the situations in which more and less civilized people usually meet prescribe that the outsider be the teacher and that the insider, willingly or unwillingly, be the pupil. In all probability it seldom occurs to the less civilized people that they have practices and values to offer to the more civilized. Possible contributions from their side they come to appreciate after greater and more intimate contact with the West provides them with an awareness of their own ways and of the defects of the West.

Family

It is unnecessary to beat the drums to proclaim the importance of the family in any society. The infant's initial helplessness, the role of the family in socialization, the economic function of the family need be mentioned only quickly in order to recall the positive affection and positive bond which almost inevitably exists between children and parents. Until they are liberated by adulthood, children must recognize the competence of parents as instructors in certain spheres and, as a result of the easy communication characterizing most family life, parents are likely to transmit, or at least make known, their attitudes toward old and new ways. As ever, "the way of all flesh" appears to triumph: as parent, so child.

Again and again, nevertheless, children do differ from their parents. The especially gifted or dull child does not follow the traditional bent of his normal family. The mobile person climbs

away from some or many but not all of his early forms of behavior. When there is social contact with a more civilized society,
will the new forms of behavior some people learn lead to differences between generations?

From one a priori standpoint, differences may be anticipated.
The motivation to become more civilized may spring from a
protest against the family or its ways; or that motivation may
arise elsewhere but, after the change has occurred, the individual
may be in conflict with his family or drift away from them as a
result of his changed interests. From another standpoint, no important differences can be expected when the parents themselves,
having become acculturated, rear their children in the new
manner. Or it is quite possible for the man of the household to
earn his living by means of some Western trade but at the same
time to cling to traditional family forms: each work day he
literally or figuratively commutes between cultures. In other
instances the changing person may differ from his peers regarding proper family practices without necessarily differing from
his own family: in becoming more civilized he can carry along
with him not only his immediate family but also his extended
and even his spouse's family.

The case for anticipating differences between parents and
children or for expecting parents and children to view family
practices differently can thus be argued either way. It all depends
—and the possibilities must be investigated empirically in each
instance of acculturation or for each group of people. It has been
pointed out, for example, that the patriarchal father among American immigrants demands and obtains the loyalty of his wife and
children and thus prevents them from becoming rapidly Americanized; but the inevitable contacts of the next generation with
America, especially in school, induce them to change their attitude toward the head of the family; with the change in this attitude, contact becomes more complete (Humphreys, 1944). Or in
another situation, according to a teacher in Uganda, parents who
have approved only the very general principle of a Western
education at a boarding school for their children are themselves
likely to be affected by unanticipated by-products of such an
education—standards with respect to clothes, food, punctuality,

cleanliness—which the children learn and then display at first sporadically during holidays and then perhaps continually after graduation (Musgrove, 1952).

For at least three reasons, however, this complicated state of affairs should not prevent a tentative hypothesis from emerging. In the first place, some change in family form or practices eventually occurs—or at least this seems roughly to have been the experience so far of societies who have adopted Western ways. Then in most instances of social contact, not one but both aspects of the Spiraled Explanation will probably function: at a particular point in time or for one group, there will be differences and also similarities. Under such circumstances, reliance can be placed upon one of the oldest and most venerable dicta of human observation and social science; beliefs learned in the family are likely to persist, especially those concerning the family itself. Such persistence ought to be evident especially in less civilized societies. For these societies, it has been suggested, tend to be characterized by a relatively absolute faith in most beliefs. In addition, the family is held in particularly high esteem because it exercises control through authorities who are close at hand and because it is the source of beliefs that are likely to be interrelated and hence associated with it. With the postulation of such a modal tendency for each society, it must follow that changes involving the family will certainly occur slowly; hence:

HYPOTHESIS 6 (consequential): People changing from old to new ways are likely to retain traditional attitudes toward family forms and practices until or even beyond the occurrence of central changes within them and their society.

This hypothesis suggests few if any differences when the attitudes toward the family of the unchanged and the changing are compared; differences ought to begin to appear when the comparison is made between the changing and the changed. Relevant evidence from the Africa-Jamaica studies appears in Table 3 (p. 285); the outstanding feature of the section titled "Family" is the few statistically significant differences between the relatively unchanged and the changing Africans. Among the Luo, assumed to be the least acculturated, differences are fewest;

among the Zulu, assumed to be the most acculturated, differences are the most numerous. Noteworthy is the consistent tendency among the latter for more of the better educated to pay tribute to the role performed by their mothers during childhood (rows 8–10)—this may reflect the fact that the father in the urban environment must work outside the home throughout the day. In all three African societies the better educated tended to refer not just to themselves but also to their families as they discussed various phases of their existence (row 19); whether the difference reflects their attitudes, their ability to verbalize their problems in social terms, or greater concern for their families in the midst of change cannot be stated. Two items suggest that traditional family ties among the Ganda may be weakening (rows 14 and 15).

Other supporting data are at hand from Africa. In the studies conducted in the secondary schools, significantly fewer Zulu boys than adults expressed a conservative view on two of five items related to the family (Table I, rows 6 and 7). The Luo and Ganda schedules contain only two such items, and here significant differences appear (rows 4 and 6). The idea that "a wife earning money may spend it as she pleases" apparently has a different appeal for boys and adults in the three societies. Among the Luo more of the boys than of the adults approve of such independence; the reverse is true among the Zulu; and the figure for the Ganda boys falls significantly between the poorly and the well educated adults. A still higher percentage of boys agreeing with this nontraditional proposal was obtained in a study not reported in Table I: 64 per cent of a sample of East African boys in an experimental school run by a very competent European headmistress gave their verbal assent. In yet another Ganda school almost all the younger and older children state that young people should submit to older people and to authority—or at least so they claimed on a questionnaire administered by adults (Table II, rows 1–2). Finally, the sample of Zulu women was asked to indicate 24 beliefs, 13 of which pertained principally to the family and family practices and the remaining 11 to miscellaneous traditional matters and values. When the more acculturated urban group is compared with the less acculturated rural group, it can be seen, in Table III, that the samples differ with respect to 7, or 64 per cent, of the traditionally interpreted "facts" but only on 4, or 31 per cent, of the items pertaining to the family.

Little information concerning the family was collected in Jamaica. If any trend is discernible, it would be that significantly more of the better educated informants show hostility toward their father as revealed by reactions to the "father" and "son" in an ambiguous drawing and the way in which they completed the sentence "Father is . . ." As befits a changed group, however, more of them also believe that their mothers helped them achieve their present status by formulating plans for them (items 20, 94, and 108 of the Schedule in Appendix B).

From two of the four measuring devices employed in the Indian-white study various measures of attitudes toward the family and toward both parents are available (Table A, rows 4–15). Hypothesis 6 is tenuously and indirectly vindicated by the fact that only three of the *rho's*—a measure of correlation or association between the ranks of the societies with respect to acculturation and the trait in question—are significant. For if attitude toward family changed with increasing acculturation, the Indian children would more closely resemble the white children and hence more of the associations would be significant. All three of the significant ones (rows 6, 10, and 13) suggest that increased acculturation is accompanied by increased hostility toward the family and toward both parents.

In the same study the large number of significant differences between the Indian groups and the Midwestern white children (columns 2 and 3) may also prove the tenacity with which the Indians cling to their traditional feelings concerning the family. The investigators themselves subscribe to the view, as they interpret the results from the Emotional Response Test, that discipline is administered in the family more frequently among Americans in the Midwest than it is among Southwest Indians and that the American mother, unlike the Indian mother, plays a more important role in children's lives than the father (Havighurst and Neugarten, 1955, p. 72). Finally, there is a consistent tendency—with one exception—for more of the children from the less acculturated than from the more acculturated Navaho community to react strongly to family matters: according to the measures employed, they roundly praise or condemn their families. Perhaps, then, here is an indication of change in Navaho society, but it seems more likely that the less acculturated children, being more isolated and hence dependent upon their families, have developed more distinctive and readily verbalizable feelings toward them.

Otherwise whatever anthropological evidence the writer has observed seems unanimously to support the view that the family, more than perhaps any other social institution, resists change after contact. Scattered illustrations will be packed into this single paragraph. From the Ivory Coast: "Le système matrilinéaire traditionnel, s'il engendre souvent de graves conflits, est bien rarement tout à fait et ouvertement renié" (Köbben, 1956, p. 183). From Ethiopia: "Wo auch immer wirre Zeiten und Zustände eintreten, hebt stets wieder das Gefühl der Sippenzusammengehörigkeit sein Haupt empor" (Frobenius, 1933, p. 236). From the Solomon Islands: "The kinship structure itself has changed very little. . . . Kinship, in fact, is the most conservative factor in native life" (Hogbin, 1939, p. 220). From a small Indian community in Mexico which in less than twenty years established numerous contacts with the Western world and which consequently changed in many respects: "The increase in size of the community and the rise to power have not changed the simple social structure of small family households grouped into patrilineal great families" (Redfield, 1950, p. 87). From a similar Indian community elsewhere in the same country: "Despite the increased city influences in the last seventeen years, the stability of the nuclear family has not been seriously modified" (Lewis, 1951, p. 436). Information of a more quantitative sort comes from a study in the city of Chicago (Caudill, 1952): by means of protocols from the Thematic Apperception Test a comparison was made between the values of 30 issei (first generation immigrants from Japan who had been living in the United States for three or four decades) and 40 nisei (the children of the issei who had been born and raised in the United States). Some of the salient results have been summarized by the writer in the first two columns of Table E (see p. 310). It is noteworthy that the only differences between the two generations that appear by means of this technique apply to motivation (rows 1 and 4); from a statistical standpoint, the two generations do not differ appreciably with respect to expressed attitudes toward the family or other people.

Inside Leaders

Attitudes toward inside leaders, like those toward the family, can be considered to be either the cause or the consequence of change. Those who are changing may feel antagonistic toward traditional authorities and seek out the new society in order to be free from their tyranny or otherwise to become superior to them. Or, having acquired new forms of behavior, they may then repudiate these leaders as symbols of the old regime or as opponents of progressive change. Other possibilities exist. People remaining loyal to the old forms may resent leaders who accept innovations from the outside. Some of these innovations—those which are segmental rather than central—can be learned without disrupting traditional ties: the tribesman may acquire the compulsion to smoke cigarettes without distrusting his chief. In addition, the changing or the changed may continue to accord some but not complete honor to the old leaders. In the Solomon Islands, for example, youths who learn some Western ways away from home are reported to feel superior rather than respectful toward the traditional elders upon their return; and yet simultaneously they know that they must remain dependent upon them for certain services, such as knowledge of magical formulas and the traditional bride price (Hogbin, 1939, p. 174). It is well to remember that less civilized people, in spite of a possible tendency to adhere rigidly to their beliefs, do not automatically accord all power and omniscience to their leaders. There is obviously great variability in political structure: in some centralized societies leaders have virtually divine and absolute power, in decentralized ones they may be markedly affected by their followers and may in fact be easily evicted.

A consequential hypothesis can be formulated, in spite of the various alternatives, by making a few assumptions. It seems probable that attitude toward leaders only rarely produces the incentive to change, for leaders by definition and as a result of the role they perform are likely to possess some prestige. Then the behavior of the leaders can be specified: they can be called devotees of the old rather than of the new. Finally, instances of segmental change can be excluded. Under these circumstances, the following hypothesis seems reasonable:

Hypothesis 7 (consequential): *People changing centrally from old to new ways are likely to feel antagonistic toward traditional leaders who do not reveal similar changes.*

Evidence in favor of the hypothesis appears in the second part of Table 3, labeled "Traditional Authorities." There the trend, without exception, for all three African societies is for more of the better educated to feel antagonistic toward the traditional leaders (rows 20–25) or to disparage their power or importance (rows 26 and 27). No difference, however, appears with respect to the qualities ascribed to ideal leaders (row 28). Row 29 refers to behavior which, according to Western principles, is to be condemned, viz., the borrowing of money by an official from the public treasury—and more of the poorly educated condone it. In all instances except rows 23–25, the African word used for leader or chief was the general one which conveyed the connotation of traditional leader. In those rows, leaders A, B, and C, however, refer to traditional authorities performing quite different roles, which can be very briefly outlined. Among the Luo, leader A is a "Location Chief," a man appointed by the Kenya government and hence acting as an intermediary between Africans and Europeans; leaders B and C are, respectively, headman and subheadman, who are survivals from a traditional system of leadership. Among the Ganda the leaders, presented in descending order of importance (Saza, Gombolola, and Muruka), are appointed by the Ganda's own king or his advisers and not only perform traditional functions but also help carry out agricultural, medical, and educational reforms of the (European) Protectorate government. Among the Zulu, leader A is a traditional or tribal chief and B a headman; their important functions are now undertaken by Europeans. Leader C is a so-called "Advisory Board

Member," a person elected by Zulu in urban Locations to represent their interests in discussions with Europeans, but without any real authority. As might be anticipated for various reasons— for example, from the assumption that less civilized people may not compartmentalize their beliefs and categories—there is a very high correlation between attitudes toward the various types of leaders. Thus for leaders A and B, the correlation is significantly positive (*phi* coefficient of $+.77$, $+.60$, and $+.69$, respectively, for the Luo, Ganda, and Zulu).

The figures of Table 3 by themselves do not reveal why more of the better educated in the three societies evidence dislike for the various leaders. Some explanation of the trend that is in accord with the hypothesis was supplied by the Africans themselves. Again and again they said with almost complete unanimity that their objection was not to the man but to the post, or else they excused the man because of his post. The post, they said, was virtually without significance since Europeans possess the real power and exercise it through the leaders; either less competent men are willing to become leaders or the competent become impotent. Among the Ganda, it has been found that more of the better educated informants, especially those who have been to the University, differ appreciably from the minor traditional leaders and from followers and thus can aggressively and realistically appreciate the reality of the situation (Doob, 1961).

The decline in the prestige of leaders in general as a function of education appears also among the African youth. With no exceptions, fewer of them than the poorly educated adults express favorable attitudes, though the differences are seldom significant (Table I, rows 9 and 10). The differences are least marked in the secondary schools run by the Ganda themselves; in fact other evidence indicates that the boys there tended to retain a highly respectful attitude toward all authority (Table II, rows 1–3). A finding from the Luo study incidentally serves as a reminder of the fact that the expression of attitude depends upon subtle operational factors. The figure of 33 per cent who subscribe to the view that "a chief should always be obeyed" (Table I, row 9) is in fact the mean or average of two groups: 44 per cent replied affirmatively when asked the question in

English, 22 per cent when asked in the native Luo language. Perhaps, it may be speculated, a respectful attitude toward leaders had a better chance of being expressed when the language of the colonial out-group, English, reminded the youths of the need to demonstrate solidarity and loyalty in front of a wandering American (Doob, 1957a).

In Jamaica no questions were asked about traditional authorities. Instead attention was paid to feelings about the society in general. Significantly more informants in the better educated group reported hostility between "rich" and "poor" in an ambiguous drawing; could provide reasons for obeying the law which referred to ethical or social considerations rather than to the desire to escape punishment; and could designate customs and practices in their country which they wished to retain in a changing world (items 18, 127, and 135 on the Schedule in Appendix B). They thus demonstrated either an awareness or frankness concerning friction that in reality exists between various groups in Jamaican society as well as a stronger identification with a country in which they themselves occupy a higher status.

The attitude toward traditional leaders was not ascertained in the Indian-white study. The children, however, did indicate their feeling toward authority by means of two items: one showed how they reacted to discipline and the other stressed their relation to parents, teachers, employers, and the Deity. For the first measure no significant differences emerge (Table A, row 16), but for the second (row 17) there is a clear-cut trend: a concern for obedience to authority increases with acculturation. Doubtless actual obedience is as strong if not stronger in the less acculturated societies or in the more isolated Navaho community; if this is so, then the finding suggests that the greater concern of the more acculturated children may reflect the conflict between the favorable attitudes they are supposed to have and the unfavorable ones greater contact with white civilization engenders.

Outsiders

Hypothesis 5, which appeared at the beginning of this chapter, suggests that favorable attitudes toward the instructor are most likely to facilitate the learning of new ways. In fact, such attitudes are not likely to exist. For almost always there appears to be some clash of interests between members of the old society and the representatives of the new. Missionaries may want people to become completely civilized, but the people themselves seek only certain aspects of civilization and reject others. People may wish all of civilization as they visualize it, but then European settlers in the area would have them acquire only selected portions of that culture now and the rest gradually, if ever. Some traits of civilization—like guns or the ability to deceive—are learned not because they are attractive per se but because they can be used against civilized outsiders and thus in behalf of the older way of life. As indicated previously, the frustrations producing, accompanying, or resulting from acquiring new ways may produce aggression against some distinguishable target like outsiders. Often the civilizing outsiders themselves represent different interests and create confusion; during the first century of contact with Europeans, for example, the Maoris of New Zealand were confronted successively with whalers and traders, missionaries, government officials, and settlers (Hawthorn, 1944).

Even without an objective clash of interests members of the old society may feel threatened and hence grow hostile. For any outsider, no matter how saintly in appearance and in deed, appears strange, and his teachings inevitably are different from traditional ones. People usually assume that their experience with old leaders provides valuable and relevant clues for understanding leaders from the outside, and indeed that experience is their only guide from the past. Such an expectation is likely to prove invalid, for almost always the goals, techniques, and personalities of the two sets of leaders differ (cf. Gillin, 1942, p. 553). The outside benefactor, too, may evoke hostility: in accepting his generosity, people admit their own inferiority, and in feeling grateful they place themselves in his debt.

Of course affection can also be felt toward outsiders. At the very least, as Hypothesis 5 indicates, the instructor's competence must be admired or he will not be chosen as a model. The tribesman may steal or buy a gun to shoot Europeans but, however grudgingly and unconsciously, he must feel some admiration for the society which has invented, developed, and forged the weapon. In addition, the same instructor may be viewed differently as his role changes: people may like the goods a trader from the outside sells but not the kind of religion or kin system he practices. Or some people from the new society may be liked but not others; for example, teachers rather than soldiers, or physicians rather than traders. It is reported that Paluan women, who ordinarily are embarrassed to be seen naked and who therefore permit only a sister or a close female relative to assist them during childbirth, allow American male physicians and Japanese midwives to examine them since the competent foreigners are considered "different" (Barnett, 1953, p. 347). Perhaps the situation is best summarized by an African who was educated in a Scottish mission school and then later said to an anthropologist: "I am very fond of the Scots. I should like my children to be educated by them. I do not think of them as Europeans" (Hunter, 1936, p. 574).

An hypothesis stressing ambivalence seems called for:

HYPOTHESIS 8 (*interactional*): *In comparison with those who remain unchanged or who have changed, people changing from old to new ways are likely to feel more ambivalent toward outsiders associated with those new ways.*

Evidence on the hypothesis from the Africa-Jamaica studies is offered in Table 4 (p. 287). For Africans only one significant difference in ambivalence toward Europeans or Asians appears when the poorly and well educated groups are compared (rows 1, 3, 5, 7, 9, 11), although the majority of the differences among the Luo and Ganda are in the direction suggested by the hypothesis. In addition, as indicated previously, slightly if rarely significantly more of the better educated feel hostile toward Europeans and Asians (rows 2, 4, 6, 8, 10, 12). The inconclusiveness of these findings, it is felt, reflects the fact that people in the three societies tend to feel somewhat ambivalent toward outsiders, especially Europeans. First, the percentage of those expressing ambivalence is relatively large in all groups; often, it can be seen in Table 4, they exceed those expressing either positive or negative feelings (row 1 compared with row 2, row 3 with row 4, etc.).

Most of the informants, moreover, claimed close personal contact with a European (row 13) or believed such contact possible (row 15). Also, local conditions can have a marked effect upon expressed sentiments. The significantly larger proportion of poorly educated Zulu who said they admire Europeans is due in part to the fact that many of the group came from a Reserve in which a European health center was rendering Africans conspicuous, noble services; whereas urban Zulu, contributing heavily to the well educated group, at the time were experiencing a form of African nationalism.

Other data from Africa lend support to the view that contact between Africans and Europeans may have mixed results. On the one hand, in comparison with adults, fewer youths in secondary schools run by Europeans, as judged by answers to two written questions, express hostility toward Europeans or a government run by Europeans (Table I, rows 11 and 12). Among the boys in a Ganda school operated by Africans, only a minority is drawn to Europeans as such, but the majority expresses a preference for European clothes and houses (Table II, rows 4–7). Among 50 East Africans who had attended Makerere College, 29 stated to an investigator that their day-by-day relations with Europeans were "good, or mixed with good predominating"; 14 reported "indifferent relations, or an equal mixture of good and bad"; and the remaining 4 called the relations "uniformly bad, or bad on the whole." Even predominantly good feelings are thus accompanied often by some bad feelings and vice versa. One of the reasons for the mixture was succinctly stated by one man who, to suggest that the friendly contact during working hours are not ordinarily extended to social situations, stated that "race relations stop at half-past four" (Goldthorpe, 1955, p. 44). In another study middle-class Africans in South Africa were asked to describe what they liked and disliked about their occupation. In comparison with clerks, significantly more of the highly urbanized, the better educated, and the professional personnel mentioned "pleasant human relations" as a source of satisfaction and "unpleasant relations with European supervisors" as a source of frustration (Sherwood, 1959). For people presumably more acculturated, some of the "pleasant human relations" must have been with Europeans, including the supervisors.

In Jamaica a very important model to follow in order to become more civilized are people with fair skins, including the British. Factually it is probable that most Jamaicans have some "African blood" which produces little or no shame: very fair people often deliberately and unnecessarily made such a statement about themselves when first meeting the writer. Virtually no color bar exists on the island. There is, nevertheless, a decided tendency for higher-status people to be less Negroid in appearance. How, then, do the different groups react to skin color, which is thus a symbol of status and hence of civilization narrowly defined? Some of the data in Table 5 (p. 288) suggest that more of the well than the poorly educated Jamaicans behave realistically in situations in which skin color plays a role. When viewing through a stereoscope photographs that simultaneously presented African tribesmen to one eye and Europeans to the other—with eye dominance adequately controlled—fewer of the well educated sample failed to refer to skin color or race (row 1) and fewer ignored the African photograph completely (row 2); but the reporting of color as such in the pictures had no relation to education. Also fewer of the better educated were willing to judge people's honesty, intelligence, and other personality traits from photographs of men and women with different skin color and features (row 3). When offered a double-barreled question, more of them paid attention to the section mentioning skin color (row 4), but—like virtually everyone in either group—they did not spontaneously mention color as a factor affecting first impressions of strangers (row 5).

The greater realism among the Jamaican informants is accompanied by less concern for skin color as a value. None of the better educated spontaneously mentioned white people among those whom they respect or from whom they seek respect (rows 6 and 7); fewer—likewise spontaneously—mentioned white people when producing fantasies about people with whom they would exchange places or when listing the important types of people in the community (rows 8 and 9); and fewer mentioned something favorable—or unfavorable either—when asked to complete the sentence, "White people always . . ." (row 10). On the other hand, insignificantly fewer of the same people say bluntly that people are not concerned with the color of a person's skin (row 11); significantly fewer say they like Americans (row 12); and their reaction to photographs of white and Negro men and women is mixed (rows 13–15).

Such data of course can be variously interpreted. Quite possibly the better educated people wished to appear sophisticated concerning skin color in front of an educated interviewer, or the poorly educated may have been attempting to curry favor with a stranger by proclaiming, for example, favorable attitudes toward white people and Americans. At the same time the not very straightforward set of beliefs and attitudes that emerges may also reflect the ambivalence of the population toward the symbols of acculturation and toward one another.

Ambivalence can sometimes be inferred from historical data, with the usual risk. The Ojibwa Indians in Wisconsin, for example, are said to have been pacific vis-à-vis white men because their initial contact with the early French explorers had been favorable and also because they had been impressed with the strength of British forces who defeated them and their French allies. These varying attitudes toward outsiders do not alone account for their behavior: on the basis of inferences derived from Rorschach data of the present day, it is claimed that they also possessed certain general predispositions (e.g., the internal "pressure to become as emotionally independent of [their] environment as possible, and to expect very little from others") which were compatible with life on a reservation (Barnouw, 1950, pp. 27, 31–4).

The last illustration suggests the critical role the reaction to the initial contact can have in future relations between two societies. If the Ojibwa had seen British explorers or colonists at first, they might not have been confined so easily to the reservation. Experience over time of course affects the attitude of future generations but there appears to be no simple relation between any one kind of experience and the ensuing attitudes. African informants in the Africa-Jamaica studies, for example, were asked whether they had ever had a European as a close friend. Of those claiming such a friend, the proportion also admiring Europeans in general was significantly higher both among the Ganda and the Zulu than it was among the Luo; thus friendship in two instances was more closely associated with friendly attitudes than in a third.

In a figurative sense, finally, there may be ambivalence within a society. Among the Navaho Indians, for example, the "prevalent attitude" toward white people is reported to be that of "distrust or active hatred," but simultaneously "the relationships of some whites and some Navahos have been marked with understanding and cordiality on both sides." It is conceivable, however, that intrapersonal differences accompany interpersonal ones. For the same investigators also indicate that the Navaho, while adjusting to white civilization with "alacrity," have succeeded in retaining many of their own ways and the "framework of their own cultural organization" (Kluckhohn and Leighton, 1946, p. 115).

Inside vs. Outside Innovators

In the discussion so far, the assumption has been made that outsiders advocate change and insiders oppose it. Under some conditions which, being of a historical nature, are beyond the scope of this book, inside leaders may be attracted to the change. Then they rather than outsiders become the models or teachers for those who are unchanged or changing. Are they likely to be more effective than outsiders? Hypothesis 5 has suggested three conditions outsiders must satisfy if they are to be influential; almost always insiders satisfy these conditions. A corollary, therefore, follows: *The proficiency with which new ways are learned is likely to be greater when the competent teachers are leaders in the old society rather than outsiders.*

One word in the corollary requires a brief explanation, viz., "competent." That adjective would indicate that the teacher himself must have the requisite knowledge to function as a teacher. The traditional leader cannot teach his followers to drive a car without knowing how to do so himself. If he knows how to drive, the corollary states, he will be a better instructor than an equally skillful driver from the outside.

The inside leader by definition possesses the "general com-

petence" referred to in Hypothesis 5, and he evokes in his followers generally favorable attitudes. The fact that he himself
has made the change, moreover, is a clear-cut indication of his
own favorable attitude toward the innovation. Other reasons for
the corollary can be piled on top of one another. His ability to
learn the new form of behavior, especially if some kind of unusual
manual or mental skill is demanded, demonstrates to his followers
that insiders are capable of such successful learning; otherwise
they might consider themselves inferior or incompetent. The inside leader, coming from the same society as his followers and
hence having to cope more or less with a similar background, is
likely to be acquainted with them and their peculiarities in the
new learning situation. He ought to be able to anticipate some
of their objections and difficulties since he himself has had to
endure the same ordeal. He if anyone ought to be able to pierce
the solipsistic case in which all people are perforce enclosed, since
he has the same language and hence can express and understand
the intricate, subtle nuances of that language. Being their leader,
moreover, he has direct access to them, and they may also have
access to him; such feedback between teacher and instructor can
accelerate learning. In contrast, an outsider may not have such
a ready channel of communication and, even when he does, both
literally and figuratively he may not be able adequately to speak
their language.

Over and over again instances are reported in which the outside expert, though a man of good will, neglects to take into
account all the beliefs and values that people feel are involved
in achieving a patently desirable goal such as improved health
or better drinking water. As a result, he may fail to win their cooperation until he acquires and utilizes the knowledge an inside
leader would never fail to take into account (e.g. Tannous, 1945,
pp. 98–100). From a practical standpoint, therefore, it appears
that such opposition and inefficiency may be avoided if the outsider provides only the principle behind the goal but not the detailed means for achieving it. If health is poor, for example, and if
it is also determined that people in the society require more protein and fewer carbohydrates, it is likely that local leaders rather
than outside experts can discover the foods that are not only rich

in protein but are also palatable and economic from the viewpoint of their countrymen. In such a situation the insider must be taught only the goal, and then he must be encouraged to work out the practical details.

Factors other than sheer efficiency, however, affect the degree to which people and their leaders initiate change. Certainly in the past, perhaps also in the present, colonial powers have sometimes been unwilling to allow less civilized peoples to exercise too much self-government. Also, in some areas the use of local leaders may have consequences beyond the particular reforms being learned. The system of "indirect" rule that British colonial officials have employed in the twentieth century deliberately utilizes indigenous institutions and leaders and thus serves to some extent to perpetuate the status quo. Sometimes, as in the Solomon Islands, people know that their chief has the "whole machinery" of European government behind him and hence come to distrust him (Hogbin, 1939, p. 143). In practice, moreover, the choice must often be made between the apparent efficiency of a master plan and the subtler efficiencies to be achieved through local initiative. There can be savings in time and money when houses are produced centrally; yet though relatively inexpensive they may prove to be unattractive to, or unsuited for, the future occupants. Decisions can be made more rapidly by a single board, but those decisions may overlook apparently small items which the people themselves demand. The outsider who would bring change to the old society may have to choose between the lesser of two difficulties: the energy to be expended in seeking to convert the leader in order to have him subsequently perform effectively among his followers versus the energy saved by not effecting his conversion which can thus be expended in actual teaching. If the leader proves especially recalcitrant, for example, perhaps efficiency dictates cooperation with marginal people because their cooperation, though not as valuable as that of the chief, at least is easily obtained. There are long-run considerations too: if people eventually are to control their own destiny, they may require practice in self-government and in producing change, and these eventual gains may compensate for momentary fumblings. Thus wards who are deprived of initiative for a long period of time may become as frustrated and as inactive as the modern Pine Ridge Sioux Indians, who now "cling" to the Federal government "for security and yet resent it because it does not permit them to be fully responsible citizens" (MacGregor, 1946, p. 120).

Securing the cooperation of local leaders is a problem which must be met and resolved in its own right if the advantages postulated by the corollary are to be obtained. Perhaps their help is enlisted because they are attracted by the civilization of the West or by one of its traits. More often, it appears, tangible positive or negative rewards have to be offered, such as money, goods, military support, or threats. The powerful king of the Ganda was persuaded to sign a treaty with the British and thus assist them in the diffusion of Western culture, according to the man who negotiated in the name of Queen Victoria, by being promised the right to a nine-gun salute: this placed him "on the same level of importance as the Sultan of Zanzibar" with whose system of protocol he was acquainted (Oliver, 1957, p. 307). Again and again, especially in the scramble for Africa, a chief whose mark was affixed to a treaty did not appreciate the extent of his commitment to act as an agent of civilization.

The potentially important role of the inside leader may produce efficient learning or may diminish some of the distress occasioned by social change, but that role makes the theoretical task of prediction more difficult. "It is a fact easily verified by observation in the field," lament two anthropologists, "that the same influences introduced into two communities culturally similar may have entirely different effects, and that within the same community at different times their results may also be dissimilar, not by reason of any change in social or economic conditions, but simply because of the rise of a new leader or of a change in the attitude of a man whom the people follow" (Culwick and Culwick, 1935, p. 169). One could question whether the two communities are in fact "culturally similar" in all respects and whether in fact a "change in social or economic conditions" has not occurred, but the writers' tribute to the leader would doubtless remain justified in large part.

Supporting Groups

Ordinarily most people in any society associate with other people who have similar attitudes and beliefs and who follow similar practices. The very existence of such similarity reduces conflict and enables them to cooperate and to feel relatively secure. When one member of a group exhibits behavior that does not conform with the usual standards, at the very least he becomes conspicuous, and it seems probable that he will also incur the wrath of those who follow tradition. Becoming more civilized in particular ways may mean that those who change will alienate themselves from those remaining unchanged. It takes real courage, therefore, to change mildly or radically when there is opposition within primary groups to becoming civilized, to adopting particular innovations, or even to associating with more civilized people. When the old society is really intact and hence provides its members with meaningful security both in their social relations and their normal demands, that courage must be all the greater: why gamble on the unknown?

Sometimes those who would change are condemned both for following and for not following the same form of behavior. Members of an African society in Northern Rhodesia, for example, once found themselves in a quandary regarding the traditional marriage ceremonies when they moved into town. If they carried out the ceremonies, other tribes in the urban area laughed at them; if they failed to do so, they were derided by their relatives in the villages when they returned there (Wilson and Wilson, 1945, p. 152).

The pioneers who change probably require more than initial courage if they are to remain changed: they must look to someone to supply the approbation and assistance which has been theirs in the old society, or else the loss of such support as well as the punishment they are likely to receive from those adhering to traditional ways may cause them to revert to the old. In some instances they may be able to join the new society, in others they may find fellow spirits and refer their behavior to a newly organized group. When the new group has been formed, then those

who have not changed because they lacked courage—whatever
courage really means in this context—or because they were otherwise reluctant or unable to incur the wrath of their contemporaries may then change: they perceive that they will be welcomed
by the already existing band of converts. Regardless of whether
people are pioneers or late-comers, then, it may be anticipated
that they will band together in new groups:

> HYPOTHESIS 9 (*interactional*): *In comparison with those
> who have remained unchanged, people changing from old to
> new ways are likely to be members. of newly established
> groups whose members demonstrate similar forms of be-
> havior.*

Evidence supporting the hypothesis consists of a series of
impressions and hence cannot be presented in statistical form.
Throughout developing areas there are clubs and associations
of people who have learned new ways and then band together
to secure mutual support. Into this category fall alumni groups,
trade associations, professional organizations, and social clubs.
In the writer's own experience, it appears that many East Africans
who once doubtless spoke fluent English during their student
days at the University in Uganda lose that fluency unless their
occupation or contact with Europeans requires them to use the
language relatively frequently. African males who have received
professional training often complain that they cannot find equiv-
alently trained females to marry; with a traditional wife, they say,
it is difficult to retain a Western outlook. At the time there are
often more compelling reasons to marry a traditional woman:
such a person expects to do manual work, especially in connection with agriculture; and her very traditionalism gives her husband's contemporaries the impression that he has not departed
too far from traditional ways and hence renders him less conspicuous and less unpopular (Goldthorpe, 1955, p. 38).

Other types of evidence fit more closely the following corollary
than the hypothesis itself: *People learn new forms of behavior
more readily when they can join new groups which encourage
them to do so and/or can desert old groups which discourage
them from doing so.* For it seems clear that significant change

occurs only when some members of the society can be literally separated from the old groups and learn new forms in an approving group. Children of immigrants, as one writer has said of Hawaiian-born offspring of Oriental immigrants, do not resist acculturation as do their parents but rather accept the new society "wholeheartedly" (Burrows, 1947, p. 208). This ability to absorb the new ways stems from many sources, including the fact that the children have experienced the old ways only for a relatively brief time at home. Absolutely crucial, however, seems to be the situation at school, in which knowledge concerning the new ways is not only taught but considered *de rigueur* in the children's peer group. To be acceptable socially for them means to learn the ways of the new society. Learning becomes even easier when children are separated from their parents not merely during school hours but throughout the entire day and night. "The only evidence of a sharp break with tradition," it is stated of a small Indian village in Mexico, "comes from the small group of boys and girls who have studied outside the village and returned imbued with new customs and ideas." Even though their number is small and their family groups oppose their new ways, "they are nevertheless extremely important since they serve as models for the youth of the village" (Lewis, 1951, p. 395).

The influence of the old group must wane, however, if those who have learned new ways are neither to abandon them nor find themselves in an unbearable situation. This point can be forcefully illustrated by considering the kind of homecoming that awaited Zuni and Navaho young men who had served with the American Army during World War II. By being in the army they had been removed from the influence of their own society, generally for the first time in their lives, and necessarily had been compelled, by drill sergeants and gentler forces, to acquire many new forms of behavior. The Zuni veterans were regarded, especially by conservative members of the tribe, as "forces for destructive change"; deliberate efforts, consequently, were made to reabsorb them into the traditional ways of the tribe by staging ceremonials which were rites of purification and thus symbolically removing some of the outside contamination. When they displayed white ways, moreover, they were made to feel conspicuous and uncomfortable through gossip, rumor, and ridicule. In contrast, Navaho authorities, even the conservative leaders, considered their veterans "potential forces for constructive change" and hence accorded them honor and prestige through ceremonies whose aim was to make them feel welcome as well as to dispel any troublesome effects from war service. The young men, furthermore, were praised when they displayed their new learning, e.g., the ability to read English. The reasons for the difference in treatment can be found in "the differing historical developments and the differing socio-cultural systems that are now current in the two tribes" and hence are of a historical nature. It seems clear, however, that under existing conditions the new forms of behavior would be retained more easily by the Navaho than by the Zuni since the former and not the latter secured the social approval of their meaningful group. In fact, many of the Zuni who were attracted to the new ways found life so intolerable within their pueblo community that they left the reservation, presumably to live in a community where, they believed, their new ways would not be punished (Adair and Vogt, 1949).

Sometimes the new condition in the old society must affect everyone. A society is defeated in war. Or it moves on to another area where the soil seems more fertile or the game more plentiful. A case in point in modern times are the Bikinians, who were evacuated by the United States Navy when their land was selected as the site at which atomic bombs were to be experimentally exploded (Mason, 1950). There appears to have been complete social support for retaining as much of the old as possible under the changed conditions.

Usually some subgroup within the society responds differentially to changed conditions and gradually develops a subculture of its own. Regardless of the reason for the initial difference in response to the change, the new ways when once established can have a tremendous effect upon the learning of future generations. In one district of Natal in the Union of South Africa, for example, there are two distinct clans whose members, in European terminology, share the same surname. The original head of clan A arrived in the area in 1878 at the age of forty and, for reasons that are "now difficult to assess," became converted to

Christianity. Twenty-two years later, a sixty-year-old man moved into the same district with two wives and their children. He believed that his first two wives had died as a result of witchcraft in the area that he was deserting. After his arrival he refused to be converted by the leader of clan A. Soon his wives left him because they found him too "quarrelsome." He retained the headship of clan B, however, because sons of his deceased wives remained near him, but—with one exception—they insisted on independent homesteads. He prospered because of his powers as a native doctor. Ever since, there have been marked differences between the descendants in the two clans. Members of A stay in school longer; prosper economically to a greater degree; maintain more spacious and cleaner homes; grow a greater variety of vegetables and fruits in their gardens; cooperate decidedly more eagerly with government officials, including an inspiring local health center; drink less alcohol; quarrel among themselves but settle their arguments, when they finally do settle them, less violently; perhaps suffer more from hypertension; and produce healthier children (Kark, 1951).

In 1955 the writer administered his regular schedule to 13 members of clan A and 12 of clan B, all males who were either living permanently on their Reserve (usually because they were old) or who were home temporarily from a job in the city or on a European farm. Most of the differences between the two groups are not large enough to be statistically significant—with such small numbers, a difference of course must be quite large not to be attributed to chance—but virtually all the significant ones and the trend of the remaining indicate greater acculturation on the part of clan A. For example, 7 out of 13 in clan A know no English; 10 out of 11 in B. The greater interest of A in Christianity is suggested by the fact that 8 out of 13 believe that "life in heaven will be better than here"; 4 out of 11 for B. Some of the differences are probably not related to acculturation; thus only 1 man from the A sample but 6 from the B expressed hostility toward Indians.

A brief schedule was also administered to all the children in both clans who were attending the two elementary schools of the area on a given day. As might be anticipated, more from clan A than B were at hand: 28 of the former could be located, but only 9 of the latter apparently were faithful pupils. When these imperfect, small samples are compared, no differences are even suggested with respect to (a) six traditional beliefs as ascertained directly; (b) attitudes toward the Zulu, Europeans, and parents as determined by the technique of incomplete sentences; and (c) feelings about father and people generally as measured by the reactions to two ambiguous drawings. Evidently the contrast in later behavior is not evident before adolescence. The children from clan A, however, did perform significantly better on a test of visual retention.

Often those who are changing exercise the new forms only in some groups and retain the old forms in others. Mexicans living in Tucson, Arizona, for example, are reported to speak Spanish with their families, to shift rapidly and frequently between Spanish and English in informal groups, and to speak English almost exclusively in formal groups and in the presence of Americans (Barker, 1947, pp. 195–6). Similarly some educated Africans in East Africa change from Western to traditional clothes when they return home from the office each evening. Were there no reference groups with opposite expectations, it is reasonably certain that old forms could be more quickly discarded and new ones more efficiently perfected.

Other People

When people choose between old and new forms of behavior, they are often, as Hypothesis 9 suggests, really choosing between different groups to which they can refer their behavior, and hence they are in fact deciding with which people they will associate. The old society contains numerous groups that claim people's devotion, but their functions usually differ and are complementary rather than competing. Goals achievable in the family are not likely to be at variance with those sought in work or occupational groups. In contrast, people undergoing acculturation are confronted with incompatible groups. They may continue, for example, either to follow a traditional occupation or to learn a new skill after subscribing to a set of new beliefs.

Attention so far has been devoted to the attitudes that changing or changed people are likely to have toward the other persons in the old and new groups with which they then do or do not associate. Now it is being contended that people who have made, or must presently make a choice between associates are compelled to observe other people rather carefully in order to discriminate between them. While it is undoubtedly true that one aim of socialization in any society is that of "inculcating in the child a regard for other people" (Havighurst and Neugarten, 1955, p. 109) and therefore people must always be sensitive to other people, the a priori case for believing that such sensitivity is increased during acculturation appears strong. The individual becoming civilized almost always has some kind of meaningful contact with outsiders. He must be ever alert to discover whether he is acceptable to his new associates or whether members of the old society are flatly or subtly hostile toward him. On the other hand, a man who remains unchanged may be sensitive only to cues from traditional people and may fail to acquire knowledge of the behavior of outsiders. This is not to say that traditional societies do not occasionally demand the perception of delicate nuances in other people; if people believe in witchcraft or sorcery, they must show grave and frequent interest in their contemporaries and so become acutely aware of changes in other people. Still, if it may be assumed that awareness not merely of others but of the contrast between insiders and outsiders is a delicate discrimination, it *may* follow that:

> HYPOTHESIS 10 (*interactional*): *In comparison with those who remain unchanged or who have changed, people changing from old to new ways are likely to be generally sensitive to other people.*

The trend of the evidence from the Africa-Jamaica studies presented in the first part of Table 6 (p. 289) appears largely to support the hypothesis. The last three items, rows 10–12, are straightforward: fairly objectively they reveal whether or not an informant includes other people within the framework of his own value judgments. The first nine indexes, being derived from projective tests, require a word of explanation. The reporting that a human being or some human detail is present in the ink blot of a Rorschach plate or in a vague line drawing is interpreted to mean that the informant is so set to respond to people that he sees them in ambiguous stimuli (rows 1–4). In Plate VIII of the Rorschach series virtually all informants claimed they saw animals, but some of them—a slightly higher proportion among the educated—also reported something human. A more doubtful measure of sensitivity, in this case sensitivity to the interviewer, was obtained through what is often called the "testing-the-limits" procedure: after his response to each Rorschach card, the interviewee was told that "most people see" something which he had not reported and he was asked whether he too could see the same thing. Note was then made whether he was "sensitive" to this suggestion immediately (row 5) or on the very next card (row 6). The results from these two measures, it can be seen in the table, are inconclusive. Finally, the failure to respond at all or to respond adequately to ambiguous figures that were labeled human beings by the interviewer indicates, it is presumed, an inability to discuss human relationships suddenly or in a strange context (rows 7–9).

Admittedly the claim that differences in the above indexes reflect differences in sensitivity to other people is debatable; and yet, it is plaintively asked, how else can sensitivity be measured? A discussion of the interpretation to be given human responses to the Rorschach plates may prove instructive: unsolved problems are apparently so numerous that the index at the moment cannot be considered very promising. First, the index in the Africa-Jamaica study is probably reflecting different sequences of events. It might be contended that the better educated Zulu who live in urban areas have little opportunity to see animals; they must respond to plates II and III in some way and hence do so by reporting the one aspect of their milieu which they frequently perceive, viz., human beings. Rural Zulu obviously also see human beings, but it may be guessed that their current interest in animals is strong enough to affect them when they observe Rorschach plates. For Zulu, consequently, varying experiences with animals are assumed to have produced the postulated difference in sensitivity to people, but the experience itself is a by-product of residence which in turn is either a cause or a consequence of acculturation.

Even on speculative grounds the same tenuous explanation cannot be employed to account for the results in the other two African societies. For there residence is probably irrelevant. Highly educated as well as poorly educated Luo and Ganda live in rural areas. In Kenya and Uganda, there is no sharp separation between urban and rural areas as there is among the Zulu: cities and towns are less numerous and "bush" conditions usually begin right outside city limits.

Results from the Rorschach test among the Ojibwa Indians not only are contrary to the hypothesis as tested by the index but they have also been quite differently interpreted by the investigator himself. More rather than fewer responses occurred among the less acculturated (see p. 309, Table D, rows 1 and 2). The obtained difference is explained not by a reference to sensitivity but in a manner similar to this book's Hypothesis 2 pertaining to aggression: in the more acculturated group "an aboriginal personality structure . . . appears to be breaking down," as a result of which "hostility in human relations" occurs (Hallowell, 1955, p. 71).

On two grounds, moreover, a difference between the less and the more acculturated Ojibwas with respect to animal responses might be anticipated. First, like the Zulu, they may have fewer contacts with animals as acculturation proceeds; therefore the more acculturated should frequently observe animals on the cards. Then the opposite prediction can be made through a chain of premises. The investigator himself shows that in several societies human and animal responses are the "predominant Rorschach categories" (ibid., p. 51); hence there should be an inverse relation between animal and human responses. Since the more acculturated Ojibwas produce fewer human responses than the less acculturated, they should report more animal responses. In fact, none of the differences between the groups in this respect are significant (Table D, row 3).

The unpromising character of the human vs. animal responses to Rorschach plates as an index of sensitivity is finally illustrated by two other observations. The animal responses of Indians from the very same Ojibwa society, which are said to be about as frequent as those commonly found in "Western society," are thought by another writer to reflect not sensitivity or a change in personality but yet a third attribute which he calls "mundane and intellectually undifferentiated thinking" (Honigmann, 1949, pp. 262–3). The Adult Section of the Indian-white study offers only inconclusive results with respect to the percentage of animal responses to the Rorschach plates (Table B, row 1).

Other problems arise when different indexes are employed. Children's interest in other people in the Indian-white study was measured in various ways—or at least the measures may perhaps be so interpreted. Subjects indicated whether they were concerned with problems involving self-restraint for the sake of others (Table A, row 18), with altruism in general or through good deeds (row 19), with interpersonal relations that proceed without friction (row 20), with shame produced by embarrassment in front of other people (row 21), and with aggression displayed toward their peers (row 22). It was also noted whether very general references to "they," other people, everybody, etc. were positive or negative (rows 23–26). When there are significant differences, and with two exceptions (rows 21 and 26), more of the children among the more acculturated Navaho reveal an interest in others. These variations, however, may not stem from the kind of experience which has been assumed in order to formulate Hypothesis 10 but may merely reflect an ecological fact, viz., the relative isolation in which the less acculturated Navaho children live. Under the same testing conditions and with no exceptions, moreover, higher percentages of the Indian groups than the Midwestern Americans turn out to be, according to the indexes, more sensitive to people. This finding suggests support for the hypothesis: Indians who observe two cultures may be more alert to others than are Americans who observe only their own society. Or, again, the explanation may be ecological: the close-knit nature of village life in a pueblo may produce greater sensitivity. Here is another illustration of the difficulties that arise when comparisons are made across cultural lines.

Another index to be derived from the same study is the extent to which the children produced sketches of people rather than, for example, animals or landscapes. When it is possible to make a comparison of the drawings from the less and the more acculturated communities within the same society, the hypothesis is supported in two societies, contradicted in one, and unsupported in a fourth. There was also a tendency in two of the societies but not in a third for children in the more acculturated communities to produce better defined drawings of people (Havighurst and Neugarten, 1955, pp. 167–8; Havighurst et al., 1946, p. 55). The authors warn that some of the differences between communities may be partly due to "fashions" in drawing: in one community, a relatively high percentage of ceremonial objects and designs were drawn as a result of influences previously exerted by an art teacher stationed there.

Among the Menomini Indians no trend appears when the available categories are observed and analyzed (Table C, rows 20–22). The one significant difference between the least and the most acculturated groups is in the anticipated direction (row 22), but the series offers no consistent tendency for the category. Such evidence in support of the present hypothesis, it is freely confessed, is like the rest of the evidence in this section: it leads, one can say by really stretching one's imagination, to the conclusion that eventually the hypothesis may be vindicated, or at least the possibility cannot be excluded.

Ideals

There are in any society certain "common human problems" whose solution determines how people judge one another and themselves (F. R. Kluckhohn, 1950). What, they ask, is the nature of man? Their answer to the question indicates the assets or liabilities they ascribe to all men at birth. Ultimately people are judged good or bad when they are thought to realize or not to realize the potentialities of which it is assumed they have been originally capable. Second, the inquiry continues, what kind of a universe must each person face—what is the nature of his surroundings? It may be believed, on the one hand, that natural forces can only be understood and then obeyed; or at the other extreme, those forces may be viewed as subject to human control. Then, after declaring their opinions of people and of their surroundings, men confront themselves with a third query: Which other human beings—living or dead—significantly affect existence and how should those beings be treated? Men pay attention to, and are perplexed by, not only themselves but also their ancestors, their descendants, and their own generation. Toward whom do they try to orient their behavior? A decision is thus reached concerning the traits people must possess if they are to be highly valued.

The questions, variously phrased and just as variously answered, have been of concern to anyone who has had the leisure and talent to ponder. Being cosmic, they are usually handled normatively: dicta are issued to specify what the ideal attitudes should be. For present purposes, the more modest objective—which is really not the least bit modest—is to ask: Can a set of Postulated Traits for civilized societies be indicated? For all the usual reasons most social scientists refuse to answer such a question, for they point to the variability from civilized society to civilized society and from stratum to stratum within a given society. The problem, nevertheless, seems hopelessly intriguing.

One sociologist, the same one whose broad schema has been utilized slightly unfaithfully in the first paragraph of the present section, has postulated the following "orientations" of what has been called the American "core culture" (ibid., pp. 382–3):

1. Human nature is thought to be "evil but perfectible."
2. Man can demonstrate "rational mastery over nature."
3. Man's relation to other men is "individualistic."
4. A man is judged "primarily on the basis of his accomplishments, his productivity."

Even within American society, different orientations in the above respects are recognized in each social class and ethnic group. In fact, the formulation at best is thought to be partially and tentatively valid only for the American middle class. But, if it were validated more conclusively and more broadly, it would then be necessary to know whether the orientation of that class resembles the dominant views in other civilized societies. For want of a better assumption and for illustrative purposes, let such a leap be semi-seriously made. Then it is possible to say that civilized peoples tend to subscribe to certain Postulated Ideals and that other peoples, in becoming civilized, necessarily learn those ideals. The ideals in turn demand that a high evaluation be placed upon certain human traits; for example:

HYPOTHESIS 11 (consequential): *After people change centrally from old to new ways, they are likely to value in others and in themselves traits which indicate initiative, independence, and self-confidence.*

The three traits selected, be it noted, are related directly to the four orientations postulated by Kluckhohn. A person displaying initiative, independence, and self-confidence can agree with the view that human nature is evil since the evil can be eradicated. He must also feel that he can exercise control over nature. His concern in interpersonal relations is more with his own accomplishments than with his ancestors, contemporaries, or descendants. Such traits, moreover, can be admired without necessarily subscribing to all of the orientations allegedly characteristic of the American middle class; hence the traits may possibly be valued in other areas of Western civilization.

Although the principal purpose of the hypothesis is to raise and not resolve the provocative problem of the ideal personality associated with civilization, the writer cannot escape the serious conviction that the Postulated Traits are not altogether imaginary. Consider briefly "self-confidence." That trait is a variant of the confidence already identified as one of the factors determining whether or not a new form of behavior will be learned (Hypothesis 4). If a person lacks confidence, he may never attempt a new task or, if he attempts it, he is likely to fail or progress very slowly. If he feels that traditional ways are inexorable and that his fate is not determined by his own desires and plans, he is not likely to try to change himself or even to imagine that the future can be different from the present or the past. The learning required to become civilized and then to adjust to civilization and produce changes therein, it is argued, demands self-confidence.

Evidence for the hypothesis from the Africa-Jamaica studies is rather trifling but it is presented in the second part of Table 6, under the heading "Conceptualization." The first item (row 13) was the following statement, with which informants were asked to agree or disagree: "People would be much happier if they talked less and worked more." Here the stress is on self-confidence: get on with the job, it may be assumed the more civilized man says, quit complaining. Does he say so? If he does, then in all three African societies the differences between the better and the poorly educated people are in the expected direction, but are too small to be significant. Likewise the other items on the table tend to point in the same direction, though not overwhelmingly. In comparison with their parents, the African boys in the high schools run by Europeans appear more ruthless and ambitious (Table I, rows 13–17). In Jamaica, the well educated informants differ significantly from the rest on all three items for which data were collected: while fewer of them condemn verbal complaints (Table 6, row 13), more of them pay tribute to ability in producing success (row 17) and refuse to shift responsibility for failure upon others (row 18).

The Indian-white study provides more convincing evidence. As already indicated, more American than Indian children seek goals for themselves rather than for the group (Table A, row 1). The authors themselves observe:

> It is as though the Midwest children were more self-centered and felt a personal sadness when not given their own way in such matters as going to a movie or getting new clothes, while the Southwest Indian children were more group-centered, feeling sad when people were aggressive or bad even though the aggression may not have been directed against them personally [Havighurst and Neugarten, 1955, p. 43].

The children's attitudes toward at least three human traits were also ascertained. In Table A, "competence" refers to a person's achievement, especially in his work (row 27); "personal virtues" to patterns of behavior, such as honesty and courage, considered important in the society (row 28); and "aggression by others" to actions by other people, such as fighting and lying, which the person himself condemns (row 29). Although these traits only remotely resemble those in Hypothesis 11, the results do establish the point that they are evaluated differently by the two Navaho communities and to a degree by the Indian and American children.

A more detailed study of 15 Navaho men provides relevant data. The anthropologist making the study first characterized what he believed to be traditional orientations in Navaho society: all of them, he thinks, differ from the American views. Whereas Americans tend to believe, as suggested above, that human nature is "evil but perfectible," for example, Navaho traditionally think that "both good and evil are ever present" simultaneously. Then he has studied the values which the 15 men expressed during interviews and in projective tests to determine whether their views are Navaho or white American. On this basis alone he classified four as "most acculturated," six as "least acculturated," and the remaining five "intermediate." Validation comes from the fact that certain other aspects of behavior which by any definition are known to be related to acculturation are associated with these three categories. Among the four "most acculturated" Navahos, there is "an overtly expressed zeal for white ways of life." The same men "speak fluent English," whereas "only one . . . in the 'intermediate' grouping speaks enough English to carry on an extended conversation with whites" (Vogt, 1951, pp. 85–9).

Not for a moment has it been contended in this discussion that the ideals of civilization are actually realized or that people believe them to be. In fact, one of the frustrations associated with changing may be an inability to reach the very goals whose existence has given impetus to the drive to change. In the Middle East study, for example, people were asked two pairs of questions that are clearly related to their feeling of self-confidence. The first pair was: "a. What is the biggest problem that people in the same circumstances as yourself face in life? b. Is there anything that you an individual can do to solve this problem?" The second pair was similarly worded but pertained to "the biggest problem that our country as a nation faces today." An index of "personal impotency" derived from the answers decreases as the estimated modernity of the six countries increases;

and within four of the lands the highest proportion of those feeling impotent occurs among the Transitionals. The two exceptions are Turkey and Lebanon, the most "modern" of the countries (Lerner, 1958, p. 100). Perhaps the actual attainment of modernity restores or creates confidence.

Chapter 6.

BELIEFS AND VALUES

EVERYWHERE men seek to explain and evaluate their environment, their associates, outsiders, and themselves. "Why do you do this?" receives the response, "I don't want to have bad luck." Here is a belief that the activity will bring disaster, and it is accompanied by the implicit value that the disaster is to be avoided. The belief and the value are facts pertaining to the person, regardless of whether they are rationally founded or valid.

The conceptual model of behavior being presented suggests that attitudes, beliefs, and values help to evoke drives and motives and then channel them into very general or specific forms of behavior. A man who believes that a brook is bewitched will not be tempted to drink from the stream when he sees it or to search for it when he is thirsty. People, it has been noted in another context, "cannot effectively carry out acts for which they have no underlying systems of belief" (Leighton, 1945, p. 292). In different words: attitudes, beliefs, and values are inferred forms of behavior that are general rather than specific and that mediate between the eternal world and the individual's observable or overt behavior. Hypotheses previously formulated to specify the conditions under which external forms of behavior are changed, therefore, are applicable to the internal forms—the beliefs and values—which are the concern of the present chapter. The patent differences between internal and external forms of behavior, however, give rise to the hypotheses of this chapter.

Verbalizable Opinions

A number of alternatives are available to a person who is asked to indicate what he believes about a particular subject. He may refuse to reply. He may express the truth as he sees it, by outlining the belief he thinks he has or by stating that he has no opinion when in fact he thinks that such is the case. Or he may lie, either by uttering a false belief (including the spontaneous expression of a belief he composes at the spur of the moment) or by falsely claiming that he has no belief. For purposes of the present discussion let it be assumed that the individual is willing to express himself and then that he either indicates his belief most faithfully or says, "I am not sure, I don't know," when he has no opinion. Why would he have no opinion? At least four possibilities suggest themselves:

1. He may never have had to face the issue, and so he lacks both the knowledge and the drive to reach a decision. A person in the jungle who has seen planes in the sky has not imagined that he himself will ever have the opportunity to fly; he has no opinion as to whether or not planes are safe.

2. He may have faced the issue without acquiring the necessary knowledge to reach a decision. The man in the jungle wonders whether planes ever fall or have accidents, but he and his people have no information on the subject.

3. He may have the necessary knowledge but be unable or unwilling to reach a decision. The man has heard of plane crashes but cannot say whether one accident after thousands of flights means that planes are unsafe, or he may have no interest in the general safety record.

4. He may have reached a decision but be unable to express himself. Within the man is the feeling that planes are or may be unsafe, but either the conviction is repressed or he cannot intelligibly verbalize it.

On all four counts it appears likely but not certain that those becoming more civilized have opinions on a variety of issues and can appropriately express themselves more efficiently than those remaining unchanged. To change, a person must be at least confronted with people who display the old and the new form of behavior. He necessarily is acquainted with the old form, and his contact with the new doubtless provides him with relevant information. Situated between the forms from the two societies, he has reached a decision concerning the form in question, and through a process of generalization he may feel compelled to make similar decisions concerning other forms. In contrast, the old society tends to have only a single set of values. Those who are unchanged, finally, may have their own beliefs so intertwined and undifferentiated—one of the assumptions concerning the attributes of less civilized people—that they cannot respond instantly to a discrete question. Evidence to be presented in the next chapter, at any rate, indicates that the changing are better equipped to express themselves verbally.

It is possible, however, to turn some of these arguments around. People who are changing and hence wavering between two societies or between alternate beliefs are in a state of conflict; one of the solutions to conflict is to avoid coming to a decision, for example, by repressing the struggle or refusing to face the situation. Even if such people make a decision and hence acquire opinions, they do not necessarily generalize the decision-making process. They remain undecided in other areas. In addition, it may be contended, those not changing may be forced to form opinions because they feel challenged or because they have considered the new and deliberately rejected it.

Perhaps the conflicting expectations may be resolved by specifying the kinds of issues concerning which beliefs are held. If a stone is thrown into a pool of water, will it sink? All sane adults in any society will agree that it will sink; nobody will say "I don't know," regardless of his state of acculturation: the experiences giving rise to the belief are universal and unequivocal. But is there a life after death? Experience does not contribute an answer to this question, rather people must depend upon their intuitive feelings and the tradition of their society. If a traditional reply is provided, the unchanging will have opinions, the ones they have been taught from the very outset; but if that traditional reply conflicts with the outside view, then those who are changing may be in a state of conflict and without opinions. Who is more important in human progress, the people or their leaders? If there is an outside but not a traditional reply to that question, then those not changing are not likely to have an opinion. Those who have had contact with the outside, on the other hand, are likely to have an opinion for at least two reasons. Their contact has enabled them to obtain the necessary information or indoctrination. And contact with the West means in part that people must ask themselves searching questions. If these considerations are correct, then the following hypothesis may be true:

> Hypothesis 12 (interactional): In comparison with those who remain unchanged, people changing from old to new ways are less likely to have readily verbalizable opinions on traditional issues and more likely to have such opinions on nontraditional issues and on issues involving self-awareness and awareness of society; those who have changed are likely to be similarly different from those in the process of changing.

Related evidence from the Africa-Jamaica studies appears in Table 7 (p. 291), where the percentages of "no opinion" are presented. For traditional issues (rows 1–7), there are no differences between the two groups in each of the three African societies; it will be noted that the figures are very low and that no trend emerges. For issues that might be called nontraditional (rows 8–31), the percentages of no opinion are appreciably larger in all groups; and the few significant differences and the trend of all the differences tend to be in the anticipated direction. Hypothesis 12 receives slightly more convincing confirmation in the third category, the "information-seeking" questions (rows 32–46): apparently when suddenly asked questions about themselves and their society, more of the better educated informants are able to supply some kind of definite answer. Likewise fewer of the better educated Jamaicans claim no opinion on a variety of questions.

The author of the Middle East study argues strongly in favor of the view that Transitionals and Moderns, in contrast with Traditionals, have opinions about themselves, the world, and contingencies that might arise. "Especially important" for the modern man in a civilized society, he says, "is the enormous proportion of people who are expected to 'have opinions' on public matters—and the corollary expectation of these people that their

opinions will matter" (Lerner, 1958, p. 51). The evidence to
support his view and hence the present hypothesis is indeed very
convincing. In the first place, as indicated previously when his
three types were described (see p. 59), inability to demonstrate "empathy" has been measured by determining whether or
not people could reply to a series of nine projective questions.
The number of no replies was found to be correlated with the
social indexes of acculturation, viz., education, urbanism, occupation, and exposure to the mass media of communication.
Then each correspondent was ranked "as a participant in the
Middle Eastern opinion arena" by means of an "opinion index"
based upon whether or not opinions were expressed in relation to
eleven questions "on different matters of large public importance." Rankings from this index were also found to be related
to the indexes of acculturation and hence to the three types when
the types were defined in terms of those indexes (ibid., pp. 71–2,
99).

The Middle East study, moreover, indicates that the Moderns
and the Transitionals not only have more opinions than the
Traditionals but are better informed about the outside world.
Except in Turkey where each group seems alert, fewer of the
Traditionals than of the other two groups named an international
rather than a local event when asked to recall "the last item of
news" that had come to their attention. Likewise, those no longer
traditional revealed that their conception of a newspaper came
closest to "the modern approved attitude" (ibid., pp. 97–8). Succinctly if glibly the investigator says: "In villages that remain
Traditional, no voices need be raised to defend traditional ways
because no other ways are on the agenda" (ibid., pp. 141–2).

Persistence

A single pin when struck by the ball may tumble without
causing any other in the set to fall; or while falling it may strike
other pins which then fall. These falling pins may drop to the
side without producing further repercussions or they may strike
the remaining members of the set and scatter them all in the
alley.

Likewise, it may be said with an apology for the analogy, a person's beliefs and values change. One belief or value may change without affecting others. Or, as in a religious conversion, the single change may have far-reaching consequences. Indeed, since beliefs and values are organized as part of the personality, normally one or more repercussions must occur. Whether the repercussions are confined or widespread, it is clear that some beliefs and values change more readily than others.

There are grounds for believing that some traditional views are likely to persist in every society or person. At least a few members of the older generation loudly or softly prophesy doom for those who do not follow ancestral ways. The convert to the new faith is perpetually reminded of the old by the ancient temple, even when the building is used for some other purpose, or by the former priest, even if he be assigned to another occupation. The man from the old society who has attended an agricultural school knows very well from the viewpoint of modern science that there is no connection between the success of a crop and the phase of the moon when its seeds were sown; but the moon will always be visible and serve to remind him of the ancient lore. On either a rational or a completely emotional basis, moreover, the individual often may find himself unable to run the risk of transgressing the old. A tribesman trained in modern science may hesitate to mistrust completely the medicine man of his society when he discovers that some herbs have their use, that psychosomatic medicine has prestige in the West, and that there are no cures, or no quick cures, for some diseases. In addition, he may observe on occasion, however rarely, that the old remedy works. A priori, common-sense convictions like these lead to the following hypothesis:

> HYPOTHESIS 13 (causal): *People who are confronted with alternative beliefs and values are likely to retain traditional ones which appear to serve a continuing need and to reject those which do not, but always to retain some of the traditional views.*

In a real sense Hypothesis 13 is a variant of a previous one (No. 4) which states that "people who are experiencing some discontent with a prevailing form of behavior are likely to accept rather than reject an alternative form when that new form," among other attributes, "has advantages which are intelligibly demonstrable in the present and which can be anticipated to continue in the future." The phrase "continuing need" in the hypothesis now under discussion is another way of expressing the "advantages" which cause people to change or not change forms of behavior. The new feature of Hypothesis 13 is its insistence that some traditional views will linger on and, in part because they *are* traditional, satisfy a real need.

In the Africa-Jamaica studies no evidence has been obtained concerning the continuing needs which traditional beliefs and values do or do not satisfy. Some of these beliefs and values are indicated for the three African societies in Table 8 (p. 294). Those which, according to formal ratings or informal opinions provided by anthropologists and other experts, are traditional have been combined into an index, the means for which are indicated in row 21. The differences are clearly significant—as great a gulf exists in Jamaica too (a mean of 6.0 for the less well educated, one of 0.8 for the well educated)—and hence it is evident that changing groups in Africa tend to reject traditional views. In a circular manner it may be argued that these groups must find that the traditional views no longer satisfy their needs, but independent evidence on the relations between the needs and the views would have to be supplied to prove that contention. There would thus seem to be little doubt that valuing cattle rather than money as a form of wealth would not be reinforced in an urban area and hence urban men—and even women— among the Zulu would appreciably change in this respect (Table III, row 20); but what then would one argue concerning the effect of urban living or acculturation upon another Zulu belief, viz., that a "man who gets a wife by abduction should be punished" (Table 8, row 9)? Table 8 does substantiate the last part of the hypothesis, which suggests that traditional views persist: in only one instance (row 5, Luo) is there a better educated group that does not include at least one person subscribing to the traditional belief or value. Likewise, traditional beliefs and values persist among adolescents in African secondary schools although the Western viewpoint is taught (Table I, rows 18–28) and among Zulu women in an urban area (Table III, rows 14–19).

Similar confirmation is obtained from the Indian-white study with reference to beliefs concerning the supernatural and animism (Table A, rows 30 and 31). Increasing acculturation among the Indian societies is accompanied by a decrease in supernatural and animistic belief; since the correlations are significant but not perfect, the conclusion must be drawn that these traditional explanations are not abandoned. Even though fewer of the children in the more acculturated than in the less acculturated Navaho community express fears concerning the supernatural and even though the former live "in a group that has largely adopted white customs and beliefs," 23 per cent of the boys and 31 per cent of the girls in the sample continue to express such fears (Havighurst and Neugarten, 1955, p. 55). With a few statistically nonsignificant exceptions, the same tendency appears not only among Navaho but also among children from communities of varying acculturation in other Indian communities. Again, with one exception, the use of animistic explanations decreases with age; and age of course is related to schooling, which in turn, for Indian children, means greater contact with the Western view of causality. In an earlier study, Hopi children between the ages of 12 and 18 in an American-type school were found, upon careful examination, to possess appreciably more animistic beliefs than roughly comparable groups of American children (Dennis, 1943). Perhaps the teachers did not provide other explanations of the phenomena, and no doubt learning in the school occurred against a home background which, for good reasons within Hopi society, favored animism; if so, then here would be the reason for the persistence of the traditional beliefs in the face of competition from the outside.

An objective knowledge of people's practices does not by itself provide an explanation for the varying persistence of beliefs. Among the Menomini Indians, for example, dependence upon native medicine, native games, native objects, and outdoor facilities decreases with acculturation, but the decrease is much more rapid for the first two than for the last two (Table C, rows 11, 12, 14, and 17). These different rates must be a function of innumerable factors in the contact between Indians and Americans, and such factors must be investigated in their own right before the beliefs accompanying the practices can be comprehended. Has the efficacy of American medicine been demonstrated; what do native games and objects mean to these Indians; can the less acculturated Indians afford an indoor privy?

Again and again those who have had contact with less civilized people report that some ideas from the West are learned more readily than others. "The deepest and most general cultural obstacle I have found in my pupils," states an Englishman who has taught in a secondary school for Africans, "is their assumption about the nature of causation, whether in the world of nature or of men." They find it difficult to comprehend "the slow and spontaneous action of nature" that produces changes on the surface of the earth; instead they would rather ascribe the changes to "the more dramatic, immediately observable results of human action or . . . of an individual man." Likewise it is easier for them to trace an historical event to a single man rather than to "a complex of interacting forces, economic, geographical, cultural, operating over periods longer than the human life-span" (Musgrove, 1952, p. 247). To evaluate these interesting observations it would be important to know whether similar difficulties are experienced by boys of comparable status in the West. The difference between African and British school boys, if validly established, would then have to be explained. Possibly the "continuing need" of the Africans involves their relative intolerance of delay in attaining goals (as indicated in Hypothesis 3): they may grow impatient and hence misunderstand or resist causal explanations which refer to long-range, intricate processes.

The view current among most social scientists that traditional beliefs are retained when they serve a psychological function is especially impressive in comprehending magic. On the surface, for example, it appears strange that often magic continues to be practiced by changing people who are working right in the midst of an industrial civilization. It has been suggested that the new civilization which hires such people also creates anxiety for them since the possibility of unemployment always exists, and unemployment in an industrial society can have more serious consequences than in the older society. That possibility arouses anxiety, the old way of dealing with anxiety was to employ magic, hence magic is now used in the new context of avoiding unemployment. Other situations creating uncertainty—such as relations with Europeans or with potential lovers—evoke the same kind of need for supernatural help (Hunter, 1936, pp. 455–8). Likewise devout converts to Christianity sometimes resort to magical practices for the same reasons and also, sometimes, to assuage a sense of guilt; for example, when the exacting taboos of the old traditions have been abandoned, people may feel that a sense of security is being too easily obtained and so, to insure protection from evil spirits, some of the old magical practices are retained (Richards, 1935b). Or the belief in magic may appear only in those situations in which actual anxiety is aroused. Thus converts to Christianity in a village in North-East New Guinea are reported to speak "with derision" of the old spirits when questioned in broad daylight, but at night they are less "positive" since they have "an inordinate dread of darkness." A woman in the same society explained to the court why she had committed adultery: "she had no alternative as the man touched her on the arm with charmed oil" (Hogbin, 1951, pp. 267–8).

Anthropologists offer evidence supporting the hypothesis when they demonstrate that some portion of the old culture is retained even under most unlikely circumstances. Slaves, for example, seldom lose all their traditions. A case in point is that of the Gullah Negroes, who live on the islands off the coast of South Carolina and Georgia. Most but not all of the West African forms of behavior perished. In some instances, however, when an old practice was compatible with behavior demanded by the owners, there emerged a new institution with "European details" but an "African stamp." The efficiency of field hands was presumably increased when they followed the African custom of hoeing side by side and often to music (Bascom, 1941).

In fact, it is difficult to find an instance of the complete disappearance of the old forms within a generation or two. Theoretically people ought to be able to forget those forms relatively rapidly if they could be removed from their old environment and shifted elsewhere into an utterly different area which would not remind them of their former homes. Actually they would then probably be compelled to make radical changes, and yet their very continuation as a group would perpetuate some of the older forms of adjustment. An illustration of such persistence is that of transplanted Bikinians mentioned in the last chapter. Even the single person who moves from his old environment and from all his old associates does not sever every psychological tie: natural phenomena like darkness at night or social ones like the cry of a child can reinstate the old feelings.

A converted Zulu, it has been suggested, "does not know all the tenets of Christianity, nor even all the pagan beliefs he is expected to abandon" (Gluckman, 1958, p. 57). Such a person does not appreciate what he must learn and unlearn, it seems evident, either because his teachers have been lax or because he himself, consciously or unconsciously, would obtain security from both pagan and Christian beliefs. In any case, aspects of the old persist within him. From a practical standpoint it is usually safest to assume that, no matter how well educated the adult in a changing society is and no matter how urbane he appears, there lurks within him some trace of a traditional belief or value.

Is it possible to state in a general way, in the words of Hypothesis 13, which beliefs and values are likely to "appear to serve a continuing need" and which ones will not so appear? Various theorists have proposed categories—such as material vs. nonmaterial innovations—in an effort to establish a sequence of change, but here only one theory, a very promising one, will be considered: "That which was traditionally learned and internalized in infancy and early childhood tends to be more resistant to change in contact situations" (Bruner, 1956, p. 194). The theory rests on the fairly solid assumption of psychoanalytic and other clinical research which suggests that experiences in early childhood can play a critical role throughout life. Hypothesis 6, which stresses the fact that changes in family forms and practices proceed very slowly, stems from the same source. The author himself adduces supporting data from the area of acculturation, such as the reluctance of people to abandon the food they have eaten since infancy. Or, he states, a religion that is taught very early in life resists change more than one that is transmitted to its adherents later in life. If forced to specify to practical people such as educators, leaders, or missionaries a supplementary corollary, one could state: *Traditional beliefs and values that have been learned at an early age, other things being equal, are more likely to appear to serve a continuing need than those learned later in life.*

Having stated this corollary, the writer must immediately concede that significant changes can occur after infancy and childhood: man's fate is not completely determined at the start. The proponent cited above recognizes this possibility: "Resistance to change," he writes, "may be a function of other factors in addition to relative age of learning, such as degree of affect and ego involvement in the learning situation" (ibid., p. 196). In effect, he is agreeing that "other things must be equal" for age per se to be the critical factor. A child ought to be able to learn a second language more readily than an old man, but only if he has some motive to learn it, only if he can create an opportunity which will give him access to it, and so on: all the factors that may be associated with learning, according to previous hypotheses in this book, immediately become relevant. It remains true, nevertheless, that forms of behavior acquired early in life are likely to be heavily reinforced. Children who are removed from the tribal milieu and placed in a boarding school, it may be predicted, will more quickly absorb civilized ways than those not so detached; yet as children they may be less efficient if they suffer from homesickness, and later on they may suffer from a conflict between themselves and their peers at home or between original and more recent impulses.

"The continuing need" which early forms serve must find expression in the adult environment. Since generations overlap, such an opportunity is likely to be created. People's own language enables them to manipulate their universe and so it is not easily replaced. In a Mexican community, for example, the Indian inhabitants have adopted many Spanish ways, ranging from Catholicism to currency, but most still retain some knowledge of their indigenous language and use it in certain restricted contexts as during ceremonials or when telling secrets or jokes (Lewis, 1951, pp. 33–4).

Another corollary, involving the question of conflict, follows from the section of Hypothesis 13 which maintains that old beliefs and values usually persist: *People changing centrally are likely to remain in a state of conflict concerning the advantages and disadvantages of both old and new beliefs and values.* Recently attention has been paid to a phenomenon which has been termed postdecision dissonance—the dissatisfaction and regret people experience *after* they have arrived at a decision (Festinger, 1957). People in a changing society doubtless experience such dissonance, especially as they are surrounded by reminders of the old society. More than dissonance, however, is involved, for these people usually are able to revert to old forms and indeed, it is suggested here, they carry within themselves remnants of the old and aspects of the new. They must not only reduce their regrets for having made the decision to change but also must decide whether they should retain the new or revert to the old. This is conflict.

The corollary would not imply that the co-existence of old and new beliefs and values necessarily produces conflict. In a Mexican community, for example, hogs have been known to die not only after the performance of the traditional ceremony which is supposed to avert disease but also after the injections of serum which scientifically prevents hoof-and-mouth disease. Under these circumstances, it is said, "no definite choice between the old and new remedy is made. Rather, the new is added to the old. If one does not work, the other is tried" (Redfield, 1950, p. 121).

Conflict is painful and is therefore either avoided or, if unavoided, resolved in some manner. Perhaps the Indians in the Mexican community are not laboriously appraising the relative efficacy of their ceremony and of injection but are avoiding a show-down between the two techniques by believing that each is useful to achieve the same end, though in a different manner. Civilized men, unacquainted with the causes of the common cold, may avoid drafts and wet feet without considering the prophylactic measures to be in conflict.

It may be that people in changing societies prefer to reduce conflict not by meeting the issue directly and rejecting one of the competing forms but by trying, like the Mexican community, to produce a synthesis based on both. This social process, known sometimes as syncretism, is illustrated by the fact that people in Brazil, Cuba, and Haiti have been able—and presumably independently of one another—to see similarities between the old African gods and new Catholic saints and thus to have little difficulty in learning to accept the latter (Herskovits, 1937). Here, it must be noted in passing, is one explanation for the fact, which will be discussed subsequently, that new forms of behavior usually undergo some modification when they enter an old society.

In a special study in Jamaica it was hypothesized that there must be a relation between attitude toward traditional beliefs and the availability of those beliefs. From one standpoint, contact with prevailing beliefs cannot be avoided regardless of attitude. In the study of the Menomini Indians, for example, it has been shown that some individuals in the most acculturated groups were familiar with "native lore and belief" (Table C, row 9), even though few if any followed traditional practices in their daily lives. Most Americans can name a number that is supposed to be unlucky without subscribing to the view that "13" inevitably brings misfortune. From another standpoint, however, it can be reasoned that the belief to which a person subscribes helps guide his behavior; a helpful belief is frequently evoked; hence that belief must be close to the surface and easily aroused. Being reminded of a traditional belief that has been rejected, furthermore, can produce anxiety—"Can 13 possibly bring bad luck?" the person in effect asks himself. Repressing or neglecting the knowledge that sets up such a disturbance, therefore, can reduce internal conflict. Or the sequence can be reversed. Frequent, perhaps involuntary contact with a traditional belief may often mean that the person simultaneously is exposed to supporting arguments; hence a frequently evoked belief is likely to secure assent.

A brief summary of the research must suffice, especially since a full report has been given elsewhere (Doob, 1959). The informants included 65 adults from the principal part of the study, and 93 school children between the ages of 11 and 15. During an interview, the availability of a particular belief was first determined by asking a question which could elicit the belief without stating it. For example: "What do some people say will happen if a woman with child drinks a lot of milk?" If the "correct" traditional reply was made, the informant was then asked whether he agreed or disagreed. If the person did not or could not supply the belief or gave an "incorrect" one, the investigator offered the "correct" view: "Some people think that, if a woman with child drinks a lot of milk, the child will be born light; what do you think?"

Among the adults ten beliefs (items 110–19 of the Schedule) were tested in the above manner, and for all ten there was a positive association between agreement and the ability to recall them correctly—one half of these associations were significantly above chance expectancy. Among the children twenty beliefs were tested, and again the association for all was positive, although only one half were significant. There is thus a clear-cut but low relation between the two factors in the direction anticipated: rejected beliefs may persist but are not at the tip of the tongue.

Since it has been previously shown that the more acculturated Jamaicans have far fewer traditional beliefs (see above, p. 151) and since assent has now been related to availability, there ought to be a negative relation between acculturation and availability. In fact, this relationship does *not* seem to exist. For the adults there was no relation between availability of knowledge and education; even though urban dwellers assented to fewer beliefs than those in rural areas, the urban dwellers could more readily recall the beliefs. For the children there was no relation between availability and grade in school (hence amount of education), general scholastic standing (hence quality of education), or performance on a test involving the ability to remember visual forms (hence, perhaps, intelligence of some sort). How, then, can there be a relation between acculturation and traditional beliefs and also between traditional beliefs and availability without a corresponding relation between acculturation and traditional beliefs? In statistical terms both of the first two relations are significant but low, too low to permit the third to emerge. It is of course possible that the particular measure of availability here employed is not sufficiently sensitive.

After this excursion a corollary may be deduced from the facts

(a) that some traditional views are likely to persist in the old society and (b) that such views affect modes of perception and judgment: *In a society undergoing change from the outside, misunderstandings are likely to arise between those who are unchanged and those who are changing and also between either of those groups and those who have changed as well as outsiders.*

In the Africa-Jamaica studies, again and again misunderstandings arose in the course of the interviews which reflected different beliefs as well as different linguistic expressions. On the question of polygyny, for example, Africans who were devout, well educated Christians could agree or disagree with the statement that "a man with more than one wife can be a good Christian" for reasons that a Westerner might not anticipate. Some said that a polygynist could be a good Christian, since the number of a man's wives is no criterion to employ to evaluate a man's religion; rather the spirit in which he lives or his devotion to God should be the determining fact. Others stated that a man with many wives must be a poor Christian, not because the Church opposes polygyny, but because constant bickering among co-wives prevents a husband from acting like a Christian. Similarly, the higher proportion of the better educated Luo agree that "people can change into animals" (Table 8, row 2). From every standpoint such a result is surprising: one must expect that a Western-type education would reduce the number assenting to a traditional "superstition." Not until toward the very end of the research was it discovered that an unknown number in the subgroup were providing a metaphorical interpretation: robbers and criminals, who were greatly feared, were thought to be acting like animals. In Jamaica it began to seem necessary to invoke subtle psychoanalytic explanations when many poorly educated informants stated that they would be eager to exchange places, if they could, with "the opposite sex" until the context indicated, and other Jamaicans subsequently confirmed, that the phrase there means people of higher social or economic status.

Many of the misunderstandings between members of the old society and outside innovators involve disagreements concerning means, not ends. People from both societies may unhesitatingly agree, for example, that a building to which sick people are sent to be killed is an intolerable abomination. To a man from the West, a hospital is an institution in which sick people receive medical care and, hopefully and actually in most instances, are discharged when they are better or a cure has been effected. To a man from some African societies, a hospital is a mysterious place to which only the hopelessly ill are consigned and from which few ever return alive. The fear of the African often prevents him from sending people to a Western clinic until they are desperately ill; hence the mortality rate may be high. But in any case the fatal illnesses are likely to be impressive. The function of hospitals as places where babies may be delivered, furthermore, is often especially difficult for some noncivilized peoples to understand. Expectant mothers, they know, are not desperately ill, and so why should they go to a place which previously they have associated with only grave illnesses? Then, as has been pointed out (Mead, 1955, p. 205), there is added terror in Burma and in parts of Africa where it is also believed that "pregnant women must never see a corpse or be in the vicinity of one." The Westerner and the non-Westerner, in short, agree that ill people and pregnant mothers should be helped, but only the former is convinced that a modern hospital can achieve that end.

The controversy between Christian missionaries and many Africans concerning polygyny can be similarly viewed. Both sides, as it were, agree that wives and children must be provided for. Both also agree that there must be fidelity for those whose marriage has been formally and ceremonially declared. Both finally agree that it is right and proper for a man to secure assistance in cultivating his land and taking care of his property. They differ only on one detail: the African finds it convenient to combine the economic and marital functions, and thus his wives provide him not only with homes and children but also with assistance in the fields. Likewise misunderstandings occur when outsiders observe only the economic aspect of bride purchase by Africans and overlook its subtle and far-reaching implications for a host of social relations (Krige, 1937, pp. 113–17).

From a practical standpoint, those who seek to help or change so-called underdeveloped peoples must be sensitive to the interpretations people persistently attach to their old ways: otherwise

innovations may be resisted. The sophisticated Westerner, for
example, views running water in a house as a great convenience
and as hygienically superior to water drawn from a fountain in
the village square and then transported home. Rural Greek
women, it is reported, sometimes refuse to have running water
installed even when they can afford the expense because they
would not be deprived of the social contacts at the fountain or,
while washing clothes, at a nearby stream (Mead, 1955, pp. 92,
238). As has been so frequently suggested in this book, less
civilized people are likely to view any activity from a variety of
angles, only some of which may be in accord with the "realism"
of the scientific innovator. Thus the way land is plowed not only
affects the ensuing harvest but also may be considered to reflect
the cultivator's private attitudes toward his ancestors or his descendants. In parts of Africa, therefore, changes in traditional
methods are resisted because they symbolically represent "a
break in continuity with the values of ancestors." Contour plowing, though foreign to sections of French Africa, became acceptable when the Africans were persuaded that thereby they would
"pass the land unharmed to their descendants" (ibid., p. 189).

It would be misleading to conclude this section without acknowledging that differences between traditional and more
civilized views sometimes involve more than a matter of semantics,
perceptions, or values and in fact include irreconcilable conflicts.
An old Zulu is reported to have made the following reply to a
European official who pointed out the disastrous effects of overstocking upon the land: "You are wrong. It is not that we have
too many cattle for our land, we have too little land for our
cattle" (Gluckman, 1958, p. 67). This was not a glib reply. The
man did not fail to perceive the effects of overstocking, nor did he
disagree that eroded land was undesirable. Instead he was thinking of the traditional method to solve the problem: there must
be neither fewer cattle nor more eroded land but more uneroded
land for more cattle. And of course, such land is not readily
available for the Zulu in modern South Africa.

Beliefs vs. Values

As has been stressed in other connections, thinkers with both theoretical and practical interests have raised again and again the problem of temporal sequence: What aspects of a society or of a person are most susceptible to change? The effort has been constantly made to find some kind of monistic solution, for it would be both comforting and convenient to be able to provide a simple proposition to which the exceptions would be infrequent and unimportant. Such a solution, it is here contended, seems impossible except on a very abstract level, and then only under particular conditions which must be assumed and specified.

Consider, for example, the ancient and somewhat tarnished view that so-called material changes are likely to be accepted more readily than so-called nonmaterial ones. In a sense this is a watered-down statement of the Marxian position which maintains that changes in the substructure of society—by which Marx himself meant economic relations, which he defined variously and not always consistently—precede changes in the superstructure (social institutions and ideologies) and that these latter changes only reflect or rationalize the basic ones. In sociological parlance "social lag" refers to the delay between the adoption of material changes and the necessary nonmaterial or institutional readjustments. If the postulated sequence be generally true, then it is necessary to determine the reasons both for its frequent occurrence and its infrequent nonoccurrence. In both instances the answer must be found in large part in the factors suggested by Hypothesis 4: new forms, it is there stated, are likely to be accepted when they are accessible, when they possess demonstrable advantages, and when they evoke confidence in people. If material traits precede nonmaterial ones, on the whole they must possess those attributes; in exceptional cases they do not. Less civilized people will accept the tools and trinkets of traders and trappers more readily than they will the newcomers' religious beliefs because learning the behavior associated with the former is made easier and more attractive than the learning of the latter; in fact, they may remain unacquainted with the new religion. In contrast, missionaries are more likely to encourage learning of new values and thus, if their own material ways are really submerged, to produce an apparent exception to the usual sequence. But suppose the traders and trappers also emphasize their religion and the missionaries praise the trinkets and tools of civilization, suppose the less civilized people thus have access to the material and the nonmaterial, then which would they choose? Under these circumstances, it should be evident, no immediate decision can be reached on theoretical grounds: it would depend upon the trinkets, the tools, the religion, the people, and the outsiders —and one can imagine varying possibilities, not all of which by any means suggest that the material traits would have priority. The outcome, in brief, depends upon the details of the pattern at hand.

At first glance it might seem reasonable to anticipate that beliefs which involve assertions concerning facts ought to be more easily modifiable than values which involve assertions concerning desirable goals. For facts can be perceived, and hence the truth or falsity of beliefs can be subjected to a test which demonstrates whether the person's expectations are realized or not. In contrast, the desirability of a goal cannot be subjected to a definitive test. In the Africa-Jamaica studies, for example, Zulu informants were asked whether they agreed or disagreed with statements like the following:

1. A traditional chief can intercede with his ancestors to produce rain.
2. A man who gets his wife by abduction should be severely punished.

The first statement involves a belief which can be tested: when a traditional chief intercedes, does it in fact rain? If it can be shown that rain does not occur after intercession and/or if the scientific explanation for rain is given, then the belief ought to change. But what can be done about the second statement, which is a value in traditional Zulu society? No proof can be offered that the rascal should be punished; instead the Zulu have or have not the conviction that he merits the punishment or that Zulu social relations will deteriorate unless the practice is prevented. The belief is testable, the value is not.

But is the belief testable? The belief turns out upon examination to involve more than empirical evidence; it includes a value pertaining to the traditional chief, and that value in turn affects the evaluation of evidence. During a relatively recent drought the Zulu held a ceremony honoring a former chief. The present paramount chief is reported to have uttered a prayer for rain; almost immediately afterwards, the drought was broken by heavy rains. This single incident was considered to be convincing evidence of the chief's ability by those who attributed the power to him; it was not thought of as a coincidence by the doubters— rather they seemed embarrassed and perplexed by it. Another belief enabling some Zulu to retain faith in the tradition is that chiefs *formerly* possessed the rain-making ability but now, after contact with Europeans, no longer do so.

In general, therefore, beliefs may be testable from the vantage point of the objective observer but they are considered sacrosanct by the firm believer. To preserve them, he may discount relevant evidence or refuse to expose himself to negative instances. Likewise values may be said at first glance to be heavily reinforced and hence not subject to change; but little energy may be required to change them, especially when they no longer prove satisfactory. For beliefs and values, alas, the argument can go either way; hence it seems necessary to conclude that:

> HYPOTHESIS 14 (*interactional*): *In a society having outside contacts, beliefs and values are likely to change at similar rates unless old ones are particularly satisfying or unsatisfying, or unless new ones are particularly attractive or unattractive.*

Evidence relating to the hypothesis from the Africa-Jamaica studies is provided in Table 8 (p. 294). The first eight rows contain "beliefs" which are theoretically testable; rows 9–15 suggest values on which the society seems to take a stand; and rows 16–20 are values for which there appears to be no official position. As the hypothesis would indicate, the results are quite mixed. Fewer of the better educated by and large subscribe to traditional beliefs or values, but no greater number of significant differences appears in one category than in the other. Sometimes the significant difference may be slightly greater for the belief than for the value (Zulu: rows 8 and 10), at other times the reverse effect appears (Luo: rows 4 and 11). With a few exceptions, Ganda and Zulu adolescents are like their relatively well educated elders in repudiating traditional beliefs; but again with an exception, Luo youth, though in school, are more similar in this respect to their less well educated countrymen (Table I, rows 18–24). In all three societies the position of the boys with reference to the few values for which comparisons are available is variable (rows 25–28).

Other evidence pertaining to the hypothesis is difficult to assemble and then to interpret. Part of the Indian-white study, for example, consisted of a detailed examination of fifteen Navaho Indians. All of them are attracted to most of the obvious material aspects of American society but lack the money to buy them. Eleven of the men say they would prefer the American-type rather than the traditional house; seven have such a home. Only one man owns a radio set. Most resistant to change are their "implicit values," e.g., that "the universe is full of dangers" or that it is necessary to place major emphasis "upon this life with little concern for what happens in the afterworld." Part of the explanation for the different attitude toward traditional houses and traditional values is supplied by the investigator. The new style of house is desired, not because it provides better protection—in fact, the reverse is true—but because people would "live in a house in the manner of the white people." In contrast, the old values are not likely to be so sharply verbalized and, since the values are indeed "the fundamental assumptions about life which run like connecting threads through large sectors of Navaho culture" and since they exist in a society which places a high premium upon individual and social harmony, they are not likely to be easily challenged (Vogt, 1951, pp. 109–16). But then it is necessary to ask why the values of a house type are more consciously verbalized than ethical values and why less disharmony occurs when the former rather than the latter are changed.

Another illustration may be taken from the broader part of the same study. If children think that they themselves may alter the rules of a game, they are said to be less subject to "moral constraint." There is a negative relation between the acculturation of the society and the degree to which such restraint is demonstrated with respect to *American* games (Table A, row 32), but on the whole, the investigators conclude, these Indians have "incompletely adopted" the white attitudes of elasticity (Havighurst and Neugarten, 1955, p. 142). Likewise the belief that "there is a power in the world which punishes people for wrong doing through its influence over 'natural' things and events" declines with increasing acculturation either when all the societies are compared or when the two Navaho communities are compared (row 33). Other values also fluctuate with acculturation, although the relation is not always regular or consistent (rows 34–38).

The intimate relation between beliefs and values which prevents change from occurring simply as a result of empirical evidence provides still another explanation for the tenacity of magic. Very often the facts of modern science are at hand, but they prove to be unconvincing or are variously interpreted. Thus the efficacy of modern medicine may not be doubted, but still it may be thought that there are enough elements of surprise and uncertainty in the critical affairs of men that it may possibly be dangerous to abandon all magical potions. The Zulu, for example, were once reported to have believed that European doctors could indeed treat "straightforward cases of diseases." Other "ills that Europeans know nothing about, and do not, in fact, suffer from," they also thought result from "the machinations of evilly-disposed persons" and hence can be treated successfully only by native doctors (Krige, 1934, p. 99). People in the Solomon Islands have assigned modern medicine not to particular diseases but to particular people: it is "all right for the white man, but our illnesses are caused by spirits." Since no man is ever immune from all disease, these people could adduce proof for their belief:

if one of their complaints were cured by modern medicine, "the spirits will only send another" (Hogbin, 1939, p. 197). Likewise it is possible to subscribe to magic without discounting the facts provided by one's senses. In the Sudan the Azande take note of the perceived circumstance of death—an enemy's spear, a wild animal, or sickness—but these are considered only secondary causes; the "true" causes involve the machinations of witches who operate through those precipitating events (Evans-Pritchard, 1937, p. 73).

It is fashionable nowadays, as this section has demonstrated, to ascribe greater importance to subjective than to objective factors. Maybe this psychological doctrine subjectively distorts the reporting of objective reality. One tale must suffice. A young Burmese once had an antidrowning tatoo inscribed upon his body. To demonstrate its efficacy, he had his hands and feet bound and he was then thrown into the Rangoon River. He drowned. Witnesses, it is stated, believed so strongly in the value of the tatoo that they ascribed his death to "some miscalculation of his horoscope, or some such unforeseen contingency" (Mead, 1955, p. 56). Now surely some of the spectators, no matter how devout they were, must have suspected that tatoos are no match for the force of gravity acting upon a bound body in a stream.

Relativism

The changing man who has had personal contact with competing beliefs and values and who then rejects some of the old and accepts some of the new is not likely to forget that alternative interpretations exist in the world. He has had to make a choice and therefore—and therefore what? Perhaps he remains slightly humble, and the humility prevents him from ever being completely certain or from ever passing eternal judgment. To resolve the conflict between the old and the new and then to be able to adhere to his choice, he may also bolster his own courage by clinging dogmatically to the new. On balance, however, it is guessed that for two complimentary reasons the change will have some liberating effect.

In the first place, it has been presumed that people in less civilized societies have a tendency to consider their values sacred and absolute; restricted as they are and deprived of any or many contacts with outsiders, fewer doubts arise and, as has been indicated in an earlier chapter, unanswerable questions are not likely to be raised. Then, secondly, it is perhaps also possible to discern in civilized philosophies a shading in favor of tolerance and relativism. The knowledge that each society occupies its present position only as a result of accomplishments in the past; that any group stresses some values and places less emphasis on others; that standards of virtually everything, from science to the explicit manifestations of morality, keep changing; that people can be ethnocentric and proud of their prejudices; in brief, the knowledge that knowledge itself tends to be tentative and subject to improvement exists in the tradition of civilization. Of course it does not exist in all men, nor does it always dominate the thinking and behavior of many individual men, but at least the spirit behind the philosophy plays some role, however inconspicuous at times. One can passionately defend one's ideas, one's values, and one's way of life and simultaneously be aware of the passion being displayed; and one can be aware of that passion without being ashamed of it as well as without being humorless about it.

Let this chapter end with a lofty hypothesis:

> HYPOTHESIS 15 (consequential): After people change centrally from old to new ways, they are a little less likely to be dogmatic concerning the validity of their own beliefs and the goodness of their own values.

Immediately the very civilized outlook of the writer makes him assert that more civilized people do not have a monopoly on tolerance. Indian groups living side by side in Guatemala, for example, appear to have a strong esprit de corps within each community and to possess fairly distinctive subcultures of their own. "To the Indians," an anthropologist reports, "cultural differences between themselves and outsiders are as much to be expected as differences in kinds of trees. . . . Indians of another town may be considered lazy or stupid, but so far as I know, depreciative epithets in terms of customs are not applied to

them" (Tax, 1941, pp. 31 and 32). Such an attitude, wherever
it is found, is doubtless noteworthy because it is rare.

It is felt, nevertheless, that the following incident illustrates
the probability of tolerance having some slight relation with
civilization. The missionary and explorer, David Livingstone,
reports to his father-in-law some of his initial impressions as he
was entering Angola:

> The clothing of the women in front is scarcely so broad as
> half this page and about twice the length. Yet they laughed
> at our [native African] men because their behinds were
> naked. We were ashamed when they came and gazed at us,
> but they stood (Eve's daughters fair) with as little sense of
> indecency as we with our clothes on [Livingstone, 1854].

Each of the three groups—the women, the men from another
part of Africa, and the Europeans—considered his mode of
dressing superior, but presumably only Livingstone—in spite of
a missionary's prejudices concerning nudity which caused him
to feel "ashamed"—had perspective enough to note the varying
reactions and indeed to be amused by them.

Chapter 7.

INTELLIGENCE AND SKILL

EVERY task is performed with varying degrees of aptitude and skill. Virtually everyone can walk, but people's gaits can be differentiated on the basis of some criterion like energy expended or speed. Differences between individuals are especially evident in connection with a manual activity such as operating a car: some drivers can park easily, others cannot; some shift gears with precision, others with such clumsiness that a good mechanic shudders.

Over and above skills that are exercised in specific situations may be some type of general ability which leads to excellence or inferiority in a wide variety of situations. Will the good walker also be a good driver? General ability is sometimes called intelligence.

Decades of research on the problems of intelligence and intelligence tests have led to almost unanimous conclusions, which will be briefly outlined and then utilized in this chapter. Specific abilities tend to be so interrelated that it is in fact fruitful to refer to general ability or intelligence. The man who walks well may not necessarily also drive well but it is probable that he will. Although such ability undoubtedly has a native or inborn component, it is also markedly affected by opportunity and experience in a social environment. Nowadays research is best summarized by saying that for most but not all behavior heredity sets wide limits within which environmental factors can be most efficacious. A very favorable environment will not convert a moron into a genius but it may help him appreciably.

Special problems arise in connection with the measurement of intelligence: a very general ability cannot be assessed at a glance.

What must be done is to secure a quick and somewhat varied sample of the person's behavior in the series of standardized situations which compose a test. The assumption is that these situations so closely resemble those facing him in real life that his future performance in the latter will be very similar to his present performance in the test. As ever, future behavior must be inferred on the basis of performance in the past.

Tests of ability, and especially intelligence tests, are frequently used to compare one person with another or one group with another. Here emphasis is placed primarily on relative performance in the test situations; but of course the implication again is that differences there foreshadow future differences in nontest situations. If the *native* abilities of two persons or two groups are to be inferred and then compared, two assumptions must be made concerning the test situations. In the first place, it must be assumed that the testing situations are equally novel to both parties; otherwise one and not the other will have the advantage gained from previous experience. Secondly, if the testing situations are not completely novel and contain elements that reflect previous learning, it must be assumed that both persons or groups have had equal opportunities to learn those elements in the past; with an equal opportunity assumed, then perhaps it can be maintained that the ability to learn is being tested by what has been learned.

The evidence is overwhelming that these two assumptions are usually without foundation. People, especially those from diverse backgrounds or cultures, do not have the same experiences or learning opportunities; as a result, the components of an intelligence test are newer or more bizarre for some than for others, and the background information that must be brought to bear on the solution of the test problems correspondingly varies. There are in addition a host of other factors which render the two assumptions invalid. The examiner, if he is a stranger or if he comes from a strange society, can influence unwittingly the kinds of replies the subjects give. Many tests must be completed within a limited time, and some people or groups react favorably, others adversely, to such external pressure. Answers considered correct, finally, often contain a cultural bias, whereas some scored as false may be quite correct from the standpoint of another group. To date, in spite of numerous and frequently ingenious efforts, no intelligence test has been devised that does not unfairly handicap someone or some group; and many distinguished investigators believe that those who would devise a truly "culture-free" test are pursuing a will-o'-the-wisp.

Often, however, the aim of the investigator or the test is not to make inferences concerning native ability but to determine whether there are actual differences in ability regardless of their genesis. Such a practical orientation is especially evident when an effort is made by means of tests to assess quickly and efficiently the skills of less civilized men before they are hired to work in modern industry, in mines, or in offices (e.g., Biesheuvel, 1952; Ombredane, 1951, p. 525). Then no assumptions need be made that the previous experience or opportunities of people from different cultural backgrounds have been equal, because one is interested in measuring not innate potential but present performance. A test that measures knowledge of French, for example, is obviously unfair to someone who has never had contact with that language, but it can be exceedingly useful if the aim is to discover who is proficient in French. As a performance test it does not indicate that, if a person fails either because he has not studied French or because, having studied it but being poor and humble, he could not afford a tutor or a trip abroad, he is natively unequal to the most capable French scholar, nor does it imply that such a person could not have learned or could not now learn the language proficiently. In brief, it enables the examiner to compare the knowledge of French possessed by various people but it does not reveal or condone the reasons for the differences which it reveals.

In exactly the same way results from tests of general ability and so-called intelligence can be utilized not to cast aspersions upon less civilized peoples or to heap praise upon the more civilized but to establish differences between societies living under different conditions and hence favoring some kinds of knowledge and some ways of learning rather than others. It is doubtless true that on the whole people score better on tests devised for themselves than they do on tests devised for other people. A New

Yorker probably could not identify the spoor of an elephant, nor could a tribesman from Central Africa correctly infer the name of the manufacturer from the radiator grill of an automobile. For many purposes, however, it is valuable to know, as it were, that the New Yorker functions better on a street than in a jungle and that the reverse is true of the African. Here is a rare instance in which the Jumping Fallacy is not unwittingly but deliberately committed: an ethnocentric interpretation is placed on the behavior of people from another society as a result of an interest in their performance within the society in which the judgment is being passed.

When the reasons for the test performance of a person or a group are legitimately sought, once again a Spiraled Explanation usually appears. At first blush the direction of the cause-and-effect sequence may seem easy to establish. The explanation of the fact that in the three samples of the Africa-Jamaica studies more of the well than the poorly educated know English (Table 1, row 1) should be perfectly obvious. English is taught in the schools, by definition the better educated have attended school longer, hence the classroom experience must account for the difference. And yet even this primitive illustration requires that other factors be considered. Since English is used throughout the three African areas, it is by no means certain that the school has played the exclusive or even the decisive role. The better educated may have been sent to school in the first place because they were more "intelligent." If this is so, then the school's responsibility for the greater knowledge of English must be considered a proximate but not an ultimate cause. Better educated Africans know English because they have been to school, and they have gone to school, perhaps, because they have had an aptitude for learning English or a desire to learn it.

Can one avoid the Spiral? The examination of individual life histories of men who have or have not changed proves unfortunately to be no closer to a solution than a purely statistical approach. The details often suggest, for example, that "chance" must have been operating to determine that one family or one son in a given family rather than another was induced to become civilized. "Chance" of course is merely a quick way of summarizing a host of complicated factors that cannot be separated. In this chapter, therefore, the emphasis will be upon pointing out probable differences between the less and the more civilized; only informal attempts will be made to account for them.

Transfer

Tests of intelligence or general ability, it has been said in effect so far, call attention to the important question of transfer or generalization: ability revealed in test situations is or is not also displayed in real-life situations, or vice versa. Likewise, when men from one society are called on to solve problems in or from another society, a similar question arises: Can they transfer their ability or knowledge from the old to the new situations? It appears that the degree of transfer depends upon at least two factors. In the first place, there is the perceived similarity of the two situations; do they seem to call for fairly similar forms of behavior? Objectively similar situations are of course likely to evoke similar responses; for example, all water, regardless of color and temperature, is so similar that a person suddenly tossed into a pool undoubtedly would begin to swim and would not engage in other behavior like opening his pen or brushing his teeth. Also, the individual may behave in a similar way not as a result of the objective similarity between situations but for reasons to be found within himself. The outgoing manner of the extrovert may be so strong that it is triggered off by almost any kind of person or situation.

It is to be anticipated that men from the old society will experience some difficulty in solving problems in the new society. A person may arrive at a solution if the new situation is sufficiently similar to ones he has already experienced and if he has the wit or ability to recognize that his past experience and way of solving problems are applicable in the new situation. People who are changing or who have changed are likely to have had the necessary experience or to have acquired the needed skill to produce transfer. In brief:

HYPOTHESIS 16 (*interactional*): *In comparison with those who remain unchanged, people who are changing or have changed centrally are likely to be more proficient in novel*

situations; the degree of their proficiency will vary with the
perceived similarity between those situations and ones in
their past experience.

In the hypothesis "novel situations" are those which either belong to an outside society or are more or less foreign to a person's
experience. Similarity is "perceived" and, as explained above,
does not necessarily reflect objective reality.

Evidence from the Africa-Jamaica studies appears in Table
9 (p. 295). The rationale behind the table is straightforward:
in the course of a long interview the informants were presented
with a group of tests which were believed to be novel to them
and which are typical of certain aptitude tests employed in
Western society. Virtually without exception the performance
of the better educated people in each society was superior. More
of them could readily understand the instructions, which directed
them to observe and then immediately afterwards to identify
geometrical figures (Benton, 1950), to locate simple figures that
were embedded in more complicated ones (adapted from Witkin,
1950), and to sort into piles pieces of cardboard that differed in
various respects (rows 1, 5, and 11); naturally the investigator
made a strenuous effort to make the task at hand comprehensible
to each informant. More of the better educated excelled on these
same three tests (rows 2, 6, and 12). Among the Ganda and the
Zulu (the exercise was not used among the Luo), more of them
too could accurately recall a communication presented earlier
in the interview (rows 21–23). In only a single test, one designed
specifically for the Jamaican informants, did the trend fail to
appear, probably because the task—noting among various piles
of blocks the one pile which had not been previously present—
proved to be too difficult for everybody (row 43).

It is possible also to see in the results from the projective
measures evidence of the superiority of the better educated.
Fewer of them tended to reject the first or subsequent cards in
the Rorschach and TAT-type series (rows 24, 25, 36, and 37),
which is interpreted here as indicating an ability to comprehend
instructions to use one's imagination. More of them responded to
each card by attempting to account for all of the blot, including

even the white spaces between the black or colored parts (rows 26 and 27); while realizing that these responses are quite differently interpreted by Rorschach experts in the West, the writer feels that such behavior again suggests thoroughness and conscientiousness in the test situation. More of them gave the impression of responding easily to the TAT-type drawings (row 38). In Jamaica, finally, more of the same group were able to respond when first confronted with the task of finishing an incomplete sentence (row 42).

Do such results lend support to the second part of Hypothesis 16, which attributes the higher proficiency of the more acculturated to perceive similarity with past experience? At hand is evidence that is impressionistic as well as some that is a little more systematic. So far as could be determined, all the tasks were novel from the standpoint of the African informants: none of them had ever seen the materials or had been confronted with the precise tasks. With the exception of some of the Ganda in the urban area who had recently been questioned in the course of a sociological survey, moreover, none of these men had been systematically interviewed by a European. And yet it cannot be argued that the superiority of the better educated was unrelated to very general experiences which they could transfer from the school situation. Certainly, it may be guessed, they had had greater opportunity to follow rather similar instructions during regular classroom sessions and especially during examinations. In school, furthermore, they may have grown accustomed to problems detached from a life-like context; remembering the shapes of geometrical forms inscribed on a card and then trying to find amid four similar drawings the exact one that had just been seen is the bookish kind of skill which schools and not tribal life is likely to encourage.

The a priori argument can be prolonged by asserting that the tasks on which the better educated were superior demand of people a fairly quick adaptation to relatively novel situations and that those who succeed are more elastic or flexible, less rigid or compulsive than those who do not. Again and again the investigator had the impression that many of the Africans were not trying very hard to understand the instructions or to perform well; here—and some of them said this—was a queer white man having them execute some meaningless tasks and answer many silly questions. It matters not whether the ability to become interested in a wide variety of tasks and questions—whose relation to reality or the self is not immediately evident—in part accounts for, or indeed results from, the fact that the person has gone to school; when once he possesses such plasticity, he is undoubtedly better able to face and try to solve the tasks a more complicated civilization poses for most people.

Less lofty than the foregoing contention but perhaps more impressive is an examination of the kinds of error which occurred in two of the standardized tests. (Only readers with a passionate interest in the tests, the kindly warning is offered, can endure the remainder of this paragraph.) Well and poorly educated Africans commit, in roughly equal proportion, errors which spring from the stimuli at hand in the Embedded Figures Test: finding not the embedded figure but its mirror image (Table 9, row 7); and following some of the lines of the concealed figure beyond the point where the tracing should shift to another line (row 8). In contrast, fewer of the well educated Jamaicans make the latter mistake. And fewer of the better educated Africans produce errors that appear to be related to an inability to carry on persistently or to adjust in this novel situation. They do not tend to deny, for example, after a long search, that the simple figure is in fact embedded and thus, instead of admitting their own failure, to claim that the investigator was trying to trick or deceive them (row 9); and they are less likely to fail to respond to tutoring (row 10). In the Visual Retention Test, mirror images rather than the correct figures are selected significantly more often by the poorly educated informants in three of the four societies (row 3). In Jamaica, moreover, an effort was made to determine whether the performance of 20 poorly educated men and women who had failed the test miserably could be improved: the original model was not withdrawn and the informant was asked simply to point out the one drawing exactly like it. Even while observing the model, 14 could not perform the task; of the 6 who responded correctly in the easier situation, only 2 could then perform better when returning to the normal procedure, 2 performed just as poorly as they had previously, and 2 were not tested.

Other data lend support to the view that schooling per se stimulates superior performance. When the Visual Retention Test was given in a school of very elite Ganda girls, the youngest girls (Primary V) had a mean of 11.0 correct out of a possible 15; the means of each grade gradually but significantly increased until a high of 13.1 was reached in the oldest group (Secondary III). Even in this select group of girls, then, the aptitude improves with schooling and/or age. Although the improvement occurs gradually and significantly on each of the 15 items of the test, the really large difference appears on the very first item, which was solved by 18 per cent of Primary V but by 61 per cent of Secondary III. This particular test is not more but much less complicated than most of the items that follow; it seems reasonable to conclude that the test taps the ability not only to recall forms but also at the outset to comprehend and execute instructions in a somewhat novel situation. That latter ability is stimulated by increased schooling and hence the children become test-wise. In this restricted sense they are better prepared for a more civilized world.

All the tests were administered in identical fashion in the four societies and—with the exception of a small group of Ganda—by the same investigator. Are there differences in performance from society to society? Clearly yes, as demonstrated, for example, in the case of the Visual Retention Test (Table 9, rows 1–3). Among the poorly educated Luo, 63 per cent could not grasp the instructions accompanying the test; among the poorly educated Ganda, only 15 per cent could not. In all four societies significantly fewer of the better educated showed no understanding, but again a higher percentage of well educated Luo failed. The Luo who did so poorly on one test, however, led the other two African societies on another test, the sorting of pieces of cardboard according to some principle (rows 11 and 12). The conclusion must be tentatively drawn, consequently, that the Luo informants brought to the test situation experiences and sets different from those of the Ganda. Although these background factors are for the moment unknown, the hypothesis at least suggests the paths along which an appropriate investigation might be made.

Data from the Indian-white study do not lend themselves to a simple or straightforward summary, but by and large they support the contention of the hypothesis that proficiency depends upon similarity in past experience (Havighurst et al., 1946). In the first place, the two intelligence tests given to the children were both performance tests and hence slightly less dependent upon schooling than purely verbal tests. On the Arthur Point Performance Scales most of the Indian groups, as has been almost always the case when such cross-cultural comparisons are made, fell below the mean of the white children (as ascertained on the same or a roughly comparable test). A less and a more acculturated community in three of the six Indian societies can be compared: in two instances (Papago and Sioux), the mean score of the children from the less acculturated one is slightly lower than that of the children from the more acculturated one; and in the third (Hopi) the reverse result has been obtained. In a fourth society (Navaho), the mean is the same in the least and the most acculturated communities, and it is lowest in the community which, though ranked between the other two with respect to acculturation, has the smallest percentage of children actually attending school (Leighton and Kluckhohn, 1948, p. 156).

On the other test, the Goodenough Draw-a-Man Test, all the Indian groups were *above* the white mean. With a single unexplained exception, furthermore, there is a low relation between the scores of the Indian children on the two intelligence tests, whereas the relation ordinarily tends to be high among white children. There must be, therefore, some aspect of Indian experience which causes them to score low on one test and high on the other, and indeed the investigators believe that Indian children have greater interest in forming "concepts of the detailed form and organization of the human body which are tested in the Draw-a-Man Test" (Havighurst et al., p. 58). Among the Sioux children, those in the more acculturated community score about the same as the white norm, but those in the more traditional community are far superior, on the average, on this test. On the other hand, the neatness of the explanation is spoiled by the fact that among the Papago and Hopi (data are unavailable for the remaining three) the reverse trend appears: the more acculturated do better on the test, though only slightly so (Leighton and Kluckhohn, 1948).

After the fact, the investigators relate differences in the performance of Indian boys and girls on the tests to the different roles the two sexes play in each society. In the Zia pueblo, for example, where boys score higher than girls, this situation prevails:

> From the time a boy can handle a pencil or a brush he is encouraged to draw and paint. . . . Parents and siblings encourage the youngsters with admiration and criticism. Girls rarely draw pictures except in school, but by the time the children start school the boys are much more advanced in their ease of handling pencils and colors and even more in their ability to put their accurate observations of animal forms and movements onto paper. The pueblo expects its boys to be able to paint animals upon the house walls at Christmas to encourage fertility, as well as to work later at painting the ceremonial masks, altars, and other ceremonial paraphernalia. Girls are expected to paint nothing but the conventionalized designs used on pottery [Havighurst et al., 1946, p. 59].

Clearly, it appears, the preparation of the boys for an intelligence test based upon drawing has been better than that of the girls.

The Indian children also confirm, not unexpectedly, the view that increasing acculturation is accompanied by greater readiness to respond with the kinds of materials that are likely to be helpful on a Western-type intelligence test. They were asked to produce "free" (i.e. unguided) drawings. With only two exceptions, the rankings of the Indian communities with respect to acculturation are the same as the rankings given the drawings with respect to proportion of content devoted to " 'native' items and 'acculturated' items" (Havighurst and Neugarten, 1955, p. 173). Likewise children in the most acculturated Navaho community who were given a modified form of the Thematic Apperception

Test mentioned "the material objects of white society" and "white persons" more frequently than those from the two less acculturated communities (Henry, 1947, p. 107).

Two of the investigators in the Indian-white study, finally, present some informal evidence relating to the problem of whether superior performance on an intelligence test is the cause or the consequence of schooling. Among the Navaho, they indicate, at least one child from each family is sent to school:

> Definite policies of selectivity are followed. In some families those who have better memories and are quicker to learn are chosen. But in at least the poorer families the prevailing tendency has been to send the more delicate and crippled children who are less useful in the home economy [Leighton and Kluckhohn, 1948, p. 63].

Those with "better memories" may be brighter at the outset, if it may be presumed that there is a close relation between memory for matters Navaho and American; and the delicate and crippled, by virtue of their handicap, may be more strongly motivated to succeed. If these interpretations are correct, then the superior in ability or motivation are sent to school and hence their proficiency on intelligence tests, as compared with that of their siblings, may be a function of factors other than experience.

In this study and in other studies of American Indians the number of "whole" responses to the Rorschach plates (W) has been noted; that measure roughly corresponds to "accounting for all of the blot," which was found in the Africa-Jamaica studies, as already indicated, to increase somewhat with acculturation. Is there a positive relation between the number of such responses and increasing acculturation? If anything, the relation is negative among Navaho children (Leighton and Kluckhohn, 1948, p. 259). It is positive in the Adult Section of the Indian-white study, since slightly but not significantly more "whole" responses are produced by the more acculturated veterans in the two Indian societies than by the less acculturated nonveterans; but both Indian groups score higher than the Mormons (Table B, row 4). The remaining studies elicit similarly contradicting data. Among the Menomini Indians the relation is positive when the least acculturated group is compared with the next-to-the-most acculturated one, but no significant differences emerge when the former group is compared either with the most acculturated one or with the white sample (Table C, row 24). In the Ojibwa study the proportion of all responses which can be classified as W's increases with acculturation (Hallowell, 1955, p. 352), but not when their mean number is noted (Table D, row 9).

The number of responses of all kinds to the entire Rorschach test may be related to some general ability. In the Indian-white study an analysis has been made of the protocols obtained from children in three Navaho communities which differ with respect to acculturation. As anticipated, children from the most acculturated community produce the highest number of responses not only on the Rorschach but also on the Thematic Apperception Test. On the former they mentioned "unusual" details "and/or" the white spaces most frequently, which again may then be taken as a symptom of their cooperativeness. On the other hand, there is little difference in the number of Rorschach responses from the other two communities, and the highest proportion of rejections in the Rorschach series comes not from the least acculturated community but from the one in the middle of the acculturation series (Leighton and Kluckhohn, 1948, pp. 257–8; Henry, 1947, p. 108). In the Adult Section of the same study the more acculturated Indian veterans do produce more Rorschach responses and they produce them more rapidly than the less acculturated nonveterans; and the two Indian groups produce fewer responses than the Mormons and produce them less rapidly than either the Mormons or the Spanish-Americans (Table B, rows 2 and 3). Other significant and confirmatory evidence comes from two other studies of American Indians (Table C, rows 27 and 28; Table D, row 4).

Elsewhere a sample of 23 carefully selected natives of Truk tended to respond slowly and with relatively few responses to the Rorschach cards. In the context of their over-all performance, their slowness is interpreted as reflecting the fact that they are not "characteristically impulsive" and so in a situation in which "they are not sure of themselves" they must first overcome their own "reluctance and self-doubt." Their small number of responses reflects their "concreteness of thinking," as a result of which they cannot assume that "a stimulus may have various significances or meanings" (Gladwin and Sarason, 1954, pp. 225–6). In general, many less civilized samples seem to produce a relatively small number of responses on the Rorschach test (e.g., Abel and Calabresi, 1951, p. 310). The stray bits of evidence presented here from the Rorschach research are, and the summary must be, suggestive but not conclusive.

On the practical level the importance of Hypothesis 16 becomes clear whenever the relative inefficiency of the native worker in a Western-type industry is established. Every man of course acquires in his own lifetime the skills he must exercise on the job. Men who have been reared and have continued to live in a nonindustrial society, however, are not likely to have had much of the relevant experience before they apply for work in a factory, and thereafter their way of life outside may not promote efficiency inside the plant. One study concludes that, in the city of Durban, Union of South Africa, "a larger number of tests and records made in the Dunlop factory suggest that the more efficient type of Native takes about half as long again to learn a particular job as a European, and that his normal rate of output is about 85% of the European's" (Department of Economics, 1950, p. 5). Other factors besides skill, of course, have contributed to produce such a condition. It is reported that "the majority of the men" were suffering from malnutrition. Because of an "acute shortage of accommodation" many lived in shacks, and some had to spend much time or money or both getting to and from work. Only 6 per cent of the married men had brought in their wives from the reserves; the very idea of trying to have a family live under such conditions was greeted by some with either "anger or contempt." Even if some of these depressing factors were eliminated by having the factories located in the reserves, as over 80 per cent of the men themselves advocated, it seems doubtful that an alien culture could forthwith produce the kind of coordination and discipline demanded by the modern factory.

The last illustration suggests the warning that more than mechanical skill is involved in the similarity which does or does not exist between previous experiences in the old society and the novel experiences demanded by the new. It has been noted that some North American Indian tribes have been able to adapt themselves more easily to the reservation than others and that one of the critical factors seems to have been their old methods of hunting: those who had hunted cooperatively made the change less readily than those who had hunted in an "atomistic" manner (Barnouw, 1950, pp. 13–16). Certainly it must have been easier for men like the Ojibwa, who were in the latter category, to learn to hunt in the new milieu: their old habits required little modification, and transfer could occur. Other factors operated simultaneously. As previously mentioned (cf. pp. 83, 124), they respected the British who had defeated them, and perhaps they had personality traits suited for reservation life. Then the very similarity between the old and the new with respect to hunting may have made the change less traumatic for them.

The generalizations of anthropologists lend implicit support to Hypothesis 16. According to one astute investigator of acculturation, "in every society undergoing change, there is a necessary time lag required for the learning and practicing of the behavior implied in the new patterns," as a result of which "there would seem to be an inevitable period characterized by some confusion and lack of stability in behavior" (Gillin, 1942, pp. 547–8). Transfer, it is being said, is not automatic: experience is needed. Officials in the modern world whose countries have recently won independence from colonial powers recognize, without blushing or apologizing, the inexperience of their countrymen with respect to administrative and technical matters. For this reason they have been often eager to retain many of the European staff during a transition period not only to keep government and private enterprise functioning efficiently but also to train local men and women eventually to be their successors.

Abstraction

If performance on intelligence tests and other tests of general ability changes as people become more acculturated, then it is useful to try to determine the kind of activity that is altered. Perhaps, it is here contended, the ability to abstract is involved.

But first let abstraction be defined as a type of detachment from perceived reality which enables a person to discern some degree of similarity in the midst of perceived dissimilarity. As semanticists are fond of saying, every object (including people) in the external world is unique in some respect, either when compared with other objects or when compared with itself over a period of time. No two dogs are exactly alike, and the same dog will be different in the future because his weight, respiratory rate, knowledge, etc. will have changed in the interim. It is possible, however, to disregard the dissimilarities and to concentrate upon the similarities. The word "dog" rests on an abstraction: the unique qualities of a poodle and an Alsatian must be ignored if the common label is to be applied to both.

Survival anywhere certainly depends upon learned abstractions. People distinguish "dogs" from "foxes" and behave appropriately after perceiving one rather than the other. On the basis of past experience, people know, or think they know, whether an animal is dangerous, whether a plant is poisonous, whether a stranger constitutes a threat to them—and they know this quickly, in fact, by often instantaneously perceiving similarities which have been isolated in the past.

Clearly, then, no group of people, no matter how civilized they are, has a monopoly on the ability to note similarities and hence to employ abstractions. The sharp distinction between less and more civilized peoples that thinkers like Lévy-Bruhl (1926) have made is not being repeated here. Even seriously faulty analogies that are current among people unacquainted with modern science spring from disregarding innumerable irrelevant attributes and concentrating upon a single relevant one. It is said, for example, that among the Zulu "a witch doctor believes the fat of the more powerful beasts will cure severe illness, lion fat being especially favored because of the lion's strength" (McCord, 1946, p. 97). To have such a belief the quality of strength must be abstracted from men and beasts. Different languages, moreover, contain varying types of abstraction. Thus Hopi is less abstract than English when it uses one word for water that is moving and another for water that is stationary, but it is more abstract when it uses the same word to refer to insects, planes, and pilots which possess in common the ability to fly (Whorf, 1940, pp. 230, 247).

Undoubtedly every person in any society abstracts when he finds it necessary or somehow advantageous to do so. It may follow, consequently, that as a result of some of the conditions prevailing in less civilized societies—and not for any innate reason —people there are a little less likely to view objects, other people, and themselves out of context. As suggested earlier, they have a tendency to unify experience. Perhaps it is fair to say that they lack systematic, scientific thinking in the sense of deliberately searching for the unknown and then being able in some way or other to cope with novelty. Like everyone everywhere, their first impulse is to use old formulas which have previously worked; they have not been trained to attempt to devise relatively new ones. They have been living, it is presumed, in a simpler society, in which it is less frequently necessary to decide between techniques or roles and hence to make concrete decisions through deliberation and thought. On the basis of such cultural considerations, the following hypothesis is formulated:

HYPOTHESIS 17 (*consequential*): *After people change centrally from old to new ways, they are likely to develop facility in abstracting.*

Again Table 9 must be consulted, for data from the Africa-Jamaica studies. The superior test performance of the better educated, already mentioned in the previous section, may be considered evidence of their ability to abstract, inasmuch as the solution to each problem can be found only by ignoring particular details. True enough, perhaps, but additional information concerning the actual process seems desirable. On the Sorting Test, the subject is confronted with sixteen pieces of cardboard, among which four colors, four shapes, and two sizes are represented; in the center of each is a small insignia—a star or an arrow which is either red or silver. To follow instructions—"Put those pieces together which seem to belong together, and they will seem to belong together when they have something in common, etc."—a limited number of attributes or a single one must be detached from the rest; some kind of abstraction must be made. African informants were given three trials, Jamaicans two.

The solution achieved or attempted on the first trial (rows 13–15) provides a clue concerning the attributes which struck the person immediately and most forcefully. Only one significant difference emerges: among the Ganda, fewer of the better educated used the insignia (row 14). No trend is discernible. The analysis of all three (or two) solutions is more productive (rows 16–19): slightly more of the better educated tend to employ varied solutions. From many standpoints such variation represents a real intellectual feat. On the first trial the individual achieves a perfect solution; for example, he sorts the sixteen pieces into four piles according to the four colors. Then, after being praised, he is asked to produce a different kind of solution, an instruction which requires him to abandon the hard-won principle and to search for another. This flexibility also affects the frequency with which the different types of solution appear; for an unaccountable reason, for example, there is a nonsignificant tendency for more of the better educated to employ shape as the common characteristic at least once.

Responses to the Rorschach plates may be said to involve abstraction. In the first place, in all four societies the model response to plates VI and VII is a reference to animals or animal skins. Such a reference is called "abstract" when the generic term for animal is provided, "nonabstract" when a specific animal is named. There is a tendency for more of the better educated Luo and Jamaicans to use the abstract category; the same tendency is evident among the Ganda and Zulu for only one of the two plates (rows 28 and 29).

Another kind of Rorschach response can be employed to test the hypothesis by making a wild assumption: the reporting of a part of a human being (e.g., a face or leg) as a response is more abstract than the reporting of an entire human being, since human parts are seen less frequently than intact people and hence, when reported, reflect the ability to isolate or detach which also appears in abstract thought. Especially among the Luo, there is a decided tendency for more of the better educated to respond in such an "abstract" way to the two plates for which human responses are frequent (rows 30 and 31). A final index of abstraction is the finding of movement in the static blots; to do this, greater effort and greater command over the stimulus materials are necessary, both of which are usually also essential in abstracting. A slight difference in the anticipated direction appears among the Luo and Ganda but not among the Zulu (row 35).

Two other measures may relate to abstraction. As indicated earlier in this chapter, more of the better educated showed proficiency in recalling aspects of a communication which had been inserted into the long interview in three of the four societies. Among the informants who remembered the communication and could recall parts of it, some incorrectly attributed to it material from other sections of the interview; for example, some said it contained one of the closed questions that had been used to test their attitude on a related or unrelated problem. Significantly fewer of the well educated Africans made the mistake (row 23). No significant difference appears among the Jamaicans since only one of them recalled an incorrect item. The other measure of abstraction is reaction time: the better educated responded more rapidly on a performance test as well as to statements testing beliefs and values (rows 4 and 39). The exception involves the Visual Retention Test, where a nonsignificant reversal occurs among the Luo: since the task in general was a difficult one for them to perform, it may be that the better educated were more conscientious and hence deliberated longer before responding.

Rorschach data from Indian societies tend on the whole to confirm the hypothesis. When human responses are analyzed in the Ojibwa study, it appears that a higher proportion in the most acculturated community referred to parts of human beings (Hallowell, 1955, p. 69; Table D, rows 1 and 2). On the other hand, no such trend appears for movement responses (rows 6–8). Among the samples of Menomini Indians there are trends indicating that increased acculturation is positively related to an increase in detailed rather than whole (animal and human) responses (Table C, row 25) and likewise in human movement responses (row 22), but negatively related to animal movement responses (row 23). In the Adult Section of the Indian-white study more movement is reported, as anticipated, by the more acculturated veterans than by the less acculturated nonveterans, and yet more (rather than less) of the same response occurs among the presumably

less acculturated Zunis than among the Spanish Americans
(Table B, row 5). The only other Rorschach category in the
study which is relevant to the present discussion of abstraction
and which produces at least one significant difference is "F%,"
or the percentage of responses determined by form alone rather
than by some other attribute, such as color or movement (row 6).
According to the investigator, "the higher the F%, the greater is
the *control* of the intellect over emotional spontaneity" (Kaplan,
1954, p. 10, italics his). If there were convincing justification here
for committing the Jumping Fallacy, as there is not, then the
finding that the less acculturated Navaho reveal less of such "control" than the Spanish Americans might be said to suggest a basis
for an improved ability to be abstract.

It would indeed be important to be able to point to general
or specific experiences of acculturating people which enable them
to learn to think abstractly more frequently. The Navaho Indians,
for example, are said to be disturbed by their dependence upon
a "distant and mysterious white institution called 'the market.'"
Formerly, "in the days of bartering raw materials, a sheep or a
sack of wool maintained a rather constant value." In contrast,
now "they never know in advance whether lamb will bring ten
cents a pound or only five cents, and they see no sense in these
variations" (Kluckhohn and Leighton, 1946, p. 116). As they become motivated to understand this puzzling market, it may be
surmised, they will have had an exercise in abstract thinking,
which they then may be able to transfer to other situations.

Time

The people of every society note in some way the passing of
time and regulate their lives accordingly. Convenient reference
points of course are the sun, the moon, the planets, and the stars;
and on the earth in the immediate vicinity are natural phenomena
such as the seasons, the tides, and the crops. Without either
quibbling or philosophizing, it can be said that the latter are
measures of objective time, that is, duration as determined by
external events. Obviously a clock, watch, and chronometer
measure objective time most precisely.

People also have a subjective feeling concerning the passing of time. As measured by some objective phenomenon—like a sunset that signals the end or the beginning of an event they fear or wish—time seems to move quickly or slowly. In the absence of external events or instruments people are able to make judgments concerning the passing of time whose objective accuracy varies considerably. In addition, many people, especially those in more civilized countries, have an attitude toward time: some seek to be punctual, others do not appear to care; some are very conscious of the passing of clock or calendar time, others are not.

Innumerable activities in the modern world are regulated by temporal considerations. People arise, eat, work, meet, play, sleep, etc. at clock times that are clearly specified and in most instances quite arbitrary. One of the symbols of civilization is the watch that the wearer must constantly consult. In contrast, people in less civilized societies often do not have to coordinate their activities too precisely. They provide temporal cues to one another; the chief, for example, has the drums sounded long before a ceremony begins, and hence each person can go about his affairs until he hears the signal. When living is confined to a relatively stable, unchanging, and simple group, furthermore, there is less need to be on one's own and hence to begin or end an activity punctually.

It is known that, with practice, Westerners can improve their subjective judgments concerning the passing of clock time but not dramatically (e.g., Gilliland and Martin, 1940). Less civilized peoples may likewise make their subjective estimates correspond more closely to natural events, but in the absence of timepieces they are less likely to have at hand a convenient and invariant criterion. Since it becomes necessary for them to acquire both timepieces and more reliable estimates after contact with Western institutions, the following hypothesis seems promising:

HYPOTHESIS 18 (consequential): *After people change centrally from old to new ways, they are likely to be more proficient in making subjective judgments of objective time intervals.*

So far as can be determined, no systematic investigation of the problem posed by the hypothesis has been carried out. An effort was made in Africa to determine whether poorly educated men could estimate clock time by asking a haphazard sample of 46 Ganda how long they thought the interview had lasted. Only 9 per cent could not make a guess; and, of those who provided an estimate and for whom the records are adequate, 52 per cent overestimated the interval, 33 per cent underestimated it, and the remaining 15 per cent were within a minute or two of being absolutely correct. The mean error was only 23 minutes.

More systematic data were collected in Jamaica, as indicated in Table 10 (p. 298). The first two columns of the table are based on the same dichotomy employed in all previous tables: the poorly educated and the better educated. The latter group includes professional people and businessmen who must follow the demands of clock time in the manner of most civilized people. In the last two columns of the table the better educated are excluded and the poorly educated are divided into two groups: an urban group that also has to pay attention to the clock and a rural group.

In the first place, the concept of subjective time is meaningful to the informants in a manner related to their educational status. They were asked directly whether "time seems to you to go slower and faster once in a while." All the well educated and a high percentage of the poorly educated urban dwellers expressed such a feeling; the figure significantly dips among the cultivators (row 1). Modally those with such a subjective impression subscribed voluntarily to the view that time pervaded with activity seems to go faster than empty time, but the better educated—as Hypothesis 17 would suggest—expressed the thought in more general or abstract terms (rows 2 and 3). Likewise almost everyone agreed that "time or the years in general seem to pass slower or faster as you grow older" (row 4). More of the poorly than the well educated indicated that this kind of time goes more slowly, and their justification therefor is like that advanced in connection with shorter intervals: "times" are worse, they said; they have grown too old to work; or as mothers they must stay home to take care of the children (row 5). Different experiences, it seems, give rise to varying impressions of time.

The three tests of temporal judgment that every Jamaican who was tested could execute, however, provide only one bit of evidence in support of Hypothesis 18. First, toward the end of the interview those informants who had looked at a watch or clock were unexpectedly asked how long they thought the session had lasted. More, but not significantly more, of the better educated, as the hypothesis demands, were quite accurate; whereas, contrary to it, more of the rural than the urban dwellers judged the interval correctly (rows 6–8). In the other two tests, the informants were deliberately examined: they estimated the length of a 15-second interval which began when the investigator said "go" and ended when he said "stop" (rows 9–14); and they themselves sought to specify a 10-second interval by indicating when they thought exactly that much time had elapsed (rows 15–20). On neither test is there a significant difference or trend in the anticipated direction. The reliable tendency for more of the poorly educated to underestimate the 15-second interval and for fewer of them to overestimate it may possibly reflect their greater ease while being interviewed, which in turn led them to feel less impatient.

It may be that increasing contact with civilization produces not greater proficiency in judging temporal intervals but a greater awareness of time and especially of timepieces. Such an awareness, it appears, is learned when people are appropriately motivated; the task—telling time from a clock or watch—is, after all, not a difficult one. Thus the Navaho Indians have their own system of reckoning time, which is dependent upon the sun, the moon, and the stars. "If a job with white people is important to a Navaho who has to depend upon 'sun time,' " two anthropologists report, "he will often arrive at work an hour or two early in order to take no chances with a system which, from his point of view, is arbitrary because it is not geared to observable natural phenomena." When the motivation to be prompt is absent, in the words of complaining white employers, "those Indians have no idea of the meaning of time. 'Right now' may be in fifteen minutes or six hours" (Leighton and Kluckhohn, 1948, pp. 108–9). Likewise people living in rural areas of modern Greece, although they traditionally prefer to regulate their lives by the sun, by their personal inclinations, and by their conception of leisureliness, soon begin to perceive that chaos or inefficency must characterize offices and factories whose employees do not arrive and leave more or less punctually. The household clock, it is stated, at first supplies only information about time and thus satisfies people's curiosity, but gradually its very presence helps give rise to a system of habits which produce punctuality and an awareness of time (Mead, 1955, pp. 70–2).

Language

Each society has a language adequate to express and reflect people's current needs and activities. Presumably when some inadequacy is discovered, for example, in vocabulary, suitable changes take place through trial and error involving many people and sometimes extending over generations. Speech performs many functions: people communicate useful information, they express private thoughts and feelings, they establish among themselves a sense of identity or security, etc. Each man, moreover, talks to himself and thus guides his behavior; and most events arouse a verbal response which, combined with actual perception, permits an interpretation.

The amount of language accompanying and/or guiding behavior varies. At one extreme are activities, such as muscular movement in an habitual coordination, which can be executed with no or virtually no linguistic accompaniment. At the other end of the continuum are activities, such as verbal argumentation, in which speech dominates. In most human activity preexisting verbal responses probably play some role in affecting overt behavior.

These responses play *some* role, but not necessarily a decisive role. A man may tell himself or be told that on the next page there is a drawing of a tiger; but he will not see a tiger there if the page contains only print—unless he is seriously deranged or hypnotized. If languages differ from one another, therefore, the people who speak them will also differ in their responses some but not all of the time.

Languages of course do differ, but are the differences likely to have critical effects on their speakers? If the referent of a noun in one language is the same as that of a noun in another language —for example, the animal called "dog" in English and "chien" in French—then the fact that the same referent is symbolized by different phonemes is not likely to have any significant behavioral consequences. On the other hand, if one language has a noun with one referent and another language does not have a noun with precisely the same referent—for example, as indicated previously, the absence of a generic term for both running and still water in Hopi—then the speakers on occasion may respond differently to the same situation. In this illustration, the English-speaking person is able to note simply whether or not the hole in the ground contains water, but the speaker of Hopi, if he is to communicate to anyone or store the information within himself, must note whether or not it contains still or running water. Different languages are likely to have differing behavioral consequences, but since linguistic responses do not always affect behavior, this general hypothesis must emerge:

HYPOTHESIS 19 (consequential): After changing people learn a new language, they are likely to perceive differently significant stimulus patterns.

The hypothesis emphasizes the process of perception for two reasons. First it would avoid the tautology of simply maintaining that people who change exhibit changed behavior. Also it would suggest that a significant change is likely to occur in the very responses which intervene between the external world and action. If he may be used once more, the Navaho who is speaking English or has forgotten or never learned his mother tongue does not have to notice whether water is still or running before naming it.

The hypothesis is not an easy one to investigate. Changes in perception, in the first place, probably interact with changes in language. A man from an underdeveloped area who has learned to operate a bulldozer or other piece of Western machinery ob-

viously observes aspects of the machine that are blurred or overlooked by his inexperienced contemporary; he also has names
for the parts; having the names he can locate the parts more
easily; knowing the parts and their functions he is doubtless able
to learn their names more readily. With such a Spiraled Explanation it is not possible to emerge with clear-cut, cause-and-effect
sequences.

Next the investigator learns about people's perceptions usually
only by hearing their verbal account of what they are experiencing. In Jamaica, for example, all informants were shown a mountain scene which contained snow: over three-quarters of the well
educated but less than one-tenth of the poorly educated referred
to that detail (Schedule, Appendix B, item 89). Since it never
snows in Jamaica, it must be assumed that the better educated
have had more experience with snow while touring abroad, with
pictures and drawings of snow, and with the word itself. But did
the poorly educated fail to perceive or merely fail to report the
snow in the picture? Casual inquiries reveal that some failed to
notice it; others noticed it but could not identify it; and others
could identify it but found other aspects of the picture more exciting to talk about.

Finally, there may be clear differences in language, but it is
not always possible to discover whether they are accompanied
by differences in perception. Again an illustration can be drawn
from Jamaica. There is a tendency in the Jamaican patois for
masculine pronouns and titles such as "sir" to be employed to
refer to females, but the reverse is never true (except that sometimes a male is called "madame"). "Where is Mrs. Jones?" The
reply is likely to be, "Him go down the road." Aside from suggesting a possible if tenuous connection with the Bantu languages
spoken by their African ancestors, this linguistic practice suggests
the following questions: Do Jamaicans who speak the patois fail
to discriminate the sex of the person to whom the pronoun refers? Do they wish—consciously or unconsciously—to emphasize
male dominance? Is there, in fact, any psychological significance
to be attached to such a twist in language? So far the writer has
been unable to think of a way to investigate the problem. In
addition a complication intrudes nowadays since most Jamaicans

have had enough schooling to become aware of "proper" English and hence are usually able to avoid the idiom in the presence of someone with superior education.

The writer has sought to circumvent these methodological difficulties in two ways. First the informants are kept constant, as it were, and the language in which they are addressed is varied. This technique requires people who are bilingual, and in three African societies—the same ones as those in the main study—it has been possible to conduct experiments with high school students who have a good working knowledge of English and with a European group of Afrikaans-speaking children who have English as a second language. Each student was given ten statements in the native language and ten in English. Each was asked to express his opinion on all twenty statements; then later—and unexpectedly—he was asked to recall as many of the statements as he could. The experiment was repeated in a Jamaican school: the patois was considered the native language and standard English the second language.

The results, given in detail elsewhere (Doob, 1957a and 1958a), indicate that the language in which a statement appears can have a pronounced effect upon the expressed attitude as well as upon the recall of the statements but that the effect is not inevitable. Among the three African groups and among the Afrikaners, there was a tendency for the native language to produce more assent than English, but the reverse tendency appeared among the Jamaicans. The magnitude of the differences, when they are significant, is noteworthy. "You should not cut your baby's hair before the baby begins to talk": 35 per cent of the Jamaican children agreed with this statement in standard English, only 13 per cent in patois; 85 per cent of those hearing the standard English version could recall it, 63 per cent of those hearing it in patois. Obviously, then, for bilingual students the language in which a statement appears conveys something besides its "meaning": sometimes but not always they observe or react to different aspects of the stimulus pattern. If such results are generalizable, it would appear that the learning of a new language, as Hypothesis 19 suggests, may have substantial consequences.

The second way to investigate the effects on perception or some other form of behavior which may accompany the learning of a second language is to use informants whose knowledge of English varies from zero to proficiency. At the outset it is necessary to identify what looks like a marked difference between English and the native language; then those knowing English can be expected to react as the characteristic of English suggests. With such a technique the differences to be anticipated may not be too marked, inasmuch as the perception of the bilingual person can be affected by either or both languages.

Colors should be useful for this purpose since some languages cut the physical color spectrum differently from others and assign labels to varying parts of the spectrum. In contrast with English, and also with the Nilotic language of the Luo, which has a rather rich color vocabulary, the Bantu languages, like those of the Ganda and the Zulu, make only gross or at least different discriminations. In Zulu, for example, *bomvu* refers to what in English would be given the designation of *red* but it also may include some shades of *yellow*. In the Ganda language, the word for *blue* has been borrowed from English: *bbululu*. This does not mean that differences between colors are not perceived. Thus in Zulu a yellow object may be called *"bomvu* like corn" and a red one *"bomvu* like blood." It was reasoned, therefore, that because their languages make fewer color distinctions, the Ganda and Zulu ought to notice color less frequently, but that the better educated among them, because they know English and have contact with English-speaking people, who make finer discriminations, might respond more readily to color.

Relevant results appear in Table 9. On the Sorting Test informants could use color as the first solution or on later trials: contrasting groups are virtually identical in both respects (rows 15 and 18). As anticipated, more of the better educated Ganda and Zulu do use color at least once on the test, but the differences are not significant and—as not anticipated—the same trend appears among the Luo. Likewise the nonsignificant trend in the two Bantu-speaking societies is for more of the better educated to report color in the Rorschach plates; but once again the only significant difference appears unexpectedly among the Luo (rows

32–34). Clearly these data do not support the hypothesis. It may be that the reporting of color under such circumstances is not related to the structure of language; in fact, the association between color responses to Rorschach plates and acculturation among Indian groups varies markedly from society to society (Table B, rows 7 and 8; Table C, row 26; Table D, row 10; Barnouw, 1950, p. 27).

Another part of the investigation, confined to the Zulu, was more successful. An assistant who herself is a Zulu presented the informants with four deflated balloons which they were to sort into two piles: "Put those together which you think belong together." By sheer chance the combinations to be anticipated from Zulu color terms—pairing green with blue and also red with yellow—would be expected to occur 33 per cent of the time. The combination actually appeared among 23 per cent of the urban Zulu and 50 per cent of the rural ones. Evidently the women who knew no English tended to employ, significantly frequently, a physical grouping in accord with the linguistic grouping. Such a finding of course is suggestive without proving that the linguistic factor is responsible. As ever, past experience must be exerting some effect, perhaps in this instance the experience associated with the language itself. The experience, however, need not be a linguistic one per se. Zulu males were shown successively pairs selected at random from a crudely drawn circle, triangle, and square and asked each time to point to the figure they liked more. The Zulu in their traditional life have a penchant for the circular form, which appears in their kraals, their dress, female coiffures, etc. In this investigation the circle would be selected by chance again 33 per cent of the time, but 47 per cent of the poorly educated and 19 per cent of the well educated preferred it. Here more frequent or more rewarding contact with the traditional form evidently influenced judgment. The influence of linguistic or nonlinguistic experience on these Zulu women and men is subtle; presumably, if Hypothesis 19 is valid, the effect it postulates occurs in a similarly subtle manner.

Other investigators have collected data that lend some support to the hypothesis. In sorting colors which were arbitrarily assigned monosyllabic names, Navaho subjects paid attention to the length of the vowel in the names and hence emerged with more piles than American subjects, who disregarded that difference in sound: the difference in vowel length can signal a difference of meaning in the Navaho language but not in English (Brown, 1956, pp. 291–5). In another experiment there was some tendency for Navaho-speaking children to match objects according to shape and size rather than color and for the reverse to be true of Navaho children whose dominant language was English; in the Navaho language more attention is paid to shape and size than in English (Carroll and Casagrande, 1958, pp. 26–30). The latter quite perfect outcome, nevertheless, is spoiled by an additional finding: comparable American children resemble the Navaho- rather than the English-dominant group among the Indians because, the authors guess, of "practice with toys and other objects involving the fitting of forms and shapes." This imperfection once again suggests a type of experience which is nonlinguistic.

Hypothesis 19 calls attention to differences in perception that may result from language differences; if it were possible to find some universal differences between the languages of less and more civilized people, then some correspondingly universal differences in perception between them might also be adduced. At the moment no such universals are evident, but it seems possible that there is a difference in the frequency with which language is used in the two kinds of societies. A distinguishing characteristic of modern civilization does appear to be a rather ready verbalism which is developed in schools and encouraged by cliques and other social groups in later life and by the mass media of communication. In contrast, it is felt, less civilized people are a little more likely to teach their children by example rather than by precept and to possess a literature which places more emphasis upon action than upon the cataloguing of internal feelings. If such differences exist, then the following must be a consequence:

HYPOTHESIS 20 (consequential): After people change centrally from old to new ways, they are likely to be more proficient in using language to describe and express their feelings and reactions to the external world.

The idea behind this hypothesis arose almost spontaneously in the course of the Africa-Jamaica studies: the better educated seemed so much more capable of giving an account of their feelings and goals. In Jamaica, for example, informants were instructed to look at some stereoscopic pictures and then to "tell me, please, what you see." Below are the protocols from two men, both in their late forties, describing the second picture they saw:

"This seems to be a view from a hill, looking down on the sea. There appears to be a peninsula or something or other in the distance, dividing the water somehow. And there is a boat in the outer harbor. In the foreground a tree, no, two trees.

I saw some trees and a house a way far off. [Do you see anything else?] Something resembles the sea. [Anything else?] No.

The first man, the head of a government bureau, had more to say and organized his impressions better than the second man, a small farmer. In general, the writer received a similar impression from all the protocols when the better educated are compared with the less well educated (Table 9, row 40). The poorly educated informants, it appears, did not always see less, they simply reported and organized fewer of their perceptions. Sometimes, after they had claimed that there was nothing more in the picture, they would be asked whether they could see a certain object; they would almost always agree that the object was there and, after further questioning, suggest that the investigator by questioning them had called their attention not to the object but to their failure to report it.

Other data are not easy to come by. As suggested in the last chapter, the tendency for more of the poorly educated to say "don't know" when asked to express an opinion, or to claim no conviction at all, may be due to an inability to express themselves. One feature of the Sorting Test does provide direct and confirmatory evidence. After an informant had sorted the pieces of cardboard into piles and, from his standpoint, had completed the trial, he was asked, "Why did you do it in that way?" and, if that question were not understood, "What do the pieces in each pile have in common?" In some instances, after a man had actually sorted the pieces of cardboard correctly, he either could not indicate the principle he had followed or else the principle he mentioned was incorrect or only partially correct. An example of a partially correct verbal explanation is the following: The pieces had been sorted into eight piles on the basis of size *and* shape, and the informant—even after repeated questioning—maintained that he had arranged them according to their size *or* shape. There is a decided tendency for fewer of the better educated informants to reveal this verbal deficiency (row 20 of Table 9).

It would not do to end the chapter by appearing to assert the superiority of more civilized men. Maybe they do talk more or express themselves more easily, but modern advertising and propaganda make one pause to wonder whether verbal facility necessarily connotes more than glibness. Can one feel profoundly without producing poetry?

Chapter 8.

EFFECTS OF PERSONALITY

THE MAJOR problem of this chapter is to begin the impossible task of trying to put together into a unified whole the various segments presented in preceding chapters. So far the people who are becoming or would become more civilized have been approached analytically: sections of their behavior have been considered in isolation. All the previously pronounced hypotheses, consequently, must be qualified with the trite but critical provision, "other things being equal." The drives, the attitudes, the beliefs and values, the skill and intelligence of men—these component parts that have been separately examined do indeed affect one another. Thus the discontent that may goad a person to change (Hypothesis 1) can produce the postulated consequence in certain situations only if he is sufficiently skillful to learn the new techniques demanded by the change (Hypothesis 16). The relating of the components to one another is a long and arduous task for which, quite bluntly, neither the state of contemporary knowledge or theory nor certainly the quivering sagacity of the writer seems adequate.

A less rigorous but, hopefully, a fruitful approach is not to construct a pattern by analyzing the numerous interactions of the components but to postulate the existence of some pattern and then to observe, if possible, the presumed effects of the pattern on those components. That pattern which organizes discrete segments of behavior is personality. And so, after these preliminary squirmings, it becomes possible to ask and attempt to answer a concrete question: In what ways do people's personalities affect their tendency to become more civilized?

203

Modal Tendencies

The thought can be expressed in various ways and the expression can be subtle or crude, but it seems perfectly clear that each person is more susceptible to learning some kinds of changes than others. He is more likely to perceive and adopt innovations which favorably affect his central interests than he is other forms which affect him unfavorably or segmentally. An individual whose values are centered in his personal reputation in the community must have a personality sensitive to the reactions of other people, and many of the significant or even insignificant changes in him undoubtedly are related to his paramount interest.

In any society people's interests and hence their susceptibility to change vary modally from group to group. The slight difference in beliefs held by men and women frequently reflects their different values and responsibilities. Among the Zulu, for example, one might expect females to be more conservative than males since they remain in the home and do not have frequent contacts with Western influences. Table III (p. 302) contains a comparison of Zulu males and females from urban and rural areas with respect to certain facts and values. In the rural community, the trend runs if anything counter to the common-sense expectation; and in the urban area the females are more traditional than the males on only one item (row 1). A methodological artifact may account for some of the differences: the females were interviewed by a Zulu female, and the males were interviewed by the writer and his interpreter. The significantly greater number of females who are skeptical concerning the powers of a native doctor (row 2) may possibly result from the greater contact of women with Western-trained health officers in connection with the bearing and raising of children. The conviction that women are more tradition-bound than men receives no support either in the rural or urban sample among the Jamaicans; there, when both sexes were interviewed by the writer, the mean number of traditional beliefs to which males subscribe was significantly higher in both areas.

Likewise, it must now be noted, certain modal tendencies

rather than others are fostered not only by groups in one society but also within each society as a whole. That each society tends to produce different kinds of people must follow from a number of convincing if a priori assumptions: the different environmental conditions in which each society operates, the different methods of socialization that societies may employ, the different institutions that characterize them at a given moment, and so on. It is to be expected, therefore, that the "typical" Frenchman will differ from the "typical" Swede, or it must at least follow either that France contains a number of "types" different from those to be found in Sweden or that there are more people in France than in Sweden who belong to a particular "type." The difficulty is to prove one of these assertions, and that difficulty largely arises from the inability to secure valid and adequate measures of enough Frenchmen and Swedes. Perhaps modal personalities are easier to discern in the more unified environments which less civilized societies usually provide.

Can all less civilized societies be lumped together and then be subject to the same kind of reasoning? If this were possible, analysis would reveal a "less civilized type of personality." The procedure, it would appear, is without flaw. In Chapter 2 it has been contended that on an abstract level less civilized societies are characterized by certain attributes. These attributes are important and hence they have significant effects upon behavior. On an equally abstract level, consequently, the resulting personality "type" ought to be discernible: the postulated attributes give rise to a modal tendency. This particular fantasy, however, must stop abruptly: at the moment neither existing evidence nor existing modes of conceptualization permit this writer, at any rate, to detect what that type is. The possibility of eventually finding the type, which cannot of course be excluded, receives here only a respectful bow before a retreat to the previous level.

If people's personalities affect what they learn and if each society tends to foster certain modal tendencies in personality, the following conclusion must follow:

HYPOTHESIS 21 (causal): New forms of behavior are likely to be learned which are in accord with modal personality traits in the old society.

Certainly Hypothesis 21 contains a tricky phrase, viz., "in accord with." Let its exposition begin with a concrete illustration. It is stated that the modern Iroquois Indians in New York are "often preferred" as ironworkers by contracting companies since they do not fear heights. In 1714 an observer reported that people from one branch of this society "will walk over deep Brooks, and Creeks, on the smallest Poles, and that without any Fear or Concern" (Wallace, 1951). It might be argued that the skill of walking on narrow supports has been transferred, but the argument would be difficult to prove: we do not know if successive generations of Indians since the eighteenth century have continued to practice that skill. It would seem rather that fearlessness in certain situations has been perpetuated as a trait and that modern members of the tribe, when faced with a number of employment opportunities and perhaps in the face of competition and discrimination, have selected the work for which they are psychologically or emotionally rather than muscularly or kinesthetically prepared. In different words, they are transferring not a specific skill but an internal trait; working on high buildings is "in accord with" modal personality tendencies in the society.

The anthropologist just cited uses the illustration to support his view that people in a society accept "forms of behavior which are psychologically congenial" and that they tend to reject the uncongenial. The thought is variously expressed by anthropologists—new traits are said to be more readily acceptable when they are "compatible" with old ones or when they "conform to the pre-existing culture pattern"—but its central feature is a commonly employed explanation of social change and acculturation. Of the 70 "major empirical studies reported by anthropologists" concerning the acculturation of the North American Indians up to the year 1952 (Siegel, 1955), about one-third appear to the present writer to provide a similar explanation. "Congeniality," "compatibility," "conformity," and the corresponding expression in Hypothesis 21 all refer to the fact that the new is sufficiently similar to the old so that learning is facilitated. The similarity may involve the nature of the skill and the behavior demanded by the old and the new situations, as Hypothesis 16 suggests; or else it may refer, as in the case of the Iroquois, to a consistent personality trait.

Is the problem that simple? No, of course not. Some of the complexities must be suggested. Innovations, it has been said, are accepted when they "fit" into the pre-existing cultural pattern or, after being accepted, they are modified so that they do fit (Bartlett, 1923, p. 195). In one sense "fit" here is again equivalent to "in accord with" or "congenial to": a man in a society has modal traits into which the innovation does or does not fit. In another sense, the fit need not be a good one for everybody in the society but—well, can it be a good fit for the society without being really satisfactory to people within the society? Up to a point, it seems to the writer, the question can be discussed exclusively in societal terms. A new religion which stresses the loving qualities of a deity is more likely to be acceptable in a society whose present gods are also benign than in the one which attributes vengeful propensities to the higher powers. Surely the new religion is or is not in accord with people's previous psychological beliefs. Under most circumstances, yes, but conceivably sometimes the fit refers not to people but to their relations. Even then some people, perhaps old leaders, must be affected. The question is not whether fit or compatibility applies to an individual or society but at which of these two levels it is more profitable to discuss a given problem. This book, being psychologically oriented, perforce must select the level of the individual, without expressing prejudice against a social frame of reference. Most usefully, for example, the latter approach may call attention to variability within a society or to nonpsychological factors which have psychological consequences. If a new form of government is incompatible, it is then necessary to discover why some members of the society cannot learn the required behavior. Parents may approve of education along Western lines for their children and yet keep them out of school: schooling usually requires attendance at regular times each day, and the children cannot be spared from performing a useful role in the family economy, such as the tending of cattle by young boys in many parts of Africa.

In this instance, children's work habits are not compatible with the school's routine and hence, in the words of Hypothesis 4, innovations from the West are not accessible to them.

Whether the analysis is made in terms of individuals or their society, the possibility of engaging in circular reasoning arises. If a new religion is accepted by the old society, then it may be argued that it must have been in accord with, or have fitted people's personalities or their institutions. What is accepted fits, what fits is accepted. In fact, a powerful leader may have been attracted to the religion for idiosyncratic reasons; thereafter he forced his followers to follow the new faith. His personality, which the new religion fitted, and his position in the society are the critical factors, not the relation of the innovation to the modal tendencies of most followers. It is conceivable, nevertheless, that even a ruthless tyrant cannot force a new form upon people unless it possesses some elements they find congenial; and yet again, people are sufficiently plastic to be able to adapt themselves to many different kinds of innovations. A Spiraled Explanation seems probable. Thus there seems to be no clear-cut escape from the circle, other than to look for traits that are common to both the old and the new forms.

That escape is the one employed a few pages ago in describing the modern Iroquois, who are descended from ancestors unafraid of heights and who themselves now display that trait. The approach appears equally useful when an effort is made to account for the selective reception of the elements in an institution from the outside. Thus the Pine Ridge Sioux have accepted Christianity reluctantly, particularly because their own very important ceremonial of the Sun Dance was suppressed by white officials. Aspects of Christianity, nevertheless, appealed to them. The Christian conception of heaven resembles their own "happy hunting grounds"; "asceticism, the torture of the crucifixion for the good of others, giving to others (especially the poor), and the high honor accorded virginity were not unconnected with [their] beliefs and cultural ways"; and "putting money into the collection plate on Sundays is still used as a means of giving honor to another person and gaining prestige for generosity in the native give-away pattern." More than a similarity in content, however, must account for the attractiveness of the outside religion. According to the same investigator, for the Sioux Christianity means "an acceptance of the deity of their conquerors and a search for his power." In practice, Christianity is "the one part of the white man's life in which the Indian was accepted as an equal." It is a religion, finally, which teaches that "happiness could be attained in a life after death, a promise which may have given some hope to the Indians when most of their happiness was being taken away from them." Christianity had elements in common with the old religion, in brief, and it also satisfied many basic traits (MacGregor, 1946, pp. 91–2).

It is to be noted that the analyst just cited makes sagacious inferences concerning the psychological responses of Indians on the basis of the religious elements which he believes appeal to them. Can the internal reactions be measured directly? In one investigation such a direct attempt has been made. Japanese Americans, born in Japan (issei) or in the United States (nisei), who did not choose to return to the Pacific coast after being released from relocation camps at the end of World War II, were able most successfully to adjust themselves to living in Chicago. The hypothesis was advanced that "Japanese and American middle-class cultures share in common the values of: politeness, respect for authority and parental wishes, duty to community, diligence, cleanliness and neatness, emphasis on personal achievement of long-range goals, shame (more than guilt) concerning non-sanctioned behavior, importance of keeping up appearances, and others" (Caudill, 1952, p. 9). The "direct continuity" between the values of the issei and the nisei and also between nisei and middle-class Americans ought to be reflected, it was thought, in performance on the Thematic Apperception Test. That test, consequently, was given to relatively small samples of Japanese in Chicago, and their responses were compared with protocols from somewhat similar samples of Chicagoans. Relevant data have been assembled by the present writer in Table E (see p. 310), in which the descriptive categories derived from analyzing the stories have been changed to fit the categories of this book; division by sex has been eliminated; and raw figures have been converted into percentages. Evidence of this kind convinces the investigator that "the ultimate destinations or goals" of nisei and middle-class Chicagoans "tend to be the same" (ibid., p. 68). In Table E, it is true, there is only one significant difference between the nisei and the comparable Chicago group (row 10). The TAT in this instance, however, may not be sufficiently sensitive since it also produces no more than two differences between issei and nisei (rows 1 and 4) and between lower middle- and upper lower-class Chicagoans (rows 1 and 7).

If the investigator's interpretation is correct, then it would appear that the nisei already possessed many of the traits of the new groups to which they were adjusting and that indeed they "strove with considerable success to be like the American middle class because middle-class values were those they felt closest to —that were most like Japanese values" (ibid., p. 17). In this respect they had little to learn, except perhaps to be less insensitive to, or less dependent upon, the reactions of their peers. Instead they could concentrate on the particular tasks at hand, such as mastering a job or a profession. Being similar to Americans, moreover, they could more easily like their teachers and, as the investigator himself emphasizes, they in turn were able to elicit favorable reactions from Chicagoans, who therefore encouraged them to become Americanized.

The last observation suggests still another approach to the problem: modal traits that appeal to outside teachers will facilitate acculturation because attractive students, as it were, elicit greater cooperation and willingness to teach. In fact such an approach has occurred to a group of writers who are concerned with the migrations of people from one Western country to another. They believe that they can adduce traits in immigrants that facilitate their adjustment, viz., "a kind of cluster which neither upsets the standards of the new group nor is skewed in any direction, so that hostility of the local group cannot be directed against a migrant because of his being different." Likewise the traits retarding acculturation are identified as those which "reduce the number of social contacts either through isolation, non-conformance, hostility, or competition." The writers then are sufficiently courageous to present two lists, which are reproduced below (Ruesch et al., 1948, pp. 26–7):

facilitating	*inhibiting*
cautious, charming cheerful, clever, constructive, conventional, cooperative, curious, enterprising, enthusiastic, friendly, generous, grateful, imaginative, kind, planful, practical, responsive, self-confident, self-respecting, self-controlling, shrewd, tactful, thoughtful	acquisitive, arrogant, assertive, autocratic, boastful, gloomy, incoherent, dissatisfied, obstructive, short-tempered, inarticulate, evasive, coarse, hostile, thankless, headstrong, dishonest, dull, jealous, mischievous, opinionated, quitting, rebellious, self-pitying, self-distrustful, sensitive, exclusive, tactless, vindictive

For the moment, since their validity has not been determined, the lists only suggest the flavor of the problem.

If speculation is tolerated a little longer, three other forms of modal personality traits with respect to which societies conceivably differ may be briefly sketched. First, it is conceivable that each society has a characteristic way of coping with adversity. When faced with some common disaster, such as a famine or an epidemic, people in one society may generally not run the gamut of psychiatric responses which have been lengthily catalogued (such as aggression, repression, displacement, masochism, sadism, rationalization), but instead may react in a traditional and rather stereotyped manner by following one or a limited number of the theoretically possible alternatives. If such a tendency exists, it would follow that people in a particular less civilized society may find it easier to learn new forms which, when adversity occurs, demand one kind of adjustment and not another. Maybe, for example, some cultures rather than others produce people better able to withstand the anonymity, the loneliness, and the uncertainties of urban living. If there were in fact a modal disposition in a society, however, it is hardly likely that the inhabitants would react uniformly to new adversity. The establishment by white men of a saw mill near the Ojibwa Indians of northern Wisconsin in 1894, for example, produced frustration. The Indians who chose to work for the mill had to devote full time to their jobs and hence could no longer satisfy their "essential needs" through the traditional techniques of hunting, fishing, and home crafts but only by buying manufactured goods at the new stores; and they soon became aware that the strangers considered them and their culture to be inferior. Two quite different reactions occurred: some of the Indians withdrew to the "Old Village" to practice their traditional forms in relative isolation, but others tried to become as American as possible (Gillin, 1942, pp. 550–1).

Societies, secondly, may also differ regarding modal methods of learning new forms of behavior. On an individual level it seems clear that people in a single society show variation in this respect. Some plunge ahead recklessly, others tend to be cautious almost regardless of the task at hand. Some demand immediate encouragements, or at least rewards in the not very distant future, whereas others can work most proficiently to attain distant goals. Some learn more efficiently in a social situation; others demand solitude. If societies have such modal tendencies, then conceivably forms of behavior that demand learning methods in accord with the accustomed techniques are likely to be acquired more readily than those dependent on other techniques.

Finally, if less civilized societies really share certain attributes and if increased civilization virtually always demands certain general forms of behavior, it may be that particular personality traits are always likely to be helpful in facilitating the learning of new forms. Thus it has been said in this book that life in more civilized areas tends to increase the number of complicated choices a person must make. Whatever combination of traits enables a person, then, to cope with complexity at an early age in his own society may become useful to him in the new context.

Hypothesis 16 has stated in effect that proficiency in new situations depends in part on the extent to which they are perceived to be similar to ones in the past. The present hypothesis argues that such proficiency also is affected by people's modal personalities which spring from responses frequently aroused in the past and which therefore probably influence future behavior. From either or both, this corollary must follow: *People from different societies are likely to be able to learn new forms with varying degrees of ease and efficiency.* Both theoretically and practically the critical problem is to ascertain the degree of similarity between the old and the new, and here is no glib task. Can the new language of the outsider or can an idea in science be learned more readily by people from one society than from another? Before either question can be answered, an empirical investigation of the societies in question must be conducted. In the first instance, it may be necessary to compare the phonemes of the mother tongues of two societies and the new language before it can be said whether the adults of one society rather than the other are likely to learn the new language more readily and to emerge with a better pronunciation. In the second case, the scientific ideas to be learned must be examined in relation to old ideas; the notion of evolution, if that be the idea under discussion, is unquestionably closer to the thinking of some nonliterate peoples than others.

This section must end by stating and then quickly resolving a paradox. It has been suggested that sometimes incompatibility rather than compatibility is a "necessary condition for acceptance" in a society if the element of "novelty" has a strong appeal (Barnett, 1953, p. 358). Incompatibility, therefore, appears compatible in this instance. In fact, the "novelty" that appeals would not appeal unless it possessed some compatible elements, and novelty is not universally alluring or alluring under all circumstances. The slightly different, in brief, must be compatible with some modal trait before it will secure adherents.

Difficult Changes

It has been repeatedly emphasized that certain traditional forms of behavior are not easily abandoned either by a person during his lifetime or by successive generations of people in a society. The tenacity with which people cling to beliefs and practices associated with the family or with their infancy and early childhood, for example, has been noted (Hypothesis 6 and the corollary on p. 156). The general security that traditional societies offer has been emphasized as one of their outstanding attributes. Eventually, however, tenaciously held forms of behavior, in spite of the strong reinforcement they have received, may change. If external compulsion does not effect the change, then the motivation for the learning must be found within those who do change. Probably the basic explanation involves the failure of the old form to bring satisfaction as well as the accessibility, potential attractiveness, etc. of the new form (Hypothesis 4). Often old forms remain satisfactory and new ones do not appear attractive until some change or changes have previously occurred. Then, since traits are organized within the personality, the more basic change may occur.

Another kind of difficult change results not from a reluctance to abandon the old but from the learning that is demanded before the new form can be properly executed. Here too a step-by-step progression is often evident; aspects, perhaps only minor aspects, of the new are first learned, more are added, and finally the complete change takes place. A single hypothesis suffices to include both difficult changes:

> HYPOTHESIS 22 (causal): A heavily reinforced form of behavior that remains satisfying is likely to change, and a new form of behavior that is difficult to learn is likely to be learned, only after some of its components have been, respectively, changed and learned.

Evidence in support of the first part of the hypothesis appears when the changes in an important custom are described. To their custom of bride price the Zulu, for example, attach very great significance for economic, social, and indeed spiritual reasons. In urban areas, it is reported, the paying of the dowry tends to disappear not because the Zulu once decided to repudiate the practice directly but because a change in one detail has gradually made the custom itself unsatisfactory. Instead of presenting cattle to the bride's family—the usual practice in traditional Zulu society—the prospective groom uses money, for obviously money rather than cattle is available in towns and cities. Money, however, changes an important aspect of the custom: "it is soon dissipated, leaving no permanent record to safeguard the stability of the marriage and to guarantee the good conduct of both husband and wife." The change in spirit produced by the change in method of payment in turn leads to another change: the bride price is now considered to be direct payment—"the grasping man or woman" who is the parent is in fact attempting to "sell" his or her daughter. Instead of promoting security for almost everyone, the remnant of the old custom begins to have an opposite effect; thus many urban Zulu have abandoned it. For them it has come to mean "the sundering of all ties between parents and child" (Hellman, 1937, pp. 420–1).

Changes in the components of an old form eventually may lead to the disappearance of the form, but sometimes it can persist for a long while after many of its components have been altered. The Pondo of South Africa who live on the farms of Europeans, it is reported, "rarely" conduct an initiation ceremony for girls because too many of its components have been either prohibited (the important dance) or circumscribed (the brewing of beer) by European law. In contrast, "much of the old ritual" for the boys survives in spite of significant changes in many important details: "the period of seclusion is curtailed, the large gatherings for feasting and dancing contests no longer take place, the technique of making the dancing skirts and masks is lost, and the whole character of the ceremony is changed when one boy is initiated alone instead of being one of an age and territorial group" (Hunter, 1936, p. 530). It may be inferred that the functional importance of the ceremony as a rite of passage toward adult duties is considered more important for boys than for girls.

There are instances in which components of the old have changed and components of the new have been learned without a significant change taking place in the heavily reinforced old form. According to the traditional view of some Indian tribes in North America, illness must be ascribed "not to breaking the rules of healthful living, as defined by white American culture, but to an infraction of indigenous morality, and often closely associated with animals." Such a belief is said to represent the survival of a "hunting world-view"; in one tribe, for example, people are thought to become ill when they offend their non-human helpers and guardians "by wanton destruction of life in any form." The Indians who have access to modern medical services no longer believe they can control the outside powers that produce disease, but they continue to maintain their "traditional belief in immanent justice and of retribution in the form of sickness" (Thompson, 1948, pp. 211–14). In spite of doctors, hospitals, and health programs, therefore, they have great anxiety concerning illness: they have lost the belief that brought them comfort and retained the one that stirs up fear. Likewise outsiders experience similar difficulties with Christianity. The Busama of Northeast New Guinea, for example, have not yet decided whether the grounds for avoiding sin should be found in their traditional religion or in Christianity. Formerly the "shame or embarrassment felt by a person discovered in irregular behavior" was the sanction that guided them; now the new religion would have them be guided by their consciences. They have acquired some of the new without changing appreciably the old:

> They are ashamed now not only from fear of the disapproval of their fellows but also from dread of the wrath of the Lord. The "inner voice" speaks to them of the all-seeing eye and of God's awareness of hidden actions; yet, if asked what is implied by their glib talk of forfeiture of grace, they tell only of the risk of hell [Hogbin, 1951, pp. 258–60].

Presumably they will emerge as Christians in spirit only after longer experience with Christian doctrine; but, the overwhelming and unoriginal thought protrudes, are many civilized Christians different from them?

It often appears as though the aspect of a new form which is most difficult to learn is what must be called its inner meaning. Again and again anthropologists warn themselves and their readers not to be misled by the appearance of symbols; for example, "the native in the lounge suit whom he [the anthropologist] had not thought of questioning turns out to be the most competent diviner in the neighborhood" (Richards, 1935a). These symbols, however, signify some change within the people concerned; thus those "who parade an alien posture before their fellows" may be doing so "for some real or supposed private advantage that it gives them" (Barnett, 1953, p. 304). The external change, however, is the first step.

The inability to learn the inner meaning of a form of behavior can be explained in terms of the problems and beliefs in the old society. Middle-class people in Jamaica, for example, express shock and amusement when a lower-class man and woman who

have been living together for years suddenly celebrate their relation with a large formal wedding to which their children come.
Such a wedding, they imply, violates the spirit of the ceremony
or sacrament. In fact, the participants appreciate the require-
ments of a respectable marriage and approve of them. They feel,
however, that they cannot meet them, and hence marriage is
postponed until they know they can. First, money is needed. The
wedding is supposed to be accompanied by all the expensive
trimmings associated with the Victorian version. The husband
is responsible for maintaining his wife and children and for their
debts. Secondly, evidence is needed that the two people are
compatible so that the marriage can follow the prescription and
be a "life-long association." Compatibility along sexual and personal lines can be tested only by a preliminary period of cohabi-
tation. Women in particular must first demonstrate that they can
be faithful, that they can be discreet, and that they can bear
children. These people, as it were, do not postpone their sexual
and emotional needs until they have enough money and are certain of one another: they surmount the difficulties by changing
some components of the institution. Indeed, during cohabita-
tion the woman is expected and also expects to work harder than
after marriage (Clarke, 1957). So far as this investigator could
detect, partners in stable common-law marriages in Jamaica continually hope that they will some day be formally married, but in
the meantime they are not ashamed of their status. Women refer
to their mates as "paramours" and men proudly acknowledge
their paternity. Indeed the discrepancy between the formal re-
quirements and the actual behavior exists virtually everywhere.
At a very formal "classical concert," the proceeds of which went
to a most respectable high school for girls, a comedian dressed
in evening clothes made the following statements, punctuated
by well-timed pauses: "My parents were very strict—they never
let me go out with girls—until I was three and a half—months—
you know my governess." The audience roared during each pause;
but would not the ancient joke appeal to almost everyone in the
Western world?

Additional evidence for Hypothesis 22 appears whenever an
investigator indicates the "stages" through which people go dur-

ing their own lifetime or through which societies over generations have gone in adopting the civilization of the West. After a
careful examination of the life histories and personalities of fifteen
Navaho Indians, for example, "four 'stages' in the transition from
Navaho to white American ways of life" have been distinguished:

1. "Minimal contact with whites": the individual "manifests
the characteristics of the traditional Navaho value system."

2. "Increased effective contacts": the individual imitates but
does not internalize "selected value patterns."

3. "Years of sustained white contact": the individual begins to
internalize "white value patterns."

4. The "final possible": the individual loses "the residuals
of Navaho value-orientations" and hence is "culturally indistinguishable from whites of the same age and sex" (Vogt, 1951,
pp. 88–9).

The above schema serves to raise at least two problems of far-
reaching consequence. Why do some people in society pass more
rapidly than others from one stage to the next? And, secondly,
is one shift more significant from a learning standpoint than
another? On the first question it must be quickly stated that all
the hypotheses presented throughout this book seem relevant, at
least in theory. For the explanation of individual susceptibility
must be found in present and past discontents, in attitudes toward insiders and outsiders, and so on. In fact, however, the
detailed study of the fifteen Navaho males just cited reveals, according to the investigator, that no single factor can account
for the stage a particular Indian had reached. Affecting him
would be social and cultural forces within his family, such as its
size, structure, and level of acculturation; his contacts with the
white world through boarding school, occupation, and service
during the war; and his personality, especially traits involving
relations with contemporaries and his personal feelings of conflict
and insecurity. No one of the factors by itself either promoted or
inhibited acculturation. The death of a parent or close relative
facilitated acculturation for three men by disrupting families
and producing "less effective socialization to Navaho values and
patterns"; but in two instances traditional socialization was

thereby strengthened because the children were reared by more conservative grandparents (pp. 90–1). Likewise feelings of conflict and insecurity led four of the men to adopt as much of white culture as possible; but two others instead became alchoholics, and three solved their problems by "an intensified return to Navaho values" (p. 107). When a plunge is made into the details of an individual's biography, the patterning of many forces and events is blatantly evident. One feels that a particular Indian would not have become so acculturated unless—and then the circumstances multiply. All is not chaos, however, for each of the circumstances could become intelligible were it to be explored in its own right. The man learned about white ways because he was drafted; he was drafted because he happened to be the right age; he was the right age because—and so on. Or he was drafted because there was a draft; there was a draft because there was a war; there was a war because—again, and so on. But once drafted his reaction to the service depended not only on circumstances which end a chain of other circumstances (such as the personality of his commanding officer or the army's policy concerning the treatment of Indians) but also his own personality, which in turn was the culmination of another long series of events.

It appears, in the second place, that the really significant shift in the acculturation of these Indians must occur between stages 2 and 3. As Hypothesis 22 suggests, components of white civilization are acquired during the first two stages: white ways are learned, but the values are not internalized. One man, whose war service had enabled him to have very satisfying contacts with white soldiers and white civilization in general, was asked how he felt when he returned to his Navaho home:

> It was too quiet around here. I left all my friends that I used to go with. It made me kind of homesick and lonesome. And it was entirely different from what we had been doing. All the time I wanted to go where there were big crowds [p. 42].

A man with such feelings was clearly in a learning mood: he wanted to become an American and was eager to learn and do whatever circumstances permitted to attain the goal. This shift, this learning of not just an additional but rather an essential component, deserves special attention in its own right: it is the subject of the next section.

Central Goals

"What would you like to do during your life that would make you happiest and most proud of yourself?" "What is the worst thing that could happen to you during your lifetime?" Among the well educated, nearly all the Ganda and every educated informant in the other three societies were able to answer these questions, which were asked in the course of the interview in the Africa-Jamaica studies. Even the poorly educated answered with dispatch; the highest number of no replies occurred among the Ganda in this category but that was only 19 per cent (Table 7, rows 36 and 37). At a minimum, therefore, people express some ideas concerning the central values they would seek or avoid; they are at least somewhat aware of the organization of their own personalities.

Any form of behavior learned from the new society can serve a segmental purpose, or it can function in support of some central value. The tribesman may aspire to read because, he says to himself, it might be interesting or important to be able to understand books and newspapers: he desires the objective per se. He may also have a much more general purpose in mind: he may seek the skill because he would thus contribute to the knowledge of his tribe and prevent that tribe, as he phrases it, from being swindled by Europeans; or, from a reverse standpoint, because he himself desires to become more like a European. In the latter case he has learned a new and central value, as illustrated by the Navaho veteran who was referred to a moment ago. Learning, it is believed, proceeds more rapidly when it serves a central rather than a segmental goal. Instead of evaluating, consciously or unconsciously, each new form of behavior in terms of the satisfaction it appears to offer, the individual who would become more civilized is drawn to all civilized forms because almost automatically he judges them to be in accord with his objective. Presumably, then, even old forms of behavior that have been heavily reinforced in the past are a little more likely to be abandoned when they are at variance with the central value. If these considerations are correct, then the following hypothesis becomes necessary:

HYPOTHESIS 23 (causal): The proficiency with which people change from old to new ways is likely to be increased when they seek a central goal that transcends the specific form of behavior being changed.

The Hypothesis has no supporting data in a rigorous or statistical sense. Over and over again, however, it is possible to observe directly or in the reports of sensitive observers that less civilized people suddenly learn civilized ways much faster when for some reason they have acquired the central value of wishing to become more civilized. A most dramatic instance is that of the Manus in the Admiralty Islands of New Guinea. In the 1930's they had been learning some Western ways but very slowly. Then during World War II:

Watching the Americans in Manus, and watching the various invading armies elsewhere, the Manus grasped the idea that there was a total civilized way of life, not an unrelated assemblage of detailed superior weapons, gadgets, and religious beliefs, etc., about which the civilized man knew and they did not.

Having thus grasped the ideal of "a total civilized way of life," they were in a mood to follow one of their own leaders and, as previously indicated, to change rapidly and drastically their mode of existence (Mead, 1956, p. 172). The new central value in their personalities did not by itself produce the revolution, but it was an essential ingredient.

The Ganda may serve as a contrasting illustration. Their contact with Europeans has been continous since the beginning of the century; they have absorbed some, in many instances numerous, European ways, but on the whole they have remained loyal to their traditions and their way of life. At first their ruling monarch was interested in acquiring some of the obviously useful impediments of civilization, such as guns and ammunition. More and more Western forms of behavior have been learned, so that today many of the urban elite have studied in England, live in Western-type houses, drive cars, drink Scotch whiskey, speak fluent English, and can quote John Stuart Mill on liberty. The learning seems to occur somewhat opportunistically or segmentally; and when challenged, the educated, verbal Ganda maintain that the particular Western innovations are useful additions to their traditional ways but that their nation must enter the modern world with its own kind of culture to which scattered Western elements are attached. Few if any of the changing Ganda, so far as could be determined, want to become Europeans; they would remain Ganda who have mastered some European ways. For this reason they do not devote full time to becoming more civilized, and one finds in fact a mixture of Ganda and European ways in the elite. Government servants and professional men seek to discharge some traditional roles while functioning in a European manner; though they live in Western-type houses and work like Westerners by day, they are distracted by their responsibilities as traditional cultivators.

Another investigator asked these African elite why they seek and obtain employment with the government or in positions demanding knowledge of European skills. They were primarily interested, he discovered, in earning enough cash to pay school fees for their children and also to build and run two houses, one in or near the city and the other in the country. In a town house they enjoyed "the amenities" of civilization and the society of other Africans as civilized as themselves; but even here they wished to have enough land to raise as much food as possible. The country home could be used to supplement the current food supply and eventually, after retirement, as a residence from which the work of hired hands could be supervised (Goldthorpe, 1955, p. 36). Again both Ganda and Western values are evident, again learning to become a complete European is difficult, indeed impossible, since the desire to do so is absent.

The Manus and the Ganda are similar in the sense that a central value still guides them. Different from both of them are the so-called "detribalized" people, men and women from the old society who have migrated to European-type cities to seek employment more or less permanently. They are no longer under the authority of traditional leaders and of their own families, and they have no intention of returning to their tribe and the security which it used to offer. Unless deliberate efforts are made to provide housing projects, they are likely to live in slums. From all over, whether the reporter be a sensitive novelist in South Africa (Paton, 1948) or a competent anthropologist in the Solomon Islands (Hogbin, 1939, p. 225), an increase in crime, prostitution, drinking, and gambling is noted. One obtains from this literature the impression that the detribalized are learning innumerable new forms without abandoning the old ones, especially traditional beliefs. What these people appear to lack is the central goal posited in the hypothesis: in one sense, they have not yet decided to become more civilized; in another sense, they have not abandoned their old society. They drift and turn to crime and drugs to ease some of their frustrations and to survive in an economic or a psychological sense. When the charge is made that Europeans have destroyed native ways without replacing them with Western civilization, the critic is referring to the miserable people in this twilight zone.

The detribalized person of course has central goals but most of them, it appears, involve only one aspect of civilization, viz. money. For, as an anthropologist has indicated, money provides "so many of the desirable things of European civilization" as well as social prestige (Hunter, 1936, p. 455). Money, especially in an urban area, can be quickly spent—pay day for the weekly or monthly wages or for the cash crop is accompanied by a riot of buying that seems more conspicuous and complete than in more civilized areas. With needs thus effortlessly satisfied after money has been arduously acquired, people are not likely to develop central goals which place a premium on subtler values of civilization such as patience or the ability to postpone gratification. Other residents in urban areas may have come to earn money for some particular purpose and plan to return home. Such people are like the Ganda. The writer has the impression that they are not subject to the same depressions as their less mobile contemporaries. They may go through a period of disorientation when they feel themselves free from the restraints of the tribal elders and when they are drawn to the delights and perversions of city life, but their primary goal of returning home as quickly as possible, if it remains a goal, keeps their morale relatively high and prevents them from becoming urbanized. Some colonial powers follow the former policy of Belgium in the Congo and prevent urban workers from rejoining their people. Families, not just individual male workers, are encouraged to leave the tribe. An effort is made to make living and working conditions so attractive that these families will wish to become more civilized and hence will efficiently learn all the forms of behavior that aid industrial productivity.

Hypothesis 23 suggests one of the reasons why mere contact between peoples does not necessarily promote acculturation: unless people in the old society are motivated to learn the new forms they perceive, learning will not occur or will be inefficient. Often each innovation is stoutly resisted not because it is likely to be unsatisfying or frustrating but because it symbolizes the outside society. Tewa Indians, for example, who have lived with the Hopi Indians on the same mesa for over 250 years have managed to retain their own cultural distinctiveness. First, they apparently have a system of negative sanctions: marriage with outsiders is prohibited and Hopi ceremonies are boycotted. Then they have fortified themselves with protective beliefs: they think that magic prevents their lore and customs from diffusing to the Hopi, and they consider themselves superior to their neighbors. Finally, they carefully retain their traditional clan and kinship systems, and they accept only innovations that do not seem to endanger existing forms of behavior (Dozier, 1951).

A specialized corollary follows from Hypothesis 23: *People who retain traditional central values are motivated to learn segmental forms of behavior that do not appear to be at variance with those values.* Trinkets, for example, are usually acceptable to people who have no desire as such to become more civilized: their ancestors are not offended, prevailing standards of decoration are not violated, the youth is not corrupted, and so on. In the introduction to a book which presents fifteen case histories of change in less developed areas, the editor believes it possible, "despite our ignorance, to support the following generalizations:

people resist changes that appear to threaten basic securities; they resist proposed changes they do not understand; they resist being forced to change" (Spicer, 1952, p. 18). In effect the sources of resistance thus enumerated refer to the motivation of those who are to be changed: the proposed change must be intelligible to them and must appear not as a frustration but as a way of increasing satisfactions. When they so view the change, they are likely to seek it and hence are in a learning mood.

The last corollary really demands another corollary to specify the conditions under which new forms do not seem to be "at variance" with the traditional central values. Paradoxically, it appears that two utterly different sets of circumstances can serve this function. On the one hand, changes may be more readily accepted within a familiar framework which itself remains unchanged: like the Ganda cited above, the head of the household may follow a new type of occupation while continuing to live at home in the traditional way. On the other hand, change may be promoted by an altogether new context; for example, "new foods may be accepted if they are introduced together with a new kind of stove or fuel" (Mead, 1955, p. 285). Why, it may be asked, are new foods likely to be more acceptable in a different context? Perhaps if the old stove or fuel were retained, it would remind people of the old food. Or maybe the old food can be rejected more easily since it tastes different when prepared differently. It is possible that two departures from tradition—the food and the stove or fuel—require no more stamina than a single change. Or the adoption of one change may be eased by the other change: the new food, if really liked, can be cooked more easily on the new stove or with the new fuel.

In addition to a corollary that indicates when new forms do not conflict with traditional values, it seems desirable at least to raise the question concerning the conditions which cause people to acquire, in the words of Hypothesis 23, "a central goal that transcends the specific form of behavior being changed"; in blunter words, When and why do people wish to become more civilized as such? Alas, the writer cannot find in existing evidence an answer that goes beyond a combination of previous hypotheses. A single corollary must serve as a summary: *People acquire the central goal of seeking to become more civilized when their traditional values no longer bring them satisfaction and/or when some experience gives them a favorable view of civilization.* The critical clauses in the corollary could be pushed further back. When, for example, do traditional values "no longer" bring satisfaction? That question is a variant of the complicated historical inquiries into the downfall of societies. Psychologically, people in declining societies must find that too few of their needs are reduced or reduced satisfactorily. They must come to reject the restrictive security they formerly enjoyed, to be unable to appreciate the rationale or the details of the old forms, to discover that absolute beliefs are, alas, fallible, or—in some way and for some reason—to lose faith in the traditional society. It is also conceivable that only important leaders experience these frustrations and disappointments and that the changes they subsequently seek also affect their followers.

In many contact situations, one of the critical factors affecting the adoption of the central goal is the attitude and behavior of outsiders: if people can assume, in the language of Hypothesis 5, that these outsiders "would have them change," they are at least likely to feel free to learn more civilized ways. This factor is especially evident in the experiences immigrants have had in American society; here "the consent of the dominant group" has almost literally had to be sought (Spiro, 1955). Indeed it has been suggested that the rate of assimilation into American life has depended upon the extent to which the cultural background and "race" of an immigrant group resembles the American pattern (Warner and Srole, 1945). Within a particular ethnic group, moreover, there are clear-cut individual differences: some persons seek assimilation, some retain primary allegiance to the old group, and others vacillate between the two extremes (Child, 1943). The solutions adopted by, or forced upon, ethnic groups or particular persons must be explained in terms of particular historical and environmental circumstances but, when they are once adopted, a host of behavioral consequences follow, as Hypothesis 23 suggests. The less the assimilation, for example, the greater the tendency for immigrant groups to cling to their original language or to form clubs and associations whose social functions perpetuate the tie to the mother country. Similarly, Italian youths who are oriented toward Italian rather than American culture are less likely to change traditional forms of cuisine, kinship, and religion. The central goal, in brief, affects discrete segments of behavior.

The central goal which facilitates learning may transcend some specific situations but not others. Since World War II, it is reported, many people in the South Pacific "feel that they have picked up by now all the tricks the white man is capable of teaching them; the result is a tendency to lapse into a new conservatism based on the fusion of native and alien ways which has been worked out in recent decades" (Keesing, 1945, p. 27). Clearly such people never had the central goal of becoming civilized. Now they are apparently less likely to acquire that goal since the adoption of some traits from the outside has strengthened their desire to retain their own way of life, which presumably they believe has thus been sufficiently improved.

The explicit assumption during the discussion of Hypothesis 23 has been that people in all stages of acculturation have central goals and that the content of these goals differs. Conceivably there is some universal element with respect to which the content varies, and also the centrality of the goals may possibly change with increased acculturation. Let there be speculation about both these themes.

First, the "universal element." Less civilized men, it has been previously suggested, tend to view the future as a repetition of the past. If people are to become more civilized, however, they must envision the future as different from the past, for in that future they will have changed, or so they hope. Accompanying the hope is the ability to tolerate delay in order to achieve the changes (Hypothesis 3). Basic to all such thinking, as Hypothesis 11 has recklessly suggested in another context, must also be the belief that men themselves—not their ancestors, not fate, not nature, not other men—are able to control their own destinies. Here perhaps is a noteworthy candidate for one of the universal attributes, for men everywhere are not likely to seek change unless they believe that change is possible.

The notion of centrality is founded on the writer's impression that less civilized people are not quite so sensitive to internal contradictions. A rural African whose *summum bonum*—as expressed after being questioned directly, and maybe indecently, concerning his goals in life—is "to have many wives and children" will also agree that he wishes to remain a good Christian, that he would prosper economically, and that he would remain a loyal member of his society. In his own mind these separate goals may be interrelated but it is difficult to get a particular informant to indicate what the interrelations are. From Hypothesis 12, which suggests that verbalizable opinions are related to acculturation, and from the above hunch, a corollary may follow: *As people change centrally from old to new ways, they are likely to be able to relate varied aspects of their behavior to consciously formulated goals.*

Once more, as indicated above, statistical evidence in support of the corollary is lacking; instead the writer would relate in some detail the impression which he received while conducting the interviews for the Africa-Jamaica studies, and which has been informally reinforced by studying his notes and doubtlessly biased sections of the literature. When anyone is asked a series of questions pertaining to his beliefs, knowledge, values, and actions, some of his replies are clearly related to one another. He offers an identical reason for subscribing to two different beliefs; or he often explicitly points out that his reason for so behaving is the same as the one "I have already mentioned a while ago." On this purely verbal level, many but certainly not all of the poorly educated appear to have the modal tendency to respond discretely: each covert or overt part of their repertoire has its own justification, and little or no effort is made to state and then refer frequently to a central goal. At the other extreme would be an African clergyman whose every thought and deed he himself relates to Christianity.

There is another dimension which, though still very impressionistic, begins to relate this kind of verbalization to behavior. From time to time the writer felt that an informant was deliberately attempting, more or less extemporaneously, to put the pieces of his behavior into a neatly appearing package in order to impress his interrogator and/or the interpreter. A minor African leader would stress his own efforts to help his people, saying in effect that his every movement—even scratching his back—is dedicated to that noble end. Or the poorly educated Jamaican, especially one belonging to a revivalist cult, would enact the role of being just too good for this world. Subsequent investigation revealed—and these are not hypothetical cases—that the African leader was in fact a selfish despot rather despised by his countrymen, and the pious lay preacher in Jamaica had sold a piece of land that had never belonged to him but on which a rather irreligious man had generously allowed him to squat. These two men were posing; but the significant fact is that they wished to and could pose.

In contrast some informants seemed unaware of the fairly coherent picture they were presenting of themselves, perhaps because they had not yet verbalized their central goal. An African clerk in Uganda, for example, would unequivocally stress strong feelings concerning his own people, but then would indicate again and again his own decided orientation toward European values. Or a cultivated Jamaican seemed to be trying desperately and sincerely during the interview to reconcile for himself—not for the investigator—some of the contradictions of modern life, such as the stress on individual achievement and the need to help one's fellow men. He was very different from the lay preacher whose glib formula provided him with a ready coherence.

In Jamaica vast differences strike one on both a very materialistic and a religious level. When the poorer people had a principle —and not all of them did—they seemed to be repeating and repeating a cliché, just as frequently as they could. "I am poor, I need money," or "We must obey God's will," they were saying over and over. In contrast, among the better educated the same views might be expressed with conscious cynicism. Other men and women showed that they were engaged in the difficult, the unending, struggle to try to fit a principle to a world that cannot be facilely described in a sentence or two; or to reconcile the demands of the body and those of the spirit.

Maybe, then, there are levels of organization on the verbal level. Most of those who are unchanged follow principles they have not had occasion to express. The more gifted among them, especially when challenged by an outsider, can be forced to become aware of the principles. During the process of changing, the central goals may be dimly perceived; or they may be blithely and not always sincerely formulated. The more civilized man follows some kind of coherent philosophy which, while fairly consistent, is not completely overpowering or rigid. Would that such statements could be satisfactorily proved!

One final corollary must be included in this section which has emphasized the importance to the learning process of acquiring a central goal, especially one which involves trying to become more civilized. Again and again, as has been indicated, that goal may prove unacceptable to outsiders. They may want "natives" to become civilized only in certain respects; or—for prejudiced or perfectly sound reasons—they may draw up a time table for the economic or political independence of a less civilized people. If the people themselves have the central goal and are discouraged or prevented from achieving it, they will be frustrated; hence, a corollary may state: *People who have changed centrally from old to new ways and who then perceive that they are being prevented from achieving some central goal are likely to learn to seek aggressively a different central goal.* The aggressiveness that, according to Hypothesis 2, changing people usually experience may be directed, under these circumstances, toward a substitute objective.

Symptoms of such a reaction, though varied, are easy to detect. There is self-glorification: we are the chosen people, men say in effect, and we are better than those who are prejudiced; we must show them that our civilization is also better or can be made better than theirs. There are revivalist cults that praise the past and offer solace in the present. There is nationalism, which is so often promoted by Westernized leaders who personally have felt rejected by colonial powers (e.g., Coleman, 1958, pp. 145–52). Of course discouragement is frequently evident. In a study previously mentioned (Caudill, 1952), the sample of American-born Japanese do not differ from another sample born in Japan and living in Chicago with respect to "discontent," but more of the former show "defeatism" and fewer of them, perhaps because they are closer to the goal of being assimilated without being permitted to attain it, project "self-motivation" upon the drawing of a young boy (Table E, rows 1 and 4).

Counter-aggression by the less civilized frequently leads to the tragedy of circularity that appears when people feel hostile toward one another: the aggressiveness of A provokes aggressiveness in B, which in turn increases the aggressiveness of A, etc. The colonial settler confers enough of the benefits of his civilization for the inhabitants of the area to acquire the urge to become more extensively or more rapidly civilized. When the group with power is reluctant to spread its gifts more widely or swiftly, the subordinated groups grow resentful. Their expression of resentment or their search for another goal appears as ingratitude to the original benefactors: "They do not appreciate what we have done for them," one hears again and again in colonial areas. Unfriendliness is felt toward the ungrateful, the ungrateful are thus further antagonized, and the hostility between the groups is strengthened. Situations like this and the corollary under discussion raise the nasty question with which the next chapter is concerned: Are people ever content to remain "partially" civilized?

Chapter 9.

REPERCUSSIONS

A MOST intriguing and perhaps also the most difficult problem of psychology and social science involves the interrelatedness of the components that form a pattern or organization. A person almost never reacts with a single response; his organized personality, as the last chapter has suggested, affects most of his behavior. Within a society institutions seldom function in isolation, for they affect and are affected by other institutions. In the modern world, societies interact economically, politically, culturally, and belligerently. The interrelatedness of each person's responses and of people themselves has important repercussions. Briefly but quite accurately summarized, this chapter would explore the fact that men and societies seem unable to add a new form of behavior without enjoying or suffering many consequences.

Modification

Every new form of behavior is literally learned uniquely, because the learner himself is unique. The ensuing behavior, therefore, must also be unique, for it is modified, however subtly, by the learner to suit his own interests, his skill, or his personality. Only by ignoring individual idiosyncrasies can it be said that the nature of the automobile itself leads to uniformity among drivers. No, each driver masters the operation roughly in his own way. Still it is pointless to become too microscopic and thus be compelled to remain forever on the level of uniqueness. Instead, in this instance, it is usually sufficient to find some point between asserting uniformity and uniqueness; for example, drivers may be thrown into rough categories such as good, average, and poor. Certainly the drivers in the "good" category differ from one another, but for some if not for all purposes their unique qualities can be ignored.

Similarly it may be reasoned that, since people in the old society differ from those in the new, they will inevitably alter somewhat any new form of behavior they learn from the outsiders. To avoid picayune distinctions, only the magnitude of the modification is here specified:

> HYPOTHESIS 24 (*interactional*): *All new forms of behavior are modified while being learned; modification is likely to be relatively slight (a) when there are marked similarities or dissimilarities between the old and new societies especially with relation to the form in question and (b) when that form inherently possesses or is permitted to possess little flexibility.*

The hypothesis suggests that modification of the new form will be slight under diametrically different conditions. If the new form resembles the old, people will presumably possess the necessary skill and experience to enable them to make the change relatively easily. If there is great dissimilarity, on the other hand, learning may not occur; but, *if* it does occur, the new form is likely to displace the old one relatively completely and hence, in the absence of competition from the past, will undergo little modification. Thus it is presumed that people who have previously plowed but not fertilized the soil will modify a new method of plowing more radically than they will a method of applying a new fertilizer.

The question of "flexibility" indicated in the hypothesis can be illustrated by a single example, the wearing of shoes. The objects as such permit little flexibility so far as their ultimate use is concerned: they must be used to protect or adorn the feet and can scarcely be substituted for gloves or handkerchiefs. In this sense there can be no modification. Some flexibility, however, is possible. The material out of which shoes are made may vary. The decorations on them can suit the tastes of those who adopt them. To cite a specific case, on Sundays some rural Jamaicans walk barefoot along dusty roads with their shoes in their hands and put them on just before entering church. Here clearly is a modification of shoe-wearing which has arisen because Jamaican roads are dusty and because rural Jamaicans are poverty-stricken.

Flexibility also includes the degree of variability permitted by teachers from the new society, especially under circumstances when the teachers are respected and have authority. The writer has the inadequately documented impression that Catholic missionaries tolerate more modification than those from Protestant sects. Among the Papago Indians of Arizona, for example, the festival of the Exaltation of the Cross (Holy Cross Day) on May 4 is celebrated by a ceremony that includes the following: "After mass a steer is blessed by the priest, then roped and killed in front of the church"; the subsequent procession is "in the style of the Spanish church ceremonies of two centuries ago." Such a mixture of pagan and Christian forms does not occur among the Protestants, it is stated, for they "demand a complete break" from traditional religious practices (Underhill, 1946, pp. 322–4). When the urge to modify Christian elements becomes exceedingly strong, perhaps people desert the established Protestant sects that tolerate no compromise and then establish institutions of their own which fuse the old and the new. A case in point is the phenomenal rise of the peyote cult among North American Indians during the nineteenth and twentieth centuries.

Illustrations of modification are not difficult to find. Even evidence from the field of archeology is relevant since material artifacts, having been manufactured by people, reflect their forms of behavior. An examination of a collection of objects from North America and Oceania suggests that social contact results either in the introduction of a new artifact or the modification of an old one. The form of the new artifact may be unaltered but it may be made to serve a different function; e.g., an imported gun replaced the bow in the grave of a departed warrior. Or at the other extreme, the form may be modified but the function remain unchanged; e.g., in the absence of steel, knives were hewn from wood. Old artifacts may be modified through the use of different materials; e.g., a harpoon head was made from iron rather than stone. Or different techniques may be used to improve old traits;

e.g., sooted lenses replaced the wooden slits in snow goggles (Quimby and Spoehr, 1951).

Inevitability

On almost every, perhaps on every, level of human behavior any change has repercussions and, as a result of the interaction between that change and other processes, the temporary effects and then the ultimate outcome cannot be easily deduced or anticipated from the change itself. It has often been remarked, for example, that among human beings the energy expended in speaking and hearing a single critical word in certain contexts has no direct relation to the kind of response that ensues. "Dead" —that whisper in some contexts evokes a flow of responses. Or slight changes in the arrangement of the external world may affect people's reaction to an entire pattern; thus the addition of one or two lines to a drawing can alter profoundly the facial expression of the character there portrayed. The converse is also true. The shout nearby is unnoticed by someone absorbed in himself. The unobservant person does not see that a frequently visited room has been repainted a different color. The shout and the new color, though momentarily ineffective, eventually may be perceived; then, if and when they are perceived, other changes consequently will occur. Why?

Additional changes do not appear to be inevitable. A person learns to ski; his newly acquired ability is then exercised in the winter when there is snow, when he would be outdoors, etc.; there need be no further repercussions. And yet, aside from the quibbling point that the amount of time now devoted to skiing he would previously have employed in some other way, it is possible also to assert that for at least two reasons the new form of behavior is likely to have more profound repercussions. Firstly, as the last and the present chapter emphasize, people are organized so that no activity in effect can function in complete isolation. The experience of skiing, therefore, is not just grafted onto the person, it is added to his personality and therefore conceivably may influence his attitudes toward outdoor exercise, sportsmen, winter, and even himself. Then, secondly, social conditions undoubtedly will conspire to effect other differences. Skiing as a sport has status; by becoming proficient he is likely to meet other kinds of people; more of his money may have to be spent on special clothing and particular waxes because these are *de rigueur* at fashionable ski resorts; etc. If you can't live alone, you also cannot ski alone.

When people's behavior is viewed through the institutions of their society, anthropologists seem to feel that always (or at least almost always) a change in one form of behavior as a result of contact with the outside is likely to produce one or both of the following consequences: (1) other modifications occur inside the society even if no additional forms diffuse from the outside; and (2) additional forms from the outside are eventually acquired. Such repercussions are especially likely in less civilized societies because of their relatively tight social organization and the tendency for behavior to be quite unified: a stone can be added to a random pile of rocks on the ground without changing them appreciably, but sensational after-effects must occur when the same stone is pushed—*if* it can be pushed—into a balanced arch. The following hypothesis, therefore, is proposed:

> HYPOTHESIS 25 (*consequential*): *A change in one form of behavior within the old society is likely to be followed eventually by other changes, but a central change is likely to have more repercussions than a segmental one.*

The kind of anthropological evidence which demands such an hypothesis can be briefly illustrated. "The introduction of the wagon, simple as the initial event was, had broad repercussions on the Papago way of life," an anthropologist who has studied this Indian society reports. "It not only displaced some parts of the technology and established new techniques and specialties; it also resulted in important shifts in the division of labor, had far-reaching effects on the economy, became for a period a strong factor for greater community solidarity, and influenced the relations of Papagos with surrounding peoples" (Bliss, 1952, p. 32). Similar reports crop up virtually everywhere; for example, changes as widespread (as among the Papago) but of a different kind occurred when missionaries provided ready-made steel axes as substitutes for stone axes in an Australian society (Sharp, 1952).

What will be the repercussions of a single change or of two or more changes? The first part of Hypothesis 25 merely states that there will be changes, and the second that under some conditions there will be more changes than under others. Wherever one looks, it seems, one finds competent and experienced people who despairingly admit that they cannot specify in any detail the repercussions of change. "There is no available body of knowledge," an anthropologist has stated while arguing against master plans for changing institutions within underdeveloped areas, "which makes it possible to predict in advance the way in which individuals will respond even to one far-reaching change" (Mead, 1955, p. 271). More specifically, for example, another anthropologist doubts whether a practical administrator could have "consciously proceeded to produce the results" which ensued when people in a Madagascan society shifted from dry to wet rice cultivation; he thus suggests ignorance concerning the interaction between economic and social factors (Kimball, 1945, p. 13). "Get them to use a pot," the trader in the bush says in effect, "and then eventually their children if not they themselves will buy an electric stove." This path from the pot to the stove is by no means an invariant one, but the cynical, if useful, aphorism suggests that one change will have consequences that may be foreseeable in very broad outline but certainly not in detail.

Such a statement becomes more compelling when specific instances of change are examined. The temple affairs of Buddhists in rural Japan, for example, are reported to be delegated to "older people in the household, especially the women." Emigrants from these areas to Hawaii find this practice must be changed. There neighboring Protestants and Catholics offer a competing faith. In order "to gather in the souls of the children" and thus prevent them from abandoning the traditional faith, the elders have adopted certain Christian forms, such as Sunday schools, hymns, and religious associations for young people (Embree, 1941, p. 109). What, then, will happen to Buddhism among these people? Will it add more outside forms? Will the essence of its religious doctrines remain intact? As an institution will it be able to survive among the descendants of these Japanese in

Hawaii? Another equally complicated illustration involves the Ganda. Adolescents, as previously indicated, tend to be attracted to European clothes and European houses, but simultaneously they admire their own countrymen and want their respect (rows 4–7, Table II). Will they be able to obtain European material objects without simultaneously valuing Europeans more and their own people and other Africans less?

Sometimes, perhaps more often than not, the very people who voluntarily have accepted some outside change are themselves surprised and even dismayed by the repercussions. The Japanese in Hawaii may have altered their religious practices as a result of outside competition, but they have modified other customs most unwittingly. When they migrated from Japan, for example, they had to leave behind many of their material possessions, including the trays used by each person at meals. In the absence of the trays, chopsticks can no longer be put into a common dish, food is wasted, and a banquet has become more like "a cross between an old Hawaiian feast and an American picnic" (ibid., pp. 30–1). Elsewhere, it has been shown, within two decades virtually all the inhabitants of a Mexican community have adopted and are enjoying the very forms of civilization which those who originally wanted changes had wished to achieve. And yet "the few people who think about the condition of their community, those who look beyond their private problems to those of the entire village, are anxious about the future." The difficulties they foresee include impoverishment of the land, poverty for some of the inhabitants, and the "vices and commercial pleasures" which will accompany the "North American or cosmopolitan urbanized life" serving as the model for change (Redfield, 1950, p. 171).

Statistical indexes from changing countries provide indirect evidence of the fact that change in one respect inevitably is accompanied by other changes. In the Middle East study, as previously indicated, factors such as urbanism, literacy, and the mass media of communication have been found to be related. More specifically, for example, the following relations emerge from data obtained in Lebanon: in comparison with those who listen only to domestic broadcasts, a higher percentage of those who also hear foreign broadcasts (1) have attended a lycée or college, (2) know some English, (3) have attained a higher standard of living, (4) have met some foreigners, (5) demonstrate some knowledge of the United Nations, (6) prefer American films and Western music, (7) see motion pictures each week, and (8) read a newspaper daily (Lerner, 1958, pp. 175–80). Such relations are interesting, provocative, but unrevealing: one is caught again in a Spiraled Explanation and has no idea what the causal or temporal sequence has been.

Hypothesis 25 does make one effort to specify not the kind but the quantity of the repercussions: "a central change is likely to have more repercussions than a segmental one." To a certain extent this formulation either begs the question or can lead to circularity, both very serious methodological sins. For it is no easy task to determine whether a change is central or segmental, and after the fact it is tempting to say that changes with many repercussions must have been central and those with few must have been segmental. The approach, however, can suggest tentative corollaries. Usually, for example, earning a living is time-consuming; frequently occurring behavior is likely to be central; hence as a corollary it is proposed that: *A permanent change within the occupations of a society is likely to produce numerous and significant repercussions.* Evidence for the corollary has already been suggested above when the change from dry to wet rice cultivation in Madagascar was cited. Similarly another investigator attributes basic changes in the Maori way of life, including their family structure and their general satisfactions, to the rise of dairy farming (Hawthorn, 1944). The introduction of fur trading in the eighteenth century, together with the horse and gun, did not have the consequence of breaking down existing institutions among the Blackfoot Indians of North America; instead this central change "acted as a stimulus to their development" (Lewis, 1942, p. 34). The change in occupation, however, must be "permanent" if there are to be many repercussions. Otherwise men may drift toward factories or mines, as they do in many parts of Africa, to obtain very specific objectives, such as money to be used directly as a dowry for a wife or indirectly to purchase a dowry in the form of cattle; but then they return to the tribal

home without necessarily being tremendously affected by the
experience. Of course the temporary change can generate a central experience; they may decide to remain in the new occupation
or, after returning home, forever after seek to become more
civilized.

Admittedly it would be more satisfactory if the precise repercussions of a change could be specified, but the possible interactions between that change and people's previous behavior as
well as the conditions of their society seem too complicated to be
encompassed at the moment. Consider, for example, the state of
affairs that exists when people are converted to Christianity. For
religion itself there might be a corollary similar to the one just
formulated for occupation: since religion usually if not always
is central, many repercussions may be anticipated. But, again,
what kinds of repercussions? Some Papago Indians have been
converted to Presbyterianism and others to Catholicism. Presby-
terian children, it is reported, reveal "an established introversion,
accompanied by a relative loss of spontaneity and a gain in
emotional control"; whereas Catholic children show "on the
average a relatively high degree of impulsivity and a tendency
toward emotional outbreaks" (Thompson, 1951, p. 113). Let two
assumptions be made: first, the difference in personality traits
resulted from the conversions and does not stem from the fact
that people with particular traits may have been attracted to one
rather than the other of the two religions at the outset; and,
secondly, Presbyterianism and Catholicism as such do not deliberately promote the world over, respectively, introversion and
impulsiveness. Then it would follow that the interaction between
some pre-existing personality traits and the two Christian religions
had quite diverse consequences upon similar people. Circumstances too affect the repercussions. Among the Zulu, for example,
one of the traditional ways to obtain a wife has been the following:
the youth abducts the girl and brings her to his own family's krall;
there she indicates her attitude by remaining or returning home,
for she is given every opportunity to escape, and the boy's father
will escort her back if she insists. An anthropologist finds "no
overt reason" why the custom should not persist among the Christian Zulu, "but in fact we have never heard of a case." Why

cannot Christians tolerate the custom? When Zulu are converted to Christianity, they are simultaneously indoctrinated with a respect for "European law and order" and they are thus taught to place greater emphasis on "the rights of the individual" (Reader, 1954). Not Christianity alone, therefore, produces this result but Christianity and the legal tradition with which it happens in this instance to be associated.

In view of the complication, anthropologists who would plot the repercussions of change have adopted one of two procedures. The more abstract, less frequently used one has been to establish the statistical probability that, among the many possible repercussions of a specific change, one general type is likely to occur. Extremely impressive and voluminous evidence, for example, has been collected which shows that "a modification in the rule of residence" that prescribes where or with whom a married couple lives produces changes in social structure and also, eventually, in kinship terminology (Murdock, 1949, pp. 221–2). In the second procedure, detailed studies are made of changes in particular societies, but what emerges seems to have limited applicability elsewhere. One anthropologist, for example, suggests after the fact that different aspects of the culture of Raroia, an atoll which is part of French Oceania, can be arranged "in a hierarchy, beginning with the most and ending with the least acculturated aspect" as follows: material culture, religion, economy, political system, language, social structure, recreation, education, and general knowledge (Danielsson, 1955, pp. 222–3). Here is an instance of factual reporting by a competent observer, but certainly the hierarchy must depend upon the particular history of this people, who, after varying kinds of contact with the West from the start of the seventeenth century, were approached by missionaries in 1870 and by French administrators in 1900. Has such an historical resultant ever occurred elsewhere?

Another example is a more complicated and skillful "configurational analysis" of a society in tropical Brazil. The writer notes eight "causes of acculturation" which range from "guaranteed protection from hostile attacks by whites or Indian tribes" to the "introduction of trade goods, cloth, salt, soap, tools, pots." These causes have seven "primary" or "immediate" effects on the society—six on the economy or economic relations and the seventh on the political system. Finally, there are eight "secondary" or "derived" effects on the society's institutions; for example, "less frequent polygyny than before." Then the investigator seeks to reconstruct history by linking each of the eight causes to one or more of the seven primary effects, and each of the latter to one or more of the eight secondary effects. The cause, "guaranteed protection from hostile attacks," helped make agriculture "important in the total economy," and that primary effect in turn helped produce an increase in occupational specialization, a greater division of labor, and a decline in polygyny. From an opposite viewpoint, the primary effect of having agriculture become important in the total economy resulted not only from the one cause cited above but from six out of the seven remaining causes of acculturation (Watson, 1952). Now obviously such an analysis, if valid, is sufficiently complicated to deal with the historical facts of this particular society. It is, however, highly unlikely that the precise sequence has ever been, or will ever be, repeated in detail.

He who for theoretical reasons would, or for practical reasons must, predict the consequences of change can be given, in essence, three bits of advice. First, expect repercussions of some kind: this is the bold and daring proposition contained in Hypothesis 25. Then if possible find a somewhat analogous situation in the past and see what happened there: this is actuarial prediction and, though most precarious, at least indicates possible outcomes or the factors to be taken into account. Finally, after collecting as many relevant data as possible, chart the future in a step-by-step manner; under the given circumstances, what is the next change likely to be? This last is the piecemeal approach of the separate hypotheses in the present volume.

Civilization?

The anthropologist who studied the Mexican community mentioned in the last section writes in his final paragraph that, in spite of the patent disadvantages of civilization from many viewpoints, the people . . . have no choice but to go forward with technology, with a declining religious faith and moral conviction, into a dangerous world. They are a people who must and will come to identify their interests with those of people far away, outside the traditional circle of their loyalties and political responsibilities. As such, they should have the sympathy of readers of these pages [Redfield, 1950, p. 178].

Similarly, modern American Indians on reservations have acquired many new ways from white people, but some tribes still manage to retain extremely important facets of their traditional life. Are such enclaves doomed "eventually" to adopt radical changes? Anyone who would dare reply affirmatively to such a question evokes indignant wrath and the charge of "ethnocentrism" from some anthropologists (Herskovits, 1938, pp. 31–2). With the very limited wisdom any one person can possess, after much soul-searching, and in spite of romantic regrets, the writer feels forced by the apparent facts to agree with the first rather than the second anthropologist; hence:

HYPOTHESIS 26 (consequential): All societies eventually become civilized in a distinctive manner or perish.

The hypothesis contains two ambiguous words, "eventually" and "distinctive." Temporal equivocation is demanded by the fact that many societies, such as those in Central Australia and in parts of South America, at the moment are effectively resisting the appeal of Western civilization and those who would bring it to them, just as within the Western world itself there are enclaves such as the Basques in France and Spain or the French Canadians. In the long run, the hypothesis maintains, such groups will succumb; unlike small and less civilized groups that have been able to reach "a working adaptation to each other" and hence to "exist side by side for many generations without any discernible tendency to fuse" (Linton, 1940, p. 510), the flow "eventually" will become one-sided and civilization will exert a dominating influence. The manner in which each society becomes civilized is said to be "distinctive," moreover, because it is inconceivable that all cultural differences will ever completely disappear. An area now considered underdeveloped, the hypothesis asserts, eventually will develop until it becomes civilized in a more or less distinctive manner, just as each country of Europe is civilized but different from its neighbors.

Explanations of the hypothesis are of two kinds. In the first place, more civilized peoples carry on crusades: they would force, persuade, or seduce others to accept more civilized forms. Then, secondly, aspects of civilization possess, it would appear, a universal appeal, as a result of which less civilized peoples by and large seek to adopt certain changes. The evidence for each must be examined in some detail.

The urge to spread civilization springs from many motives. Clearly there are economic objectives. Less civilized areas frequently contain minerals and produce agricultural commodities such as rubber and coffee. The strategic ores are especially important at a time when the so-called civilized countries of the West are concerned with their own "national security." Workers in less civilized sections can usually be employed at lower rates so that raw materials can be gathered and in some instances transformed into manufactured products less expensively. Potentially, too, the people themselves are a market for the products of the West *when* a demand for those products has been created.

To create such a demand less civilized people must be made more civilized. According to the view of commercial interests in the West, they must be taught to seek Western products. What they then offer in return is their raw materials, their crops, or their labor. Once a man has decided not to concentrate his land on satisfying the diversified needs of his own group but to raise a cash crop that will be purchased by a middleman to be sold and eventually consumed abroad, he is caught up in a stream of interdependence from which there seems to be no possibility of turning back. For then he must reorganize his life to some degree and become dependent upon others for some necessities. Ultimately the number of his needs increases.

At the present time the motive of governments which would diffuse civilization is often only secondarily economic and primarily "strategic": the support of the people must be won by helping them solve their problems so that they will not cooperate with the potential enemies of the benefactor. Those enemies should not be granted land for military bases, should not be assisted in time of war, and should not serve as a model for form of government or ideological values. The help that in turn is proffered ranges from guns through dam-building to civil service schools, but in all instances it is accompanied by the practices and tenets of Western civilization as a whole.

Likewise the driving power behind the earlier forms of imperialism was never simple. Economic, yes, but also nonmaterialistic. Political leaders sought to spread more widely their own country's influence, for more land as symbolized by the spread of a nation's colors on the globe gave expression to genuine patriotism. The men who endured the deprivations and often the horrors of exploration and conquest seem to have been variously driven: some were attracted to the thrills and the perils, others sought to demonstrate to themselves their ability to cope with danger, others wished to secure immortality and fortune, and others—such as Cecil Rhodes—fought to realize what they came to believe was their own personal destiny. The great missionary movements from the West were probably motivated almost completely by religious, philanthropic, and humanitarian convictions. Often the missionary preceded the trader and the government official, not as their agent (which is the anti-imperialist stereotype) but as representative of an independent organization; later he may have had to call on them for protection from hostile natives. Under nonreligious auspices, too, subjugation and annexation have occurred for highly ethical reasons, for example, to wipe out the slave trade engaged in by the people themselves or others from the outside. The desire to carry the white man's burden has not been an empty slogan: moved either by genuine compassion or a not necessarily evil feeling of superiority, Europeans of the nineteenth and early twentieth century made real and often incredible personal sacrifices to bring to less civilized peoples an assorted sample of what they sincerely believed to be the best of the material and spiritual aspects of their own civilization. Colonists or settlers have their own motives for leaving home: ambition, adventure, escape, etc. When once they have established themselves abroad, they and especially their children grow attached to the area: it becomes their native land.

These representatives from the West, whether they come temporarily as experts to provide technical assistance or permanently as colonists, bring with them to the new land their way of life. At first they may be interested only in achieving a particular objective, but they soon discover that, to survive or to live comfortably, they must surround themselves with many of the appliances to which they are accustomed. "It must be remembered that in the heart of savagery white men could not wander about preaching and living in native huts," it has been pointed out in describing the period when Livingstone was a missionary in Central Africa. "They were forced, if they were to live and work effectively in tropical Africa, to make clearings in the bush; to build houses, churches, schools and stores; to buy and to grow food; to hire labour and to bring up from the distant coast all the equipment they needed for this and the cloth and other trade goods which were the bulky currency of the interior" (Perham, 1956, p. 94). Thus a somewhat complete civilized model is provided for those who would or must learn new forms.

This urge to civilize less civilized peoples need not embrace all aspects of civilization. In fact it is probably true that some of the old colonial powers—e.g., the Netherlands in the East Indies (Kennedy, 1943)—prevented many civilized forms from diffusing for reasons that cannot be called the least bit idealistic; as has been indicated in a previous chapter, contact between peoples is usually regulated or restricted in some way. The conclusion, nevertheless, must be that more civilized peoples in the modern world continue to carry on some kind of crusade. The desire to civilize is not weakening; its expression is being altered. Modern missionaries, for example, are now interested not only in people's religion but also in their medical, educational, scientific, and political institutions. Colonial areas secure their independence in a political sense, but their officials deliberately, laboriously, and quite thoroughly retain intimate contacts with the modern world.

The appeal of civilization to people almost everywhere is offered as the second kind of evidence in support of Hypothesis 26.

The material aspects seem especially attractive. Nineteenth century explorers in Africa usually carried with them beads and cloth which they knew could be exchanged for food or protection and, in some instances, for a treaty that gave them or their home government innumerable rights. Western clothes, housing, transportation (especially in tropical areas at the outset, the bicycle), plumbing, and weapons seem virtually irresistible. "The inhabitants of the Plains are so advantageously situated that they could live very happily independent of our assistance," a clerk in the Northwest Company stated in 1794. "It is then our luxuries that attract them to the fort and make us necessary to their happiness" (quoted by Lewis, 1942, p. 34).

Why do the material aspects of Western civilization have an almost universal appeal? They appear economical and efficient: less energy needs to be expended to move about, to protect one's body, or to kill or injure one's enemies when the contraptions of civilization are utilized. The gains, as Hypothesis 4 suggests, are immediately and easily demonstrable, although in the longer run they may also prove to be in part illusory. The tin roof so many Africans seek for their huts is better than thatch in two respects: it does not catch fire and it lasts longer. It is less efficient too: it does not shield people nearly so well from the sun since it conducts heat much more readily; and it costs money. Perspective comes later, if ever.

Another aspect of modern civilization, though less dramatic at first glance, inevitably is desired by all peoples: medical knowledge and therapy. As indicated previously, the public health officer in less civilized areas has to overcome more resistance than the physician who ministers effectively to people's present pains. Eventually—the word reappears—it becomes evident that disease and infant mortality decrease and that life expectancy increases. Of course, civilization also brings new diseases and some civilized practices have debilitating and disastrous effects, but again there are the counteracting and easily perceptible gains.

Then, when once some changes of a material or medical sort are accepted, as Hypothesis 25 suggests, repercussions occur—a few steps on the path produce forward-pushing motion. On a

seemingly petty level it is possible to observe how the Hutterite
groups of North America, which resisted outside influences for
so long and retained the essential aspects of Anabaptist traditions from the sixteenth century, are now gradually succumbing
to the surrounding culture:

> Tradition required the use of hooks and eyes to fasten clothes
> until 1926, when it was decided that buttons on winter
> clothes *"could be retained."* The *ex post facto* regulation ac-
> knowledging this change also set clear limits: "Only black
> buttons could be used, except on white garments, where
> there should be white buttons." But the tendency to use
> buttons in colors contrasting to the cloth persisted, and
> twelve years later the 1926 regulation had to be virtually
> repealed [Eaton, 1952, p. 336].

Note the words italicized by the present writer: they indicate
that the change to buttons occurred in spite of the society's
elaborate mechanisms to resist outside influences. The winter
clothes were purchased on the outside and hence arrived with
buttons which then could be immediately utilized, whereas hooks
and eyes could be added only with effort. Black buttons, finally,
produced an acceptance of all buttons. The Serpent had entered
the Garden.

Contact with civilization may in fact produce the need to become civilized in a very specific sense. It has been noted that
the "cultural equipment of any single society does not provide
its members with the means of adjusting themselves to all possible circumstances or for the solution of every possible problem
that may arise" (Hallowell, 1955, p. 315). Traditional enemies
may have been formerly repulsed, but more civilized men with
superior weapons are invincible. People know how to survive
occasional shortages, but they cannot cope with the permanent
reduction in food supply that occurs when those same weapons
make hunting more ruthlessly efficient. Then novel solutions are
sought, and the outsiders responsible for the innovation are observed—why not get guns like theirs or eat food out of tins?

It would be unfair to civilization, as well as to the facts of the
case, however, to suggest that people inadvertently get pushed

into becoming more civilized after they have accepted a few trinkets, after they enjoy better health, or after they are compelled to face apparently insoluble problems. They may be genuinely and positively attracted by some practices and institutions of civilization. They soon see that technological advances and diversification of occupations permit an increase in productivity to a point where a surplus can be set aside to meet the emergencies created by pestilence and drought; being consequently dependent upon a world market over which one has no control is the disadvantage accompanying such security. The more substantial houses brought by civilization are an investment for the future.

Variety, too, may be attractive. Instead of drawing upon a limited number of foods, people, recreation devices, occupations, etc., suddenly a large number of alternatives is at least exhibited. In theory the old and the simple, if satisfactory in the past, ought to continue to be appealing. In fact, those ways may satisfy the older generation; but, perhaps because they have more energy, probably because they have been indoctrinated for a shorter period, and undoubtedly because through contact they experience the new either at home or abroad, younger people may seek out the complicated and the more diverse. Indeed, some individuals may acquire the central goal of wishing to become more civilized not necessarily for purely materialistic reasons but for less tangible ones (such as the ideals behind the procedures embodying "British justice" which people everywhere, however belatedly, have come to appreciate); thereafter, as Hypothesis 23 suggests, learning is likely to be more rapid. At any rate, it appears that on both the level of society and of the individual a retreat from newly acquired complications back to older simplicities is rarely observable.

Sometimes, it seems fair to say, the movement toward more civilization comes not from the vast majority of people but from a small group of leaders in the old society. When once they have the urge to be civilized, they are likely also to seek civilization for their whole society. Why? Here is a fascinating topic in its own right, for which few data, other than the biographies of liberators, are available. Nowadays, the guess may be hazarded, many leaders who have received higher education in Europe or America wish to demonstrate to friends abroad their importance at home; they seek to make a contribution of historical importance as judged first by Western standards and then by their contemporaries. One of the great rallying symbols of the modern civilized world has been political independence. That symbol—in consequence, one suspects—has been adopted by leaders in virtually every colonial country. Such rampant nationalism raises innumerable questions. Are these leaders reflecting their own personal desires as well as those of the least sophisticated of their countrymen? At what point is a society that has been a colonial dependency "ready" for independence?

The past, the present, and the future impulses of the more and the less civilized people interact; the net outcome is more civilization for the latter; and yet no single factor can be held responsible for the process that is set in motion. Why do Africans in South Africa, for example, continue to migrate or at least try to immigrate to urban areas where, from one standpoint, so much misery awaits them? At first some of the males were attracted by adventure and by the goods money could buy, such as the trinkets and devices of the West, food during a poor harvest, and cattle for the purchase of a wife. These motives, however, were insufficient to produce a flow of labor which would satisfy the needs of Europeans; in different words, Western civilization by itself was an inadequate inducement. To increase the supply of labor, at least two other motives of a negative sort apparently were necessary. In the first place, Europeans imposed a hut tax which, though small, could only be paid with money. Then there has been "a disruption and decline of the subsistence economy found widely in rural areas" (Stent, 1948, pp. 168–70). Why? Because the soil has been used improperly: great areas are now impoverished and are eroding. Why? Because the soil has been overcultivated and overgrazed. Why? In part because the steel plow has been introduced and this implement, as one African chief is reported as saying, is equal to the work of six wives. But why have people sought to increase their crops and their herds? Because the population both in an absolute and relative sense has increased. Why? In an absolute sense, because the life expectancy has increased, because tribal wars have been outlawed; relatively because less land is available for Africans. Why has life expectancy increased? Because medical techniques from the West have diffused somewhat. Why have they diffused? Obviously this story can continue backwards more or less indefinitely, but enough links in the chain have been pointed out to establish once more the thesis that the origins of socially significant behavior are numerous and complex.

The situation is equally intricate in the urban areas of South Africa, but again increased civilization is the final consequence. Some Africans remain in town because urban life is attractive to them, others because they prefer not to return to the difficult conditions in the rural Reserves, and still others because they feel they have no choice or at least they never face the problem of deciding. Except for adherents to one particular version of apartheid, moreover, the Europeans wish to have them remain in towns not so that they can become totally civilized but because they are needed as workers in industry, in homes, and on public works.

This long, rather elaborate discussion suggests that Hypothesis 26 must have some validity; and it is in line with a more specialized and more important proposition that has been stated concisely by one writer: "industrialization is not a reversible process." In support of the view, she argues very convincingly that, although their earlier cultural bases were different, countries in the West and Japan have had very similar demographic experiences after the advent of industrialization. Both in the West and in the East "substantial" populations have been involved but in each instance "the social and psychological transformations implicit in industrialization result eventually in a lessened rate of reproduction and a slowing growth." The transformations, once they have occurred, cannot be discontinued because people have become dependent upon new institutions for "procuring the subsistence essential to the maintenance of life." Cultural factors may limit the kinds of changes which are tolerated, but the alternatives to continued industrialization—subsidy from the outside, lowering of living standards already achieved, and the elimination of the surplus population—are subsequently considered either temporary or undesirable (Taeuber, 1950).

In theory it might be argued that, while it may not be feasible to march back to an earlier form of civilization, some society ought to be able to halt its own movement toward the West. The possibility of course cannot be excluded, but the evidence indicates, at least to this writer, that few if any instances of isolation persist indefinitely. The hypothesis being discussed, however, does not suggest that all aspects of the old culture must be lost: societies, it is stated, become more civilized "in a distinctive manner." In fact, it seems highly likely that some features of the old society are retained. While it may be true, for example, that more people throughout the world are becoming acquainted with a second language (usually a European one) for purposes of communication with the outside, it is also clear that native languages show no tendency whatsoever to die out. If anything, with the increased emphasis on nationalism, there are organized movements not only to preserve mother tongues but to revive ones that tended to atrophy as practical languages (such as Gaelic and Hebrew).

Another important reason why societies become civilized in a distinctive manner can be traced to the differences among the civilized countries that function as models and teachers. Wherever they have had their colonies, it would appear that England and Portugal have pursued different policies and have produced correspondingly varied institutions and, eventually, correspondingly varied independent countries. Even when the civilized model is identical—British policy, for example, has been reasonably uniform and British colonial officials have certainly been trained in similar traditions—each society responds differently because of its own background.

Cultures seem to vary, it must be added, with respect to the "brittleness" they display when they come in contact with the West. Some of them, such as societies in Asia, are said to resist cultural inroads more successfully than others, such as those in Africa and Australia. If the issue is only the speed with which the societies become more civilized in the Western sense, then the validity of Hypothesis 26 is not being questioned. But if some societies really can and do retain their distinctiveness more or less permanently, however, then that would be evidence running contrary to the hypothesis.

Reluctantly this section must end by concluding that, during the twentieth century at any rate, less civilized peoples are likely to become more civilized. Some of them will retain a greater number of their own unique characteristics than others, but all will share to a certain extent some core attributes of civilization. It is important in this connection to inquire whether the countries already civilized are moving toward greater unity or greater diversity. Arguments can be advanced on both sides. The great channels of transportation and communication, on the one hand, break down the barriers that an era of nationalism and ideological rivalry tend to build up. For similar reasons one cannot be sure whether the culture being developed by the less civilized societies will vary greatly or just a little from the models that now exist. But, without doubt, they will vary.

Chapter 10.

CHANGES IN PERSONALITY

As MEN become more civilized they change their forms of behavior, just as the societies in Western civilization have been
modified during recorded history. The changes in one sense represent variations on the limited set of themes which are the needs
of human beings. In comparison with the Romans, modern Europeans eat different kinds of food, talk somewhat different languages, and ride in different vehicles. But the same impulses remain. People then and now use vehicles to move from place to
place: the objective of a chariot and a motor car are the same;
only the techniques and speeds are different. Are Romans and
modern Europeans or Americans basically different?

So much clearly depends upon the definition of the term
"basic." If less and more civilized people differ in all the respects
suggested by the hypotheses outlined in previous chapters, then
their differences must indeed be numerous. At some point, as
dialectically inclined philosophers note, a series of quantitative
differences, no one of which by itself may be especially significant, reaches a climax and produces a vast and significant qualitative difference. More than flowery language is involved in making such a declaration. You meet a person in a less civilized area
and you assume, because of good will and experience, that he is
human and hence like yourself. But soon you discover that he
sees the world so differently and seeks so many different objectives that you must consider him "generally" or "basically" different. The sum of many differences, it should be said quite
simply, is a basic difference.

Such a view is admirably clear-cut. In fact it would be better
to say no more, for all the rest is fuzzy. But the fuzziness results

from some intriguing problems, and these must be explored. The problems largely arise from a conception of personality that has been repeatedly emphasized in earlier chapters: behavior is seldom completely hit-and-miss but is usually organized or integrated. Then it follows that, if many changes in discrete behavior occur in the course of becoming more civilized, then these changes must be organized with relation to one another and hence personalities must be basically different. The forms of behavior change, as a result of which the organization—the personality—must also change. The ultimate function of a chariot and a motor car may be the same in terms of transportation, but the drivers of each must have different skills, can express themselves while driving in different ways, and thus must be different people. A little glibly and not altogether satisfactorily it is being asserted that, when the less and the more civilized are compared, there must be some kind of a basic difference, but its nature is not specified.

A more definite approach consists of naming some important aspect of behavior and then deciding empirically whether or not it has been changed. By definition an "important" aspect exerts a significant influence upon much of a person's behavior and hence is perhaps closer to the personality around which his responses are organized. Relations with one's fellow men, for example, are always of great significance: if a change in attitude toward other men were detectable during acculturation, the conclusion would have to be drawn that a basic change had occurred. Are modern men less cruel than their ancestors, who seem to have frequently sacrificed human life needlessly, even capriciously?

A reference to cruelty makes one pause. On an empirical level it is too evident that some forms of cruelty surely persist. The modern world is not without wars, concentration camps, human jealousies, crimes, and evident inequalities. Are people, then, more or less cruel than they used to be? With what kind of hedonistic calculus is it possible to determine whether there is more sadism in an initiation ceremony of Central Australia or in a prize fight in New York City? There can be no quantitative escape by seeking to measure the amount of blood that is lost on each occasion, first because the measure is impractical and second because the intention or the reaction of the participants —and not the gore—are more sensitive indexes of cruelty. In different words, more than behavior must be assessed; have the underlying traits of personality changed?

It is largely on this level, nevertheless, that the question of basic changes in personality will be examined: do men regulate their significant behavior differently as they become more civilized? The crisply stated empirical question cannot receive a crisp reply, for empiricism as ever demands measurement, and measurement requires an instrument. How does one measure the traits regulating behavior? For reasons previously indicated, the favorite device has been the Rorschach test, and the Rorschach test—for reasons also previously pronounced—is quite imperfect, especially when employed in societies outside the West. Hopes must be low as the empirical evidence is surveyed.

Evidence

Without the usual introduction, let it be immediately said that existing empirical evidence, spotty and imperfect as it is, seems in substantial agreement with the following hypothesis:

HYPOTHESIS 27 (*consequential*): *Basic changes in personality are likely to occur as people become adequately civilized.*

Three kinds of interrelated evidence exist. First, it is asserted negatively, people become maladjusted and hence really do not cope "adequately" with civilization unless such basic changes do occur. Secondly, data are offered which purport to show differences in personality between societies that differ with respect to degree of civilization. Finally, similar differences are suggested between people within the same society who are variously civilized.

Without changes in personality, according to the first approach, the people of a changing society face serious difficulties. An investigator of the Sioux Indians reports this subjective impression from her field work:

The major administrative problem . . . is not primarily one of absence or poverty of natural resources, nor is it one of poverty of human resources. Rather, it is one of lack of connection between the human and natural resources. In general, the Sioux are not at present sufficiently interested in resolving their living problems to mobilize their inner and outer resources to cope with it. This is a question, not of intellectual adequacy, but of emotional energy and its organization and focus.

The Sioux are at least as intelligently gifted as the average group of Americans, but in general their minds are not being applied to tribal problems. Rather, their vital energies are tied up in attitudes of dependency, formerly creatively harnessed to powergiving religious beliefs and practices suitable to their lifeway, but now transferred to a notoriously unreliable government which is regarded as a conqueror and former enemy. Most Sioux, however, are not now reacting against an apparently unfriendly environment. On the contrary, they are submitting passively to it. The poor health of the Sioux is probably also a factor in their characteristically apathetic and uncreative personality orientation [Thompson, 1951, pp. 87–8, italics omitted].

If the Sioux have been correctly observed, then their troubles must spring from some defect in their personalities. Their inability to cope with the present environment may result not from failing to acquire the necessary trait that produces energy and drive but from actually acquiring the described trait that produces passivity and apathy. In either case, however, there is trouble.

A second way of attempting to determine whether acculturation changes personality is to compare two societies which have had varying degrees of contact with the West. Rorschach protocols have been obtained from 70 informants out of a total of 352 adults among the Tuscarora Indians of Niagara Falls, New York. A special analysis of the protocols that are virtually identical with respect to 21 Rorschach measures has been made in an effort to detect psychological trends. The high percentage of whole responses with a vague form and the relatively few detailed responses displayed by this homogeneous sample of highly acculturated Indians is said to be "characteristic of a deductive, perceptually inflexible type of personality, which simply cannot see reality-situations except in terms of some broad, inclusive generality" (Wallace, 1952, p. 72). This "modal personality type" is considered to be associated with acculturation since it is revealed in significantly fewer Ojibwa Indians, whose tribe has a similar culture and a similar historical background but is less acculturated. The difference in "personality" between the two societies, however, may not be due to varying degrees of acculturation. The Rorschach itself was administered to samples of the Tuscarora and Ojibwa in a manner that differed in nine respects (ibid., p. 97), and the traits of the two peoples may have been different before contact with white civilization.

As indicated in Chapter 3, when the nature of the Spiraled Explanation was first illustrated, Rorschach tests have been given on the Island of Saipan to Chamorros and Carolinian children. The more acculturated Chamorros are said to reveal a pronounced tendency to "repress all emotional expression," as a result of which they have "little surplus" energy for responding to the external environment. In contrast, the less acculturated Carolinians use their energy "in impulsive response to the immediate environment," and so each person appears to be "dependent on his environment from moment to moment for his emotional tone" (Joseph and Murray, 1951, pp. 303–4). Once again, the differences are not necessarily due to contact with civilization, for the authors themselves have pointed out variations in culture which existed before contact with Europeans and which may have originally given rise to different personality types.

The third and final approach to changes in personality—comparing groups of varying contact within the same society—is methodologically attractive. The very differences in culture that make cross-cultural comparisons so difficult and unsatisfying in interpreting a test like the Rorschach are precisely the factors which, according to such an approach, should be measured. For variously acculturated groups in the same society indeed have their own subcultures, and thus the degree of acculturation is grasped when the effects of those subcultures are ascertained. But is this so? It would be so if one could argue that the differences in subcultures are the sole determinant of the differences in personality; yet by now it should be evident that a Spiraled Explanation intrudes. The possibility that the personalities of some people or of their ancestors have induced them to choose the new subculture cannot be excluded. In spite of this reciprocal relation between people and culture, a number of studies comparing subcultural groups may be profitably reviewed.

Without offering the detailed evidence on which their judgments are based, investigators in the Indian-white study claim that the Rorschach and TAT responses of Navaho children in the most acculturated of three communities are more "complex" than those obtained in the other two communities. Although these children are said also to possess "greater sensitivity, a greater range of emotional possibilities, and more different nuances of feelings in response to life experiences," the greater social pressures to which they are subjected makes them appear less spontaneous in their reactions (Leighton and Kluckhohn, 1948, pp. 181–2). Another investigator, who has used only the Thematic Apperception Test, characterizes his Navaho subjects similarly: the most acculturated children seem to "gain greater possibilities for personality elaboration and with it greater creativity and development of a more functional use of inner life-control" while simultaneously losing "naive spontaneity" (Henry, 1947, pp. 112–13). In an equally impressionistic manner it is contended that the Rorschach protocols of Hopi children from a more acculturated community reveal greater "spontaneity" than those from a very isolated one (Thompson and Joseph, 1944, p. 111).

Five subgroups of Menomini Indians at varying stages of acculturation and a group of white Americans, as previously indicated (p. 56), have been compared. Some of the salient Rorschach results are offered in Table C (rows 20–28). To study the patterning of the various indexes, the investigator has constructed a "group psychogram" for each subgroup by plotting on a bar graph the median frequency with which many of the Rorschach responses appear. After commendable hesitation, he adopts "the standard hypothesis" to interpret the patterns; that is, with complete insight and because he can find no better alternative, he decides to commit the Jumping Fallacy and to use incompletely documented interpretations from Western society.

The best example of the procedure can be found in a contrast between the two extreme groups, A (the least acculturated) and E (the most acculturated). The single sentence summarizing the differences from the Rorschach test is quoted below in the column on the left; the interpretations the author immediately appends in five successive sentences are quoted to the right (Spindler, 1955, p. 156):

In contrast with Group A, those in Group E exhibit	*In contrast with Group A, Group E*
[1] a faster reaction time,	[1] reacts more quickly to new problem situations,
[2] a larger number of total responses,	[2] is intellectually more productive,
[3] fewer percepts in the animal content area,	[3] and exhibits a broader range of interests.
[4] a larger absolute number of human-movement responses,	[4] [Group E] exhibits more self-projective imaginative creativity,
[5] proportionately fewer animal-movement responses in the total record,	[5] with a relative decrement in the free expression of biologically oriented drives.
[6] more inanimate-movement responses,	[6] [Its members] reveal more tension, or conflict awareness. . . .
[7] a more frequent emphasis on the bright color component in the shading plus achromatic color to bright color ratio, and	[7] [They] less frequently exhibit . . . "contact shyness." . . .
[8] a more frequent use of bright color in percept formation.	[8] [They] follow through with a consistent psychological shift from the native base.

In different and more concise terms, perhaps the most important conclusion of the study has been phrased as follows:

The progressive shift from something that may be called quiescent stoicism, represented by the native-oriented personality configuration [group A], through the disturbed emotionality and regressive breakdown of control functions characteristic of the Peyotists [group B] and transitionals [group C], to the controlled and channelized emotional responsiveness characteristic of the elites [group E], appears to be the most consistent and dramatic aspect of the psychological adaptation accompanying the socio-cultural changes [ibid., pp. 197–8].

Since they have been living in the "relatively favorable" environment resulting from the establishment of a lumber industry on their reservation and the "attendant possibilities for responsible self-government," people in the most acculturated group (E) now have personalities basically different from those of their ancestors and of their less acculturated contemporaries. The modal person among them, the investigator concludes, is therefore "in effect a successfully adjusted middle-class American, with practically nothing logically identifiable as 'Indian' " (ibid., pp. 198–9).

The situation among the Menomini is in marked contrast to that among "culturally similar" Ojibwa. The investigator of the Menomini believes that the Rorschach protocols from the least acculturated Menomini and the least acculturated Ojibwa are "very much" like each other (ibid., p. 137). Basic changes in personality have not occurred among the Ojibwa, and hence they are not adjusted. The student of Ojibwa society, after an elaborate analysis of protocols from the three communities at different stages, states that "the most striking fact is the continuity of the same psychological pattern through these stages of acculturation." "There is," he thinks, "a persistent pattern core of generic traits which can be identified as Ojibwa. . . . There is no evidence at all of a fundamental psychological transformation" with increased contact. The most acculturated group, it is felt, is experiencing psychological problems of a fundamental kind: people reveal "an introversive personality structure being pushed to the limits of its functional adequacy" and are now functioning "with a great paucity of inner resources" (Hallowell, 1955, pp. 351–2). The validity of the finding is suggested, the investigator states, by his own observations; and it seems in accord with the observations of others who have also worked with the Ojibwa (Gillin and Raimy, 1940). The actual discrete Rorschach measures summarized by the present writer in Table D, however, reveal some differences among the groups; hence, if the analysis as a whole indicates "a persistent pattern core" in spite of increased acculturation, the details call attention to changes, for better or worse, within that core. On a more general level, the investigator advances the proposition that "the modal personality structure of a society may be expected to persist until conditions arise that *enforce* change" (Hallowell, 1955, p. 309, italics his). Neurosis and misery may indeed be the effective if not the exclusive goads for such drastic change, provided—well, provided many or most of the conditions specified in the hypotheses of this book are favorable.

Innovators

Since the three direct approaches to studying changes in personality have not yielded conclusive results, it is legitimate to ask whether insight might not be gained by means of a less direct method. An analysis of innovators, the people who accept and perpetuate new forms of behavior, may provide a clue. For, if they differ in personality from the noninnovators, it might be argued that their personality traits are the ones more civilized societies require.

Are there in fact differences between innovators and noninnovators? In one sense the hypotheses have provided an answer. The causal ones have suggested that those who are first attracted to innovations are the people who see in the changes the possibility of securing greater satisfaction, who have a favorable attitude toward the instructors, whose skill is adequate, etc. The consequential ones have stated that people who are attracted then acquire certain attributes. Such answers, it should be evident, involve in effect the form of behavior being learned or unlearned: people with certain characteristics are attracted or, when attracted, acquire them. The *who* and the *what* are thus made opposite sides of the same coin. Once more, however, such an approach concentrates on segments of behavior and avoids the issue of personality.

Efforts have been made to characterize, not the personality of innovators, but a few of their traits. A brief intellectual scuffle between two American anthropologists may serve as an illustration. One (Barnett, 1941) examined four Indian societies, three in California and one in British Columbia, and concluded that, besides the young, it was "the disgruntled, the maladjusted, and the incompetent [who] are preeminently the accepters of cultural innovations and change" and that it was "the ranking members in the social hierarchy [who] were the conservatives." The other anthropologist (Adams, 1951) found that in a community in the Central Sierra of Peru the innovators have been "persons of eminence" and that the changes introduced by the "maladjusted" were rejected. The conclusions of the two anthropologists are clearly different, but so were the conditions in the societies where the innovators functioned. As suggested by Adams, the four Indian groups "were breaking down as integrated cultures," whereas the Peruvian community at the time of the investigation was "still essentially stable." In addition the changes adopted by the innovators were different. In North America, for example, the marginal people of one tribe were converted to a Christian sect and moved to another community where they renounced many of their traditional customs; in Peru the elite introduced material traits such as alfalfa and the bicycle and nonmaterial ones such as a new fiesta society and an association that changed the caste system. At this point in the controversy it would appear that an historical level of analysis has been reached and hence the proponents are dealing with unique phenomena. The only abstraction on their horizon must involve motivation: both the marginal Indians in North America and the leaders in Peru needed something. The innovators, regardless of their position in society and regardless of other stresses and strains within them, shared unsatisfied needs. The investigator of the North American Indian societies himself has made a similar generalization when at a later date he published a detailed and skillful analysis of the entire problem of the innovator (Barnett, 1953, pp. 328–410).

The way the quarrel between the anthropologists has been synthesized, however, does not enable one to say whether certain personality traits are associated with increased civilization. Likewise, other conceptualizations of the innovator look as though they might be fruitful, and then eventually produce little. Anecdotes, for example, support the view that in many instances peo-

ple do not themselves decide to become innovators but are selected by outsiders to learn the changes. The native who looks
"promising" is offered a job by the Westerner. The latter may or
may not be considering basic personality traits when he makes
the judgment of "promising"; he may be regarding only the man's
strength or his cleanliness or the smile on his face. Possibly a
survey of many Europeans' conceptions of "promising" might reveal some unanimity, possibly not.

Evaluation

Now finally there can be a return to the main theme: the differences in personality between less and more civilized people
that have been ascertained. The survey in a previous section has
demonstrated the insubstantial nature of the data. In large part
this state of affairs reflects the imperfection of the Rorschach test
and other measures of personality. Just as the search for a culture-
free intelligence test has proved futile, is it also likely that new
approaches in the field of measuring personality will lead nowhere? The answer should not be prejudged. One writer has advanced the interesting hypothesis that some of the Rorschach
responses, such as those involving form or animals, may be "relatively independent" of cultural factors and acculturation, whereas
others, such as the reporting of movement or color, are "more
sensitive" to those influences (Kaplan, 1954, p. 17). The merits
of the particular suggestion need not be examined, but its rationale deserves comment. The assumption is being made that
certain characteristics transcend culture and that changes in personality, if they do occur, must be restricted to areas that are
plastic enough to be affected by culture. Nothing mysterious is
thus averred. An undisguised person is likely to be perceived as
a human being by anyone in any society; the ways in which he
is judged and appreciated will vary, especially if his appearance
is ambiguous.

It appears that the most promising lead, after one has fully
utilized the omnibus approach of some undiscovered instrument
that represents an improvement over the Rorschach test, is to postulate a central personality trait and then to discover empirically

whether more or less civilized peoples differ in that respect. The example of "cruelty," previously used in this chapter, is perhaps misleading because, as indicated then, no clear distinction can be made between the trait and the behavior to which it gives rise, nor can the behavior itself be casually measured. Instead it seems feasible to confine the inquiry to a trait, to some central determinant of behavior within people.

What should that trait be? Even before a reply is hazarded, it must be anticipated that the significance of the trait will vary from person to person and hence too from society to society, because any trait is affected by other traits operating simultaneously. It may be, for example, that those who change are more frustrated than those who do not (Hypothesis 1); but what effects does discontent have on their personalities? One consequence can be the kind of apathy that, as indicated a few pages back, characterizes the modern Sioux Indians. Among the Ganda, however, there is a wisp of evidence suggesting that the better educated, though more discontent, may have found ways of coping with adversity. The numbers in the samples are too small for each of the differences to be statistically significant, but a lower proportion of the university-educated consistently report behavior which in Western society is often considered neurotic: difficulty in getting to sleep; the emotional tone of dreams; unknown fears; tendency to become angry; and concern with health (Doob, 1961). As a starting point, nevertheless, it may be useful to know that increasing civilization has brought grief to people as diverse as the Sioux and the Ganda, even though differences in their contact with European civilization as well as other causes have produced for the moment different outcomes.

In such a spirit it may be seriously proposed that a trait that differentiates less from more civilized peoples, regardless of its eventual consequences, is the individual's conception of himself. From an objective viewpoint, criteria of civilization can be set up, such as a certain standard of literacy or the use of impedimenta from the West. Similarly sociologists and others speak of assimilation when strangers as a group so thoroughly learn the ways of the host society that they become for most practical purposes indistinguishable from the original inhabitants. The critical psychological question, however, involves the identification of the person: does he think of himself as a member of the old or the new society? In other terms, to which of the two societies does he refer his behavior when he judges himself and others? Which group does he aspire to please? With which group does he desire to reside? From which group would he or his son select a wife or his daughter a husband? These are the kinds of criteria which have been considered when efforts are made to draw up scales of assimilation or acculturation (e.g., Chief, 1940; Gillin and Raimy, 1940). For the person who thinks of himself as becoming more civilized, it is stated in Hypothesis 23, the learning of discrete segments of civilization is vastly accelerated. With such an approach, at least a bare minimum emerges: a civilized trait of personality is to consider oneself civilized.

There ought to be, nevertheless, a more subtle criterion, one that does not avoid but rather includes a value judgment. It is evident, as has been said so often in these pages, that men change as they become more civilized. In one area it is perhaps possible to maintain that the change has been progressive, indeed desirable—the area of physical health. Physical health may be defined variously—in terms of infant mortality, life expectancy, or incidence of disease—and by and large improvement is evident with the advent of civilization. Is there such a value in the field of personality? The words "adjustment," "satisfaction," and "happiness," slip from one's tongue. Although they are unctuous concepts, they call attention to *the* secular problem for whose solution men in all ages have been groping: to lead a "better" life by "improving" society. Perhaps the awareness of being civilized, which carries with it—or should carry with it—the realization that civilization means impermanence and change, makes people sensitive to the eternal quest for a finer future which is poorly defined but very, very meaningful.

For "civilization," as well as the brave and trite words that must be used to describe and evaluate it, is never satisfactorily defined connotatively and certainly not denotatively. People have often thought intuitively that the kind of civilization that has evolved is better than its predecessors and hence they must be better people. Almost equally frequent has been another intuition, which can arise no doubt only among more civilized people, viz., that civilization and civilized people have become too complex and that the simplicity of the "blessed savage" produces for him a more satisfactory existence and hence makes him a happier, probably also a better, person. The guesses and interpretations of Rorschach experts; the fumblings of observers, both competent and incompetent; yes, even the noble hypotheses of the present volume, nevertheless, ought to give rise to a compelling thought. But can a compelling thought be squeezed out of a morass of skepticism and negativism? Civilization, let it be whispered and shouted, requires people to exercise self-control, and such control is achieved by forfeiting some other tendency, such as spontaneity. We cannot be certain that to become more civilized is beneficial in an ultimate sense, however much we would like to cultivate the belief. It is certain only that we are destined or doomed to be civilized. We must rejoice or console ourselves with the conviction that we do survive by changing, maybe superficially, hopefully basically.

REFERENCES

ABEL, Theodora and Calabresi, Reneta A. The people from their Rorschach tests. *In* Oscar Lewis, *Life in a Mexican village: Tepoztlan restudied.* Urbana: University of Illinois Press, 1951, pp. 306–18, 463–90.

ADAIR, John and Vogt, Evon. Navaho and Zuni veterans: a study of contrasting modes of culture change. *American Anthropologist*, 1949, *51*, 547–61.

ADAMS, Richard N. Personnel in culture change: a test of a hypothesis. *Social Forces*, 1951, *30*, 185–9.

ADORNO, T. W.; Frenkel-Brunswick, Else; Levinson, Daniel J.; and Sanford, R. Nevitt. *The authoritarian personality.* New York: Harpers, 1950.

BARKER, George C. Social functions of language in a Mexican-American community. *Acta Americana*, 1947, *5*, 185–202.

BARNDT, R. J. and Johnson, D. N. Time orientation in delinquents. *Journal of Abnormal and Social Psychology*, 1955, *51*, 343–5.

BARNETT, H. G. Personal conflicts and culture change. *Social Forces*, 1941, *20*, 160–71.

——— *Innovation: the basis of cultural change.* New York: McGraw-Hill, 1953.

———; Broom, Leonard; Siegel, Bernard J.; Vogt, Evon Z.; and Watson, James B. Acculturation: an exploratory formulation. *American Anthropologist*, 1954, *56*, 973–1002.

BARNOUW, Victor. Acculturation and personality among the Wisconsin Chippewa. *American Anthropological Association, Memoirs*, 1950, *32*, No. 72.

BARTLETT, F. C. *Psychology and primitive culture.* Cambridge: Cambridge University Press, 1923.

BASCOM, William R. Acculturation among the Gullah Negroes. *American Anthropologist*, 1941, *43*, 43–50.

BEALS, Ralph L. Urbanism, urbanization, and acculturation. *American Anthropologist,* 1951, *53,* 1–10.

BECK, Samuel J.; Rabin, Albert I.; Thiesen, Warren G.; Molish, Herman; and Thetford, William N. The normal personality as projected in the Rorschach test. *Journal of Psychology,* 1950, *30,* 241–98.

BENTON, A. L. A multiple choice type of the visual retention test. *A.M.A. Archives of Neurology and Psychiatry,* 1950, *64,* 699–707.

BIESHEUVEL, S. The study of African ability. *African Studies,* 1952. *11,* 105–17.

BILLIG, O.; Gillin, John; and Davidson, W. Aspects of personality and culture in a Guatemalan community. *Journal of Personality,* 1947, *16,* 153–87; 1948, *16,* 326–68.

BLISS, Wesley L. In the wake of the wheel. *In* Edward H. Spicer (ed.), *Human problems in technological change.* New York: Russell Sage Foundation, 1952, pp. 23–33.

BOAS, Franz. *The mind of primitive man.* (Revised ed.) New York: Macmillan, 1938.

BROWN, Roger W. Language and categories. *In* Jerome S. Bruner, Jacqueline J. Goodnow, and George A. Austin, *A study of thinking.* New York: Wiley, 1956, pp. 247–312.

BRUNER, Edward M. Cultural transmission and cultural change. *Southwestern Journal of Anthropology,* 1956, *12,* 191–9.

BURROWS, Edwin G. *Hawaiian Americans: an account of the mingling of Japanese, Chinese, Polynesian, and American cultures.* New Haven: Yale University Press, 1947.

CARROLL, John B. and Casagrande, Joseph B. The function of language classifications in behavior. *In* Eleanor E. Maccoby, Theodore M. Newcomb, and Eugene L. Hartley (eds.), *Readings in social psychology.* (3rd ed.) New York: Holt, 1958, pp. 18–31.

CAUDILL, William. Japanese American personality and acculturation. *Genetic Psychology Monograph,* 1952, *45,* 3–102.

CHIEF, Elizabeth Howe. An assimilation study of Indian girls. *Journal of Social Psychology,* 1940, *11,* 19–30.

CHILD, Irvin. *Italian or American?* New Haven: Yale University Press, 1943.

CLARKE, Edith. *My mother who fathered me: a study of the family in three selected communities in Jamaica.* London: Allen and Unwin, 1957.

COLEMAN, James S. *Nigeria: background to nationalism.* Berkeley: University of California Press, 1958.

COLLINS, June McCormick. The Indian Shaker Church: a study of continuity and change in religion. *Southwestern Journal of Anthropology,* 1950, *6,* 399–411.

CULWICK, A. T. and Culwick, G. M. Culture contact on the fringe of civilization. *Africa,* 1935, *8,* 163–70.

DANIELSSON, Bengt. *Work and life on Raroria: an acculturation study from the Tuamotu group, French Oceania.* Uppsala: Almqvist and Wiksells, 1955.

DAVIDSON, Helen H. *Personality and economic background.* New York: King's Crown, 1943.

DAVIS, Allison and Dollard, John. *Children of bondage.* Washington, D.C.: American Council on Education, 1940.

DeGRANGE, McQuilkin. *The nature and elements of sociology.* New Haven: Yale University Press, 1953.

DENNIS, Wayne. Animism and related tendencies in Hopi children. *Journal of Abnormal and Social Psychology,* 1943, *38,* 21–36.

Department of Economics, University of Natal. *The African factory worker.* Cape Town: Oxford University Press, 1950.

DOLLARD, John; Doob, Leonard W.; Miller, Neal E.; Mowrer, O. H.; and Sears, Robert R. *Frustration and aggression.* New Haven: Yale University Press, 1939.

DOOB, Leonard W. The effect of language on verbal expression and recall. *American Anthropologist,* 1957a, *59,* 88–100.

——— An introduction to the psychology of acculturation. *Journal of Social Psychology,* 1957b, *45,* 143–60.

——— The use of different test items in nonliterate societies. *Public Opinion Quarterly,* 1957–58, *21,* 499–504.

——— The effect of the Jamaican patois on attitude and recall. *American Anthropologist,* 1958a, *60,* 574–5.

———— On the nature of uncivilized and civilized people. *Journal of Nervous and Mental Diseases*, 1958b, *126*, 513–22.

———— Attitudes and the availability of knowledge concerning traditional beliefs. *Journal of Abnormal and Social Psychology*, 1959, *59*, 286–90.

———— Ganda leaders, followers, and attitudes toward leadership. *In* L. A. Fallers and Audrey I. Richards (eds.), *Studies in leadership in modern Buganda.* London: Oxford University Press, 1961.

———— and Sears, Robert R. Factors determining substitute behavior and overt expression of aggression. *Journal of Abnormal and Social Psychology*, 1939, *34*, 293–313.

DOZIER, Edward P. Resistance to acculturation and assimilation in an Indian pueblo. *American Anthropologist*, 1951, *53*, 56–66.

EATON, Joseph W. Controlled acculturation: a survival technique of the Hutterites. *American Sociological Review*, 1952, *17*, 331–40.

EGGAN, Fred. Some aspects of culture change in the Northern Philippines. *American Anthropologist*, 1941, *43*, 11–18.

EMBREE, John F. Acculturation among the Japanese of Kona, Hawaii. *American Anthropological Association, Memoirs*, 1941, *43*, No. 59.

ENSMINGER, Douglas and Sanders, Irwin T. What extension is. *In* Edmund deS. Brunner et al. (eds.), *Farmers of the world.* New York: Columbia University Press, 1945, pp. 1–7.

EVANS-PRITCHARD, E. E. *Witchcraft, oracles, and magic among the Azande.* Oxford: Clarendon, 1937.

FESTINGER, Leon. *A theory of cognitive dissonance.* Evanston: Row, Patterson, 1957.

FREUD, Sigmund. *Civilization and its discontents.* New York: Jonathan Cape and Harrison Smith, 1930.

FROBENIUS, Leo. *Kulturgeschichte Afrikas.* Zurich: Phaidon-Verlag, 1933.

GILLESPIE, James M. and Allport, Gordon W. *Youth's outlook on the future.* Garden City, N.Y.: Doubleday, 1955.

GILLILAND, A. R. and Martin, Richard. Some factors in estimating short time intervals. *Journal of Experimental Psychology*, 1940, *27*, 243–55.

GILLIN, John. Acquired drives in culture contact. *American Anthropologist*, 1942, *44*, 545–54.

────── Parallel cultures and the inhibitions to acculturation in a Guatemalan community. *Social Forces*, 1945, *24*, 1–14.

────── and Raimy, Victor. Acculturation and personality. *American Sociological Review*, 1940, *5*, 371–80.

Gladwin, Thomas and Sarason, Seymour B. *Truk: man in paradise*. New York: Wenner-Gren Foundation, 1954.

GLUCKMAN, Max. The kingdom of the Zulu of South Africa. *In* Meyer Fortes and E. E. Evans-Pritchard (eds.) *African political systems*. London: Oxford University Press, 1940, pp. 25–55.

────── Analysis of a social situation in modern Zululand. *Rhodes-Livingstone Papers* No. 28, 1958.

GOLDFRANK, Esther S. Historic change and social character: study of the Teton Dakota. *American Anthropologist*, 1943, *45*, 67–83.

GOLDSTEIN, Kurt and Scheerer, Martin. Abstract and concrete behavior. *Psychological Monographs*, 1941, *53*, No. 239.

GOLDTHORPE, J. E. An African elite: a sample survey of fifty-two former students of Makerere College in East Africa. *British Journal of Sociology*, 1955, *6*, 31–47.

GREENBERG, Joseph H. Some aspects of Negro-Mohammedan culture-contact among the Hausa. *American Anthropologist*, 1941, *43*, 51–61.

HALLOWELL, A. Irving. *Culture and experience*. Philadelphia: University of Pennsylvania Press, 1955.

HARRIS, Jack S. The White Knife Shoshoni of Nevada. *In* Ralph Linton, *Acculturation in seven American Indian tribes*. New York: Appleton-Century, 1940, pp. 39–118.

HATCH, D. Spencer. Extension experience in India. *In* Edmund deS. Brunner et al. (eds.), *Farmers of the world*. New York: Columbia University Press, 1945, pp. 61–77.

HAVIGHURST, Robert J.; Gunther, M. K.; and Pratt, I. E. Environment and the Draw-a-Man test: the performance of Indian children. *Journal of Abnormal and Social Psychology*, 1946, *41*, 50–63.

—— and Neugarten, Bernice. *American Indian and white children.* Chicago: University of Chicago Press, 1955.

HAWTHORN, H. B. The Maori: a study in acculturation. *American Anthropological Association, Memoirs,* 1944, *46*, No. 64.

HELLMAN, Ellen. The native in the towns. *In* I. Schapera (ed.), *The Bantu-speaking tribes of South Africa.* London: Routledge, 1937, pp. 405–34.

HENRY, William E. The thematic apperception technique in the study of culture-personality relations. *Genetic Psychology Monograph,* 1947, *35,* 3–135.

HERSKOVITS, Melville J. African gods and Catholic saints in New World Negro belief. *American Anthropologist,* 1937, *39,* 635–43.

—— *Acculturation: the study of culture contact.* New York: J. J. Augustin, 1938.

HILGARD, Ernest R. *Theories of learning.* New York: Appleton-Century-Crofts, 1948.

HOERNLÉ, A. W. Magic and medicine. *In* I. Schapera (ed.), *The Bantu-speaking tribes of South Africa.* London: Routledge, 1937, pp. 221–45.

HOGBIN, H. Ian. *Experiments in civilization: the effects of European culture on a native community of the Solomon Islands.* London: Routledge, 1939.

—— *Transformation scene: the changing culture of a New Guinea village.* London: Routledge, 1951.

HOLMBERG, Allan R. The wells that failed: an attempt to establish a stable water supply in Viru Valley, Peru. *In* Edward H. Spicer (ed.), *Human problems in technological change.* New York: Russell Sage Foundation, 1952, pp. 113–23.

HONIGMANN, John J. *Ethnography and acculturation of the Fort Nelson Slave.* New Haven: Yale University Publication in Anthropology, No. 33, 1941.

—— *Culture and ethos of Kaska society.* New Haven: Yale University Publication in Anthropology, No. 40, 1949.

HOVLAND, Carl I.; Janis, Irving L.; and Kelley, Harold H. *Communication and persuasion*. New Haven: Yale University Press, 1953.

HUMPHREYS, Norman D. The changing structure of the Detroit Mexican family: an index of acculturation. *American Sociological Review*, 1944, 9, 622–6.

HUNTER, Monica. Methods of study of culture contact. *Africa*, 1934, 7, 335–50.

——— *Reaction to conquest: effects of contact with Europeans on the Pondo of South Africa*. London: Oxford University Press, 1936.

JOSEPH, Alice and Murray, V. F. *Chamorros and Carolinians of Saipan*. Cambridge: Harvard University Press, 1951.

KAPLAN, Bert. A study of Rorschach responses in four cultures. *Papers of the Peabody Museum of American Archaeology and Ethnology*, Harvard University, 1954, 42, No. 2.

KARK, Sydney L. Health centre service. *In* E. H. Cluver, *Social medicine*. South Africa: Central News Agency, 1951, pp. 661–700.

KEESING, Felix M. Extension work in the Pacific islands. *In* Edmund deS. Brunner et al. (eds.), *Farmers of the world*. New York: Columbia University Press, 1945, pp. 19–36.

——— Cultural dynamics and administration. *Proceedings, Seventh Pacific Science Congress*, Auckland, 1953, 7, 102–17.

KENNEDY, Raymond. Acculturation and administration in Indonesia. *American Anthropologist*, 1943, 45, 185–90.

KIMBALL, Solon T. Diversity and change in the culture of non-literate peoples. *In* Edmund deS. Brunner et al. (eds.), *Farmers of the world*. New York: Columbia University Press, 1945, pp. 8–18.

KLUCKHOHN, Clyde and Leighton, Dorothea. *The Navaho*. Cambridge: Harvard University Press, 1946.

KLUCKHOHN, Florence R. Dominant and substitute profiles of cultural orientations: their significance for the analysis of social stratification. *Social Forces*, 1950, 28, 376–93.

KÖBBEN, A. *Le planteur noir*. Mâcon: Institut Français d'Afrique Noire, 1956.

KORZYBSKI, Alfred. *Science and sanity*. Lancaster, Penn.: International Non-Aristotelian Library Publishing Co., 1945.

KRIGE, Eileen J. Some social and economic facts revealed in native family budgets. *Race Relations*, 1934, *1*, 94–108.

———— Individual development. *In* I. Schapera (ed.), *The Bantu-speaking tribes of South Africa*. London: Routledge, 1937, pp. 95–118.

LEIGHTON, Alexander H. *The governing of men*. Princeton: Princeton University Press, 1945.

LEIGHTON, Dorothea and Kluckhohn, Clyde. *Children of the people: the Navaho individual and his development*. Cambridge: Harvard University Press, 1948.

LERNER, Daniel. *The passing of traditional society: modernizing the Middle East*. Glencoe, Illinois: Free Press, 1958.

LESHAN, Lawrence. Time orientation and social class. *Journal of Abnormal and Social Psychology*, 1952, *47*, 589–92.

LÉVY-BRUHL, Lucien. *How natives think*. London: Allen and Unwin, 1926.

LEWIS, Oscar. The effects of white contact upon Blackfoot culture, with special reference to the role of the fur trade. *American Ethnological Society Monograph*, 1942, No. 6.

———— *Life in a Mexican village: Tepoztlan restudied*. Urbana: University of Illinois Press, 1951.

LINTON, Ralph. *Acculturation in seven American Indian tribes*. New York: Appleton-Century, 1940.

LIVINGSTONE, David. Unpublished letter to his father-in-law, dated May 19, 1854.

LOOMIS, Charles P. Extension work in Latin America. *In* Edmund deS. Brunner et al. (eds.), *Farmers of the world*. New York: Columbia University Press, 1945, pp. 117–37.

McCORD, James B. *My patients were Zulus*. New York: Rinehart, 1946.

MacGREGOR, Gordon. *Warriors without weapons: a study of the society and personality development of the Pine Ridge Sioux.* Chicago: University of Chicago Press, 1946.

MAIR, L. P. The study of culture contact as a practical problem. *Africa,* 1934, 7, 415–22.

MALINOWSKI, Bronislaw. *The dynamics of culture change: an inquiry into race relations in Africa.* New Haven: Yale University Press, 1945.

MASON, Leonard. The Bikinians: a transplanted population. *Human Organization,* 1950, 9, No. 1, 5–15.

MEAD, Margaret (ed.). *Cultural patterns and technical change.* New York: Mentor Books, 1955.

MEAD, Margaret. *New lives for old: cultural transformation, Manus, 1928–1953.* New York: Morrow, 1956.

MITCHELL, Philip. *African afterthoughts.* London: Hutchinson, 1954.

MURDOCK, George P. The common denominators of culture. *In* Ralph Linton (ed.), *Science of man in the world crisis.* New York: Columbia University Press, 1945, pp. 123–43.

——— *Social structure.* New York: Macmillan, 1949.

MUSGROVE, F. A Uganda secondary school as a field of culture change. *Africa,* 1952, 22, 234–49.

NOTCUTT, L. A. and Latham, G. C. *The African and the cinema.* London: Edinburgh House Press, 1937.

OBERHOLZER, Emil. Rorschach's experiment and the Alorese. *In* Cora DuBois, *The people of Alor.* Minneapolis: University of Minnesota Press, 1944, pp. 588–640.

OLIVER, Roland. *Sir Harry Johnston and the scramble for Africa.* London: Chatto and Windus, 1957.

OMBREDANE, André. Principes pour une étude psychologique des noirs du Congo Belge. *Année Psychologique,* 1951, 50, 521–47.

PATON, Alan. *Cry, the beloved country.* New York: Scribner's, 1948.

PERHAM, Margery. *Lugard: the years of adventure, 1858–1898.* London: Collins, 1956.

QUIMBY, George I. and Spoehr, Alexander. Acculturation and material culture. *Fieldiana, Anthropology*, 1951, *36*, 107–47.

RADIN, Paul. *The world of primitive man*. New York: Henry Schuman, 1953.

READER, D. H. Marriage among the Makhanya. *International Archives of Ethnography*, 1954, *47*, 69–107.

REDFIELD, Robert. *A village that chose progress: Chan Kom revisited*. Chicago: University of Chicago Press, 1950.

———— *The primitive world and its transformations*. Ithaca: Cornell University Press, 1953.

———— *Peasant society and culture: an anthropological approach to civilization*. Chicago: Chicago University Press, 1956.

————; Linton, Ralph; and Herskovits, Melville J. A memorandum for the study of acculturation. *American Anthropologist*, 1936, *38*, 149–52.

RICHARDS, Audrey I. The village census in the study of culture contact. *Africa*, 1935a, *8*, 20–33.

———— A modern movement of witch-finders. *Africa*, 1935b, *8*, 448–61.

RUESCH, Jurgen; Jacobson, Annemarie; and Loeb, Martin B. Acculturation and illness. *Psychological Monographs*, 1948, *62*, No. 292.

SANDERS, Irwin T. Characteristics of peasant societies. *In* Edmund deS. Brunner et al. (eds.), *Farmers of the world*. New York: Columbia University Press, 1945, pp. 37–45.

SCHACHTEL, Ernest G. Notes on Rorschach tests of 500 juvenile delinquents and a control group of 500 non-delinquent adolescents. *Journal of Projective Techniques*, 1951, *15*, 144–72.

SCHAPERA, I. Field methods in the study of modern culture contacts. *Africa*, 1935, *8*, 315–28.

———— Cultural changes in tribal life. *In* I. Schapera (ed.), *The Bantu-speaking tribes of South Africa*. London: Routledge, 1937, pp. 357–87.

SCHNEIDER, Louis and Lysgaard, Sverre. The deferred gratification pattern: a preliminary study. *Social Forces*, 1953, *18*, 142–9.

SCHULTES, Anton. *Die Nachbarschaft der Deutschen und Slawen an der March.* Vienna: Oesterreichisches Museum für Volkskunde, 1954.

Sharp, Lauriston. Steel axes for stone age Australians. *In* Edward H. Spicer (ed.), *Human problems in technological change.* New York: Russell Sage Foundation, 1952, pp. 69–72.

SHERWOOD, Rae. The Bantu civil servant. Unpublished manuscript. Johannesburg: National Council for Social Research, National Institute for Personnel Research, 1959.

SIEGEL, Bernard J. *Acculturation: critical abstracts, North America.* Stanford: Stanford University Press, 1955.

SINGH, Rudra Datt. The village level: an introduction of green manuring in rural India. *In* Edward H. Spicer (ed.), *Human problems in technological change.* New York: Russell Sage Foundation, 1952, pp. 55–67.

SPICER, Edward H. (ed.). *Human problems in technological change: a casebook.* New York: Russell Sage Foundation, 1952.

SPINDLER, George D. *Sociocultural and psychological processes in Menomini acculturation.* Berkeley: University of California Press, 1955.

SPIRO, Melford E. The acculturation of American ethnic groups. *American Anthropologist,* 1955, 57, 1240–52.

STENT, G. E. Migrancy and urbanization in the Union of South Africa. *Africa,* 1948, *18,* 161–83.

STEWARD, Julian H. *Theory of culture change: the methodology of multilinear evolution.* Urbana: University of Illinois Press, 1955.

TAEUBER, Irene B. Population increase and manpower utilization in Imperial Japan. *Milbank Memorial Fund Quarterly,* 1950, 28, 273–93.

TANNOUS, Afif I. Extension work among the Arab fellahin. *In* Edmund deS. Brunner et al. (eds.), *Farmers of the world.* New York: Columbia University Press, 1945, pp. 78–100.

TAX, Sol. World view and social relations in Guatemala. *American Anthropologist,* 1941, *43,* 27–42.

THOMPSON, Laura. Attitudes and acculturation. *American Anthropologist,* 1948, *50,* 200–15.

———— *Culture in crisis: a study of the Hopi Indians.* New York: Harpers, 1950.

———— *Personality and government: findings and recommendations of the Indian Administration Research.* Mexico City: Ediciones del Instituto Indigenista Interamericano, 1951.

———— and Joseph, Alice. *The Hopi way.* Chicago: University of Chicago Press, 1944.

Thurnwald, Richard C. *Black and white in East Africa.* London: Routledge, 1935.

Toynbee, Arnold J. *A study of history* (abridged), 2 vols. New York: Oxford University Press, 1946.

Underhill, Ruth. *Papago Indian religion.* New York: Columbia University Press, 1946.

Vandenbosch, A. The effect of Dutch rule on the civilization of the East Indies. *American Journal of Sociology,* 1943, *48,* 498–502.

Van Der Post, Laurens. *The dark eye in Africa.* New York: Morrow, 1955.

Vogt, Evon Z. Navaho veterans: a study of changing values. *Papers of the Peabody Museum of American Archaeology and Ethnology,* Harvard University, 1951, *41,* No. 1.

Wallace, Anthony F. C. Some psychological determinants of culture change in an Iroquoian community. *Smithsonian Institution, Bureau of American Ethnology,* 1951, No. 149, 55–76.

———— The modal personality structure of the Tuscarora Indians. *Smithsonian Institution, Bureau of American Ethnology,* 1952, No. 150.

Warner, W. Lloyd and Srole, Leo. *The social systems of American ethnic groups.* New Haven: Yale University Press, 1945.

Watson, James B. Cayuà culture change: a study in acculturation and methodology. *American Anthropological Association, Memoirs,* 1952, *54,* No. 73.

Weber, Max. *The Protestant ethic and the spirit of capitalism.* New York: Scribner's, 1930.

WERNER, Heinz. *Comparative psychology of mental development.* New York: International Universities Press, 1948.

WHETTEN, Nathan L. *Rural Mexico.* Chicago: University of Chicago Press, 1948.

WHORF, Benjamin Lee. Science and linguistics. *Technology Review,* 1940, *42,* 229–31, 247–8.

WILSON, Godfrey and Wilson, Monica. *The analysis of social change: based on observations in Central Africa.* Cambridge: Cambridge University Press, 1945.

WISSLER, Clark. *Man and culture.* New York: Crowell, 1923.

WITKIN, H. A. Individual differences in ease of perception of embedded figures. *Journal of Personality,* 1950, *19,* 1–15.

ZIMMERMANN, Carle C. Euro-American rural society. *In* Edmund deS. Brunner et al. (eds.), *Farmers of the world.* New York: Columbia University Press, 1945, pp. 138–52.

APPENDIX A *Tables*

TABLES 1 through 10 are based upon a long interview administered by the writer to adults in three African societies and in Jamaica. All the figures, unless otherwise noted, are percentages. The meaning of the column headings and of the symbols is uniform and is explained in the text, pp. 49–51. An asterisk signifies that the difference between the pair is statistically significant ($p < .05$). The number in parentheses after a number sign ($\#$) refers to the item in the Schedule, Appendix B, on which the row is based.

Tables I through III contain supplementary data from the same African societies. All the figures are percentages.

Tables A through E are based on data collected by other investigators. Table E summarizes a study of people of Japanese origin in Chicago, the others concern themselves with American Indians. The meaning of the figures is indicated either in the title of the table or in an attached footnote.

TABLE 1. *Validity of Education as an Index of Acculturation*

	LUO		GANDA		ZULU	
	low	high	low	high	low	high
Maximum number of informants	24	23	63	70	69	37
1. No or almost no knowledge of English	71 *	9	74 *	23	79 *	0
2. Occupation: cultivator or unskilled (#1)	42	26	59 *	16	82 *	6
3. Urban residence	0	0	24 *	68	50 *	92
4. Religion: "pagan" (#6)	30 *	0	1	3	29 *	0
5. Christians: per cent Roman Catholic (#6)	25	9	46 *	19	18	8
6. Claims a European friend (#40)	63 *	96	53	65	39 *	61
7. Demonstrated ability to smoke European cigarettes	50 *	91	29	38	48	58
8. Age (mean years) (#4)	52	49	44 *	35	50	45
9. "Acculturation" (mean, five-point rating by competent authorities)	1.2 *	2.7	2.1	2.7	1.4 *	3.5

TABLE 2. *Motives and Goals*

	LUO low	LUO high	GANDA low	GANDA high	ZULU low	ZULU high	JAMAICA low	JAMAICA high
Maximum number of informants	24	23	63	70	69	37	89	23
DISCONTENT								
1. Person in ambiguous drawing looks "unhappy" (#21)	33	46	9 *	32	46 *	70	38 *	65
2. Dislike of present occupation (#35)	8	22	9	19	20 *	51	66	57
3. Anticipated nongratification in occupation (#24)	4	5	5	13	32	44	30 *	9
4. Agrees: "Life seems to be getting worse" (#25)							53 *	26
5. Agrees: "World seems to be getting worse" (#26)							46 *	22
AGGRESSIVENESS								
6. "Chief" in ambiguous drawing "dislikes" the "follower" a (#18)	17	39	10	16	14	26	45 *	78
7. "Follower" in ambiguous drawing "dislikes" the "chief" a (#18)	43	52	26	34	17	37		
8. "European" in ambiguous drawing "dislikes" the "African" b (#19)	5	0	6	6	27	22	9	9
9. "African" in ambiguous drawing "dislikes" the "European" b (#19)	18	22	8	20	30	36	10 *	30
10. "Father" in ambiguous drawing "dislikes" the "son" (#20)	5	9	9	11	7	14	12 *	35
11. "Son" in ambiguous drawing "dislikes" the "father" (#20)	5	9	7	8	6	25	2 *	30
12. Dislike of Europeans (#36)	4	22	23	23	21	36		
13. Dislike of Indians (#37)	30	44	36	53	35	53		
14. Dislike of leader A c (#32)	17	35	13	29	17 *	51	24	38
15. Dislike of leader B d (#33)	22	35	17	22	20 *	54	18	13

283

Table 2. (cont.)

	Luo low	Luo high	Ganda low	Ganda high	Zulu low	Zulu high	Jamaica low	Jamaica high
16. Dislike of leader C e (#34)	13	36	7 *	23	17	30		
17. Agrees: "World is dangerous, people are evil" (#61)	75	87	59	49	70	83		
18. Agrees: "Failure results from secret plots of others" (#79)	50	39	53	58	70	69	66 *	22
POSTPONEMENT								
19. Agrees: "A waste of time to plan for future" (#50)	42	17	22	16	66 *	34	14	4
20. Claims to plan for a year or more (#22)	92	100	65 *	44	75	77	79	77
21. Prefers to spend £5 now rather than invest or receive £50 in a year (#29)	32	14	52 *	31	24	11	45 *	17
22. Indicates only vague plan for spending a windfall of £500 (#30)	29	17	22	20	43 *	17	18	4
23. Completes "Money is . . ." with "to spend" (#97)							21 *	0
24. Inability to anticipate life five years hence (#23)	29	17	5	8	60 *	35	34	13
25. Inability to foresee, or have preferences concerning, the country's future (#133)							32	9

a. For Jamaica: unfriendly atmosphere between "rich" and "poor" Jamaicans in ambiguous drawing.

b. For Jamaica: substitute "shopkeeper" for "European" and "customer" for "African."

c. For Jamaica: "rich people" (#128).

d. For Jamaica: "rich people," incomplete sentence (#96).

e. For Zulu: one urban area only.

TABLE 3. *Attitudes Toward People in the Old Society*

	Luo low	Luo high	Ganda low	Ganda high	Zulu low	Zulu high
Maximum number of informants	24	23	63	70	69	37
FAMILY						
1. "Father" in ambiguous drawing "dislikes" "son" (#20)	5	9	9	11	7	14
2. "Son" in ambiguous drawing "dislikes" "father" (#20)	5	9	7	8	6	25
3. "Son" in ambiguous drawing expresses hostility (#20)	4 *	26	16	29	11 *	39
4. Father judged "kindest" (#9)	32	15	20	14	11	13
5. Father "taught" most (#10)	41	45	25	22	22	23
6. Father "loved" most (#11)	14	29	16	11	13 *	0
7. Father "respected" most (#12)	36	52	23 *	45	40	33
8. Mother judged "kindest" (#9)	18	45	20 *	38	24 *	47
9. Mother "taught" most (#10)	5	20	18	28	21 *	47
10. Mother "loved" most (#11)	23	19	30	45	40 *	63
11. Mother "respected" most (#12)	9	5	7	5	8	13
12. Recalls no special person for childhood quarrels (#14)	63	30	64 *	30	44	39
13. Agrees: "Brothers can never be friends" (#54)	13	30	40	30	39	46
14. Agrees: "Kinship is closer than friendship" (#65)			85 *	59	59	37
15. Agrees: "Wife earning money may spend it as she pleases" (#66)	13	4	8 *	42	39	31
16. Agrees: "Proper for cross-cousins to marry" (#60)					5	11
17. Agrees: "Groom's family should offer special gifts" (#60)					90	77
18. Agrees: "Eloping woman disgraces her village" [a] (#57)	96	83	60	68	91	86
19. Claims to seek group rather than individual goal (#27)	73	82	61 *	89	42 *	82
TRADITIONAL AUTHORITIES						
20. "Chief" in ambiguous drawing "dislikes" the "follower" (#18)	17	39	10	16	14	26
21. "Follower" in ambiguous drawing "dislikes" the "chief" (#18)	43	52	26	34	17	37
22. "Follower" in ambiguous drawing expresses hostility (#18)	8 *	43	18	25	13 *	39

TABLE 3. (*cont.*)

	LUO		GANDA		ZULU	
	low	*high*	*low*	*high*	*low*	*high*
23. Dislike of leader A (#32)	17	35	13	29	17 *	51
24. Dislike of leader B (#33)	22	35	17	22	20	54
25. Dislike of leader C b (#34)	13	36	7 *	23	17	30
26. Agrees: "A chief should always be obeyed" (#62)	58 *	9	76 *	44	94 *	80
27. Agrees: "Leaders are more important than followers" (#69)	75	50	87 *	64	46	34
28. Stresses leadership qualities of "a good chief" (#39)	18	35	19	7	29	23
29. Agrees: "Chief may use public funds privately" (#80)	33	21	22	16	73 *	31

a. For Ganda: "Eldest son should be father's heir" (#58). For Zulu: "Man getting wife by abduction should be punished" (#56).

b. For Zulu: one urban area only.

TABLE 4. *Attitudes Toward Out-Group*

	LUO		GANDA		ZULU	
	low	high	low	high	low	high
Maximum number of informants	24	23	63	70	69	39
1. "European" in ambiguous drawing evokes ambivalence (#19)	32	48	80	66	42	58
2. "European" in ambiguous drawing "dislikes" the "African" (#19)	5	0	6	6	27	22
3. "African" in ambiguous drawing evokes ambivalence (#19)	64	55	27	13	42	42
4. "African" in ambiguous drawing "dislikes" "European" (#19)	18	22	8	15	30	36
5. Ambivalence toward Europeans (#36)	22	39	28	41	33	27
6. Dislike of Europeans (#36)	4	22	23	23	21	36
7. Ambivalence toward Asians (#37)	26	57	25	29	38	31
8. Dislike of Asians (#37)	30	44	36	53	35	53
9. Ambivalent admiration of Europeans (#42)	29	52	19	33	4 *	17
10. Admiration of Europeans (#42)	46	22	41	39	52 *	29
11. Ambivalence toward receiving admiration of Europeans (#43)	26	31	35	35	26	11
12. Seeks admiration of Europeans (#43)	24 *	0	23	16	32	17
13. Claims to have European friend (#40)	63 *	96	53	65	39 *	61
14. Claims to have Asian friend (#41)	25	22	46	43	16	31
15. Agrees: "Possible for African to have European friend" (#81)	46	64	78	81	52	63
16. Rated cooperativeness during interview	95	95	81	87	79	85

TABLE 5. Reactions Concerning Skin Color in Jamaica

	low	high
Maximum number of informants	89	23
1. No reference to skin color in stereoscopic pictures (#89)	57 *	30
2. Ignores picture of African in stereoscopic alternation [a] (#89)	22 *	1
3. Willingness to judge people by skin color (#124)	72 *	35
4. Skin color singled out in double-barreled statement (#122)	44	73
5. Claims to note skin color in first impression of a person (#98)	1	0
6. Spontaneously expressed respect for "white people" (#42)	16	0
7. Seeks respect from "white people" (#43)	12	0
8. Claims wish to be "white person" (#99)	33 *	4
9. Attributes importance to "white people" (#101)	19 *	0
10. Completes pleasantly: "white people always . . ." (#91)	40 *	17
11. Agrees: "People here don't worry about skin color" (#122)	48	25
12. Claims to like Americans (#136)	89 *	30
13. Favorably disposed toward photograph of "white man" (#124)	31	47
14. Unfavorably disposed toward photograph of Negro men (#124)	65 *	32
15. Favorably disposed toward photograph of "white woman" (#125)	51	40

a. Excludes those revealing eye dominance.

288

TABLE 6. *Attitudes Toward Other People*

	LUO		GANDA		ZULU		JAMAICA	
	low	high	low	high	low	high	low	high
Maximum number of informants	24	23	63	70	67	37	89	23
SENSITIVITY								
1. One human response to Rorschach Plate II (#71)	0	17	23	18	18	23		
2. One human response to Rorschach Plate III (#72)	55 *	83	57	66	37 *	71		
3. One human response to Rorschach Plate VIII (#74)	29	58	28	34	16	29	6	17
4. One human response to ambiguous drawing (#21)	17	41	35	49	52 *	76	18 *	44
5. Immediate "suggestibility" on Rorschach test (#72–74)	83	83	54 *	76	70	73		
6. Delayed "suggestibility" on Rorschach test (#73–74)	62 *	22	20	28	32	23		
7. No or ambiguous response to drawing of "chief-follower" (#18)	21	4	20	13	54 *	22		
8. No or ambiguous response to drawing of "European-African" a (#19)	29 *	4	23	19	42	31	0	0
9. No or ambiguous response to drawing of "father-son" (#20)	22	13	23	13	58 *	17	0	0
10. Claims preference for group, not individual, goal (#27)	73	82	61 *	89	42 *	82	19	36
11. Seeks to avoid unpopularity (#28)	0 *	35	3	5	3	5	1	8
12. Wants people to behave decently for "social" reasons (#129)							31	44
CONCEPTUALIZATION								
13. Agrees: "People should talk less and work more" (#76)	91	100	75	83	81	91	81 *	41

289

TABLE 6. (cont.)

	Luo		Ganda		Zulu		Jamaica	
	low	high	low	high	low	high	low	high
14. Agrees: "People should think of cheerful things if worrying" (#70)	88	87	7 *	32	54 *	80		
15. Agrees: "People should be successful in spite of others' jealousy" (#49)	25	22	54	61	36	23		
16. Agrees: "People should speak only well of a rival" (#63)	91	91	91	94	66 *	20		
17. Agrees: "Ability is more important than luck" (#57)			22 *	44	8	9	20 *	87
18. Agrees: "People should conserve soil or be punished" b (#64)	33	26	40	42			17 *	74

a. For Jamaica: "rich-poor people."
b. For Jamaica: "People should not blame others for troubles" (#31).

TABLE 7. *Expression of No Opinion*

	LUO		GANDA		ZULU		JAMAICA	
	low	high	low	high	low	high	low	high
Maximum number of informants	24	23	63	70	69	37	89	23

TRADITIONAL STATEMENTS

	LUO		GANDA		ZULU		JAMAICA	
1. Some people can change into animals [a] (#53)	14	4	9	2	9	0		
2. Some animals (stones) can talk [b] (#56)	0	3	5	3	12	11		
3. Eloping woman disgraces her village [c] (#57)	5	4	3	2	5	3		
4. Professional prophets can foretell future [d] (#58)	0	0	14	7	8	3		
5. Chief should always be obeyed (#62)	0	0	3	2	3	3		
6. Ghosts can produce sickness [e] (#65)	13	17			9	11		
7. Wife earning money may spend it as she pleases (#66)	0	0	4	3	12	3		

NONTRADITIONAL STATEMENTS

	LUO		GANDA		ZULU		JAMAICA	
8. People should succeed in spite of others' jealousy (#49)	71	74	4	2	55	71		
9. A waste of time to plan for future (#50)	4	0	2	0	21 *	0		
10. People were happier in old days [f] (#51)	13	8	15	4	4	3		
11. Polygynist can be good Christian (#52)	4	4	5	2	8	0		
12. Brothers can never be friends (#54)	4	0	2	0	5	6		
13. Anticipation is worse than punishment (#55)	8	4	7	2	20 *	0	11	4
14. Ability is more important than luck (#57)			2	0	22 *	9	19	4
15. Life in heaven is better than life on earth (#59)	21	36	33	25	37	43		
16. World is dangerous, people are evil (#61)	13	0	5	4	24 *	6		

291

TABLE 7. (cont.)

	LUO		GANDA		ZULU		JAMAICA	
	low	high	low	high	low	high	low	high
17. People should speak only well of a rival g (#63)	4	0	2	0	5	9		
18. People should conserve soil or be punished h (#64)	4	17	0	0	13	3		
19. Kinship is closer than friendship (#65)			2	7	9	14		
20. Steadfastness is better than opportunism (#67)	8	0	2	2	11	0		
21. For good farming use modern ideas rather than experience (#68)	17	4	9	4	11	3		
22. Leaders are more important than followers (#69)	21	22	7	6	15	3		
23. People should think of cheerful things if worrying (#70)	8	9	2	3	28 *	6		
24. People should talk less and work more (#76)	4	0	7	2	17	17	1	0
25. Liars will be punished in next world (#77)	4	17	27	16	17	9		
26. Government favors rich (#78)	8	4	7	5	11	3		
27. Failure results from secret plots of others (#79)	17	4	13	7	14	6	66 *	22
28. Chief may use public funds privately (#80)	13	4	2	0	6	6		
29. Possible for African to have European friend (#81)	17	0	2	0	11	3		
30. Judge should treat criminal brother like any other person (#82)	13	0	4	0	0	0		
31. Better to work in city than on farm i (#83)	21	9	5	10	11	3		
"INFORMATION-SEEKING" QUESTIONS								
32. Receive £5 now or £50 a year from now? (#29)	8	8	7	3	22 *	0	0	0
33. How spend a windfall of £500? (#30)	29	17	22	20	43 *	17	18	4

Table 7. (*cont.*)

	Luo low	Luo high	Ganda low	Ganda high	Zulu low	Zulu high	Jamaica low	Jamaica high
34. Plans for self and family? (#22)	9	0	46	60	36	34		
35. What doing five years from now? (#23)	29	17	5	8	60 *	35	34	13
36. What would make you happiest and most proud? (#27)	8	0	5	6	12	0	2	0
37. Worst thing that could happen to you? (#28)	4	0	19	6	13	5	7	0
38. What kinds of people believe in ghosts? (#130)							11	0
39. With what kinds of people would you change places? (#99)							7	4
40. What kinds of people are important here? (#101)							24 *	9
41. What kinds of people want you to get ahead? (#102)							18	10
42. Do you have a chance to get ahead? (#103)							22	13
43. Why should people obey the law? (#127)							2	0
44. What will happen to Jamaica in the future? (#133)							78 *	13
45. What would you like to see change in Jamaica? (#134)							42 *	9
46. What would you like not to see change in Jamaica? (#135)							36	14

a. For Zulu: "Wealth in money is better than wealth in cattle" (#51).
b. For Zulu: "A chief can make it rain" (#53).
c. For Ganda: "Eldest son should be father's heir" (#58). For Zulu: "Man getting wife by abduction should be punished" (#56).
d. For Ganda: "Cook can use medicine to get wages raised" (#60). For Zulu: "A native doctor can treat any disease" (#58).
e. For Zulu: "Sick may die if seen by 'unclean' persons" (#63).
f. For Zulu: "Groom's family should offer special gifts" (#60).
g. For Zulu: "Proper for cross-cousins to marry" (#60).
h. For Zulu: "Good-tasting food is healthful" (#64).
i. For Ganda: "Industries will help the country" (#83).

TABLE 8. *Beliefs and Values*

	LUO		GANDA		ZULU	
	low	*high*	*low*	*high*	*low*	*high*
Maximum number of informants	24	23	63	70	63	37
BELIEFS						
1. Polygynist can be good Christian (#52)	58	57	38	42	49	66
2. Some people can change into animals (#53)	21	44	43	33		
3. Some animals (stones) can talk a (#56)	25	26	32	19	46 *	20
4. Professional prophets can foretell future b (#58)	92 *	61			79 *	40
5. Cook can use medicine to get wages raised c (#60)	25 *	0	29	22	66 *	20
6. Ghosts can produce sickness (#65)	46 *	9				
7. Brothers can never be friends (#54)	13	30	40	30	39	46
8. Good-tasting food is healthful (#64)					92 *	62
VALUES						
9. Eloping woman disgraces her village d (#57)	96	83	60	68	91	86
10. Groom's family should offer special gifts (#60)					99	77
11. Chief should always be obeyed (#62)	58 *	9	76 *	44	94	80
12. Wife earning money should not spend it as she pleases (#66)	54 *	91	69	49	49	66
13. Improper for cross-cousins to marry (#60)					85	78
14. People were happier in old days (#51)	46	39	46	46		
15. Life in heaven is better than life on earth (#59)	69	70	33 *	57	57	43
16. World is dangerous, people evil (#61)	75	87	59	49	70	83
17. People should think of cheerful things if worrying (#70)	88	77	7 *	32	54 *	89
18. People should talk less and work more (#76)	91	100	75	83	81	91
19. Liars will be punished in the next world (#77)	83	78	64	65	81	74
20. Failure results from secret plots of others (#79)	50	39	58	58	70	69
21. Index of "traditionalism" (mean)	3.7 *	2.1	2.7 *	1.9	4.3 *	2.6

a. For Zulu: "A chief can make it rain" (#53).

b. For Zulu: "A native doctor can treat any disease" (#58).

c. For Zulu: "Sick may die if seen by 'unclean' persons" (#63).

d. For Ganda: "Eldest son should be father's heir" (#58). For Zulu: "Man getting wife by abduction should be punished" (#56).

TABLE 9. *Skill, Reasoning, and Abstraction*

	LUO		GANDA		ZULU		JAMAICA	
	low	*high*	*low*	*high*	*low*	*high*	*low*	*high*
Maximum number of informants [a]	24	23	63	70	63	37	89	23
VISUAL RETENTION TEST (#47)								
1. Inability to grasp instructions	63 *	22	15 *	3	44 *	6	25 *	0
2. Number correct (mean)	3.3 *	7.9	5.4 *	10.1	7.1 *	9.9	6.6 *	11.2
3. Three or more mirror images	0	6	41 *	16	29 *	6	39 *	9
4. Completion time (mean, in seconds)	108	140	149 *	126	153 *	120	84 *	58
EMBEDDED FIGURES TEST (#84)								
5. Inability to grasp instructions	83 *	30	30	11	65 *	21	46 *	0
6. Perfect score or one error	0	13	4 *	36	2 *	21	7 *	48
7. One or more mirror images	17	13	20	9	16	15	32	13
8. Distracted by lines	41	38	33	31	35	33	62 *	4
9. Denies existence of embedded figure	41	24	41 *	18	45	48	6	4
10. Performance improved during series	0	14	20	34	8 *	32	4	9
SORTING TEST [b] (#48)								
11. Inability to grasp instructions	8	0	18 *	4	16 *	3	6	0
12. Number correct (mean)	1.9 *	2.9	2.0	2.6	2.0	2.7	0.9	1.8
13 First solution: one attribute only	63	74	50	47	56	53	62	67
14. First solution: small insignia	40	52	43 *	22	40	35	33	24
15. First solution: color	32	17	29	38	26	12	38	19
16. Three solutions: varied	20	57	36	43	7	23	52 *	82

TABLE 9. (*cont.*)

	Luo		Ganda		Zulu		Jamaica	
	low	high	low	high	low	high	low	high
17. Three solutions: insignia at least once	67	91	75	82	83	90	34	52
18. Three solutions: color at least once	73	95	83	98	69	77	38	57
19. Three solutions: shape at least once	27	61	18	37	14	23	38 *	90
20. Perfect verbal description	36	65	41	54	26	47	36 *	64
RECALL OF COMMUNICATION c (#46, 75)								
21. Inability to recall anything			44 *	11	42 *	18	25	18
22. Correct recall of two or more ideas			7 *	57	34	41	50	18
23. One or more false attributions, among those recalling			78 *	43	83 *	23	0	5
RORSCHACH TEST d (#71–74)								
24. Rejects first plate	8	0	9	9	27	29	17	4
25. Rejects one or more plates	17	4	32 *	19	44	35		
26. Accounts one or more times for entire plate e	79 *	100	88	96	63	75	37 *	65
27. One or more S responses	42	65	30	42	17	29	2	0
28. Plate VI: response of animal without specifying type	11 *	47	32	50	51	68	24	43
29. Plate VIII: response of animal without specifying type	4 *	30	44	44	63	56	23	44
30. Plate II: response of human part, not whole human being			67	67	18	50		
31. Plate III: response of human part, not whole human being	0 *	36	4	17	11	33		

TABLE 9. (cont.)

	LUO		GANDA		ZULU		JAMAICA	
	low	high	low	high	low	high	low	high
32. Color responses (mean)	0.7 *	1.2	0.8	0.9	0.7	0.5		
33. Shading responses (mean)	0.4 *	1.2	0.5	0.7	0.5	0.7		
34. One or more color or black-and-white responses	79	96	78	81	60	76	36	43
35. One or more movement responses	50	74	60	75	59	56	22	26
DRAWINGS (#18–21)								
36. Rejects first card	4	0	22 *	4	9	0	0	0
37. Inability to respond to very vague drawing	14	4	26 *	8	27 *	2	17	0
38. Responds with difficulty (rating)	14	0	22	13	58 *	19		
MISCELLANEOUS								
39. Time to make value judgments (mean, in seconds) (#49–70)	14.4 *	10.7	10.0 *	7.9	11.8 *	8.3		
40. Stereoscopic pictures: provides organized impressions (#89)							26 *	74
41. Stereoscopic picture: refers to snow (#89)							9 *	78
42. Rejects first sentence-completion task (#90)							10	0
43. Ability to note new blocks added to old collection (#126)							11	8

a. Percentages showing detailed behavior are based upon informants able to carry out the test in question.

b. For Jamaica: based upon two solutions only.

c. For Jamaica: based upon only very small samples of the poorly educated informants, so that "low" here means 3 years of education or less, "high" between 4 and 6 years.

d. Based upon three plates for the African societies, two for Jamaica.

e. For Jamaica: Plate VIII only.

TABLE 10. *Judgments Concerning Time in Jamaica*

	low	high	rural	urban
Maximum number of informants	89	23	46	43
SUBJECTIVE TIME				
1. Experiences difference between subjective and objective time (#44, 45)	86	100	77 *	94
2. Claims time passes slowly when little to do, and vice versa (#44)	7 *	64	6	8
3. Claims time passes slowly in "bad" times, and vice versa (#44)	47 *	0	62 *	33
4. Claims time passes differently as age increases (#45)	97	95	94	100
5. Claims time passes more slowly as age increases (#45)	30 *	5	36	23
ESTIMATE OF LENGTH OF INTERVIEW (#85)				
6. Correct or within 10 minutes	38	59	51 *	25
7. Underestimates	11	12	15	7
8. Overestimates	76	48	66	84
ESTIMATE OF 15-SECOND INTERVAL (#86)				
9. Literally correct	6	4	7	4
10. Underestimates within 4 seconds	11	9	9	13
11. Underestimates (total)	48 *	22	49	49
12. Overestimates within 4 seconds	6	9	5	7
13. Overestimates by more than 1 minute	9	4	12	7
14. Overestimates (total)	44 *	74	33	47
REPRODUCTION OF 10-SECOND INTERVAL (#87)				
15. Literally correct	4	0	7	0
16. Underestimates within 2 seconds	11	9	9	13
17. Underestimates (total)	58	70	56	61
18. Overestimates within 2 seconds	11	9	7	15
19. Overestimates by more than 30 seconds	5	0	7	2
20. Overestimates (total)	37	30	35	39

TABLE 1. *Beliefs of African Children and Adults*

	LUO			GANDA					ZULU		
					boys[b]						
Maximum number of informants	*low*[a]	*boys*	*high*[a]	*low*	*young*	*old*	*boys*[c]	*high*	*low*	*boys*	*high*
	24	101	23	57	118	97	113	69	67	101	35
MOTIVES											
1. World is a dangerous place	75	72	87	59	32	36	23*	49	70	72	83
2. Waste of time to plan	42	28	17	22*	46	33‡	16	16			
3. Threat of punishment is more painful than the punishment itself	63	70	74	80*	54	65	66*	86	58	63	63
OLD SOCIETY											
4. Brothers can never be friends	13	17	30	40	40	30	16*	30	39	42	46
5. Kinship is closer than friendship									59	50	37
6. Wife earning money may spend it as she pleases	13	30*	4	8*†			21*	42	39*	23	31
7. Groom's family should offer extra gifts									90*	69	77
8. Man getting wife by abduction should be punished									91	81	86
9. A chief should always be obeyed	58*†	33*	9	76*	66	58	32	44	94*†	73	80
10. Leaders are more important than followers				87*†	66	73		64			
OUT-GROUP											
11. Impossible for African to have European friend	38*	16	27	20			11	19	37	25	31
12. Government helps only the rich	38	26	48			23			84*	51*	80
OTHER PEOPLE											
13. People should talk less and work more	91	86	100	75	52	52	78	83	81	78	91
14. Should be successful in spite of others' jealousy	25*	58*	22	54		52	72	61	36*	77*	23

Table I. (cont.)

	LUO			GANDA					ZULU		
	low[a]	boys	high[a]	low	young[b]	old[b]	boys[c]	high	low	boys	high
15. Should speak only well of one's rival	91*	69*	91	91*	72	89	67*	94			
16. Should conserve soil or be punished	33*	72*	26	40	56	47	55	42			
17. Ability is more important than luck				22†	41	30		44			
BELIEFS											
18. Polygynist can be good Christian	58	38	57	38*	31	24	7*	42			
19. Some people can change into animals	21	21*	44	43	16	11	16	33			
20. Some animals (stones) can talk	25*	52*	26	32	16	8	8*	19			
21. Cook can use medicine to get wages raised[d]	25†	23*	0	29	21	16	31	22	79*†	38	40
22. Chief can make it rain	46*†	29*	9						46*†	8	20
23. Ghosts can produce illness[e]									66*†	13	20
24. Good-tasting food is healthful									92*†	41	62
VALUES											
25. Eldest son should be father's heir	46	42	39	60‡	40	30‡	16*	68			
26. People were happier in old days				46‡	41	24	16*	46	57	66	43
27. Life in heaven is better than life on earth	67*	43*	70	33*†	70	72	68	57	81	70	74
28. Liars will be punished in next world	83	63	78	64			81	65			

* Significant difference between figure so marked and one immediately to its right.

† Significant difference between "low" and "high" adults.

‡ Significant difference between figure so marked and the second one to its right.

a. Adults divided into the same educational groups as on Tables 1–9.

b. Boys from a secondary school run by African authorities, divided on basis of years of schooling.

c. Boys from a secondary school run by missionaries.

d. For Zulu: "A native doctor can treat any disease."

e. For Zulu: "Sick may die if seen by 'unclean' person"

TABLE II. *Beliefs, Values, and Fears of Ganda Secondary School Boys*

	Grade	
	Lower	Upper
Maximum number of informants	118	97

AUTHORITY

	Lower	Upper
1. A younger person should never contradict an older one	79 *	92
2. Children must learn to obey and respect authority	92	98
3. A leader should never change his mind	81	78

EUROPEANS

	Lower	Upper
4. I want respect from Europeans more than from Africans	10	15
5. I admire Europeans more than Africans	20	29
6. European clothes are more attractive than African	64	74
7. I prefer European to African style of house	61	61

FEARS AND PROBLEMS

	Lower	Upper
8. I often find it difficult to get to sleep	29	26
9. I am often afraid without reason	40 *	54
10. I tend to worry about death a great deal	52	44
11. I often wish to strike an unkind friend	17	12
12. Most of my dreams are unpleasant	36	40
13. I worry about my health a great deal	63 *	80
14. I remember happy rather than unhappy events	70	68
15. I work better when praised than when scolded	60	71

* Differs significantly from the figure to the right.

TABLE III. *Beliefs of Zulu Women*

	Stable Urban	Urban	Rural
Maximum number of informants	70	56	36

FAMILY PRACTICES

	Stable Urban	Urban	Rural
1. Groom's family should offer special gifts	89 (84) [a]	95	100 (91) [a]
2. Wife earning money may spend it as she pleases	31 * (30)	7	8 (45 †)
3. A man may choose wife without his own parent's consent	56 *	0	6
4. A woman should be married by her dead husband's brother	39 *	22	81
5. Second child should not arrive before weaning of the first child	100	98	100
6. A husband should never beat his wife	90	83	86
7. An unmarried woman should not have a child	97	100	94
8. An unmarried son should give father his earnings	97	96	100
9. Women should want many children	67	79	97
10. A married woman should never have a lover	89	100	100
11. A woman should never marry someone from her own clan	99	96	100
12. Poor, helpless relatives must be supported	75	94	92
13. A woman should respectfully avoid her parents-in-law	81 *	93	100

"FACTS"

	Stable Urban	Urban	Rural
14. Chief can make it rain	37 (20 †)	39	49 (82 †)
15. Native doctors can treat any disease	29 (50 †)	13	46 (100 †)
16. Sick may die if seen by "unclean" persons	44 * (32)	54	77 (91)
17. Deceased ancestors can cause child's illness	60 *	69	100
18. Illness may result from intercourse with menstruating woman	71 *	93	94
19. Character eventually depends upon training by older children	93	91	97

TABLE III. (*cont.*)

	Stable Urban	Urban	Rural
20. Wealth in money is better than in cattle	73 * (73)	61	9 (18)
21. Polygynist can be a good Christian	21 * (57 †)	34	51 (73 †)
22. A lie is always wrong	74 *	86	100
23. Zulu women should not brew beer for sale	76 *	89	97
24. Stealing is never justified	99	98	100

* Differs significantly from rural group.
† Difference between males and females is statistically significant.
a. Figures in parentheses are for comparable males.

303

TABLE A. *Indian-White Study*

(Based on Havighurst and Neugarten, 1955, pp. 187–9)

	(1) [a] Accultura- tion	(2) Midwest vs. Southwest	(3) Midwest vs. Sioux	(4) Navaho Mt. vs. Shiprock
GOALS				
1. Individual achievement (1) [b]	+.19	MW	MW	O [c]
2. Self-gratification (1)	+.64 *	MW	MW	S
3. Self-restraint (2)	+.48	MW	MW	S
FAMILY				
4. Positive emotions toward family (1)	−.17	MW	O	NM
5. Negative emotions toward family (1)	+.11	MW	MW	NM
6. Praise of family (2)	−.64 *	? [d]	?	NM
7. Condemnation of family (2)	−.11	?	?	O
8. Positive emotion toward father (1)	−.46	SW	O	S
9. Negative emotion toward father (1)	−.04	O	O	O
10. Praise of father (2)	−.56 *	SW	O	NM
11. Condemnation of father (2)	−.40	SW	O	NM
12. Positive emotion toward mother (1)	+.29	O	SX	O
13. Negative emotion toward mother (1)	+.53 *	MW	O	O
14. Praise of mother (2)	+.16	SW	SX	NM
15. Condemnation of mother (2)	+.22	SW	SX	NM
AUTHORITY				
16. Discipline of others (1)	−.25	O	O	O
17. Obedience (2)	+.52	MW	MW	S
OTHER PEOPLE				
18. Regard for others (2)	−.01	O	SX	S
19. Service to others (2)	−.33	SW	SX	S
20. Smooth personal relations (1)	−.41	SW	SX	S
21. Embarrassment before others (1)	−.69 *	SW	SX	NM
22. Aggression toward peers (2)	−.07	O	SX	O

304

TABLE A. *(cont.)*

	(1) [a] Accultura- tion	(2) Midwest vs. Southwest	(3) Midwest vs. Sioux	(4) Navaho Mt. vs. Shiprock
23. Positive emotions toward people (1)	+.34	SW	SX	S
24. Negative emotions toward people (1)	+.32	SW	O	S
25. Praise of people (2)	+.50 *	?	?	O
26. Condemnation of people (2)	+.15	?	?	NM

CONCEPTUALIZATION OF PEOPLE

27. Competence (2)	−.65 *	SW	O	NM
28. Personal virtues (2)	−.21	O	O	NM
29. Aggression by others (1)	−.14	SW	SX	S

EXPLANATIONS

30. Supernatural (1)	−.50 *	SW	SX	NM
31. Animism (4)	−.84 *	?	?	NM

VALUES

32. Unchangeability of rules (3)	−.57 *	?	?	?
33. Immanent justice (4)	−.48	?	?	NM
34. Property (2)	+.01	SW	SX	S
35. Possession (1)	−.31	SW	O	S
36. Work (1)	−.36	O	O	NM
37. Work (2)	−.61 *	SW	SX	NM
38. Stealing (2)	−.03	SW	SX	O

* Significantly above chance.

a. Figures in column (1) are *rho's;* for an explanation of the other columns, see pp. 55–6.

b. Numbers in parentheses refer to the tests from which each measure has been derived; see pp. 52–6 of the text.

c. O = no difference; or difference not statistically significant.

d. ? = no data provided.

TABLE B. *Mean Number of Rorschach Responses:*
Adult Section of the Indian-White Study [1]
(Based on Kaplan, 1954, pp. 11, 13, 18)

	Navaho			Zuni			Spanish-Americans			Mormons		
	Non-Vet.	Vet.	Total	Non-Vet.	Vet.	Total	Non-Vet.	Vet.	Total	Non-Vet.	Vet.	Total
1. A%	55	50	53 a	55	61	59 a	70	57	63	59	52	55
2. T/R* (seconds)	113	91	98 ab	79	63	70 a	56	63	59 c	54	41	48 bc
3. R	19	28	23	23	25	24	18	23	20 a	25	34	30 a
4. W%	28	32	30	28	31	30	31	27	29	24	21	22
5. M*	.8	2.6	1.5	1.7	2.5	2.1 a	.7	1.3	1.1 ab	2	2.6	2.3 b
6. F%	33	39	37 a	48	40	44	46	51	48 a	45	40	43
7. FC*	1.4	3.0	2.4	.7	3.0	1.9 a	.9	2.7	1.7 b	3.0	3.6	3.3 ab
8. CF*	1.8	2.6	2.1 abc	.9	1.2	1.1 a	.9	.9	.9 c	.8	1.8	1.2 b

* Difference in this row between all nonveterans and veterans is significant or approaches significance.

1. See p. 56.

a, b, c. Difference between pairs in a row with the same letter is significant.

TABLE C. *Menomini Indians* [a]

(Based on Spindler 1955, pp. 111, 113, 213–24)

	A	B	C	D	E	W	rt [b]
Number of informants	17	13	15	10	13	12	
BACKGROUND							
1. Father "poorly" educated	100	100	100	80	54	75	.75 *
2. Non-Christian father (at birth)	100	85	100	20	23	0	.67 *
3. Non-Christian mother (at birth)	100	85	80	30	31	0	.62 *
CONTACTS							
4. "Poorly" educated	65	54	33	10	15	42	.77 *
5. Movie attendance: seldom or never	65	62	33	10	31	33	.55 *
6. No radio	65	46	33	0	0	17	.70 *
7. Church attendance: seldom or never	0	0	42	20	0	0	.59 *
8. "Full" knowledge of native language	88	54	40	30	31	0	.60 *
BELIEFS							
9. Familiar with native beliefs	100	85	67	10	31		.89 *
GENERAL PRACTICES							
10. Occupation: native, irregular, etc.	59	46	40	20	0	17	.56 *
11. Use of native objects	100	85	33	10	23		.88 *
12. Playing of native games	71	50	15	0	0	0	.88 *
13. "Excessive" drinking	59	31	53	50	0	17	.18
14. Largely dependent upon native medicine	35	46	0	0	0		.82 *
PRACTICES IN HOME							
15. Native house, hut, or shack	41	23	13	0	0	0	.64 *
16. Homemade furniture	53	23	20	10	0	0	.65 *
17. Outdoor or no privy	94	77	60	60	23	58	.62 *

TABLE C. *(cont.)*

	A	B	C	D	E	W	rt [b]	A vs. D [c]	A vs. E [c]
18. No pump or running water	59	54	13	0	0	0	.83 *		
19. Iron space heater	100	69	67	40	8	42	.70 *		
RORSCHACH TEST									
20. Human response to Plate III	59	31	47	50	54	58			
21. Human movement responses equal to or greater than animal responses	6	53	13	0	15	42			
22. Few human movement responses	88	46	67	100	46	50			.04
23. Few animal movement responses	29	77	73	80	77	83		.04	.05
24. Few W responses	59	38	47	10	46	67		.05	
25. Part and whole animal and human responses: low proportion of detail	65	85	40	50	38	50			
26. No main color responses	71	15	20	10	23	8		.05	.01
27. Slow mean reaction time	59	46	33	10	15	0		.03	.05
28. Number of responses (mean)	17	20	21	20	27	28			.001

* Significantly above chance.

a. Figures in the first six columns are percentages; see pp. 56–8.

b. Tetrachoric correlations based upon a comparison of groups A and B with groups C, D, and E.

c. Statistically significant *p*-values based upon the investigator's own calculation of chi-square or *t*.

TABLE D. *Mean Number of Rorschach Responses: Ojibwa Study* [a]
(Based on Hallowell, 1955, pp. 350, 352)

| | Berens River | | | Lac du Flambeau |
	Inland	Lakeside	Total	Total
Maximum number of informants	44	58	102	115
1. H	6 *	4 *	5	1
2. Hd	4 *	3 *	4	2
3. A%	49	47	50	53
4. R	25 *	29 *	27	17
5. % R to last three cards	38 *	40 *	39	33
6. M	4 *	3 *	3	1
7. FM	3 *	3	3	3
8. m	.02	.3	.2	.2
9. W	5	5	5	5
10. Sum of C	.5	1.7 *	1.2	1

* Significant difference between the figure so designated and that for Lac du Flambeau, as determined by chi-square and not by comparing the given means.
  a. See p. 58.

TABLE E. TAT Responses of Japanese and Americans in Chicago [a]
(Based on Caudill, 1952, tables 3, 4, and 5)

	Issei	Nisei	Lower Middle White	Upper Lower White
Maximum number of informants	30	40	40	20
MOTIVES				
1. Self-motivation in male [b]	93 *	58	75 *	35
2. Self-motivation in female	43	55	47	30
3. Upward mobility	67	50	60	
4. Defeatism	20 *	43	23	25
5. Discontent	57	62	45	65
FAMILY				
6. Favorable attitude toward mother	20	25	45	
7. Favorable attitude toward father	53	58	70 *	35
8. Favorable attitude toward parents	37	25	10	5
OTHER PEOPLE				
9. Male aggression against female	70	62	70	
10. Favorable attitude toward female	93	78 *	53	60
11. Female aggression	23	40		

* Differs significantly from the figure to the right.

a. See p. 209.

b. Each item refers to a response to a particular TAT drawing; in this instance, for example, the investigator's own caption mentions Picture 1 and reads: "Boy is self-motivating to be a violinist (a long-range goal)."

APPENDIX B *The Interviewing Schedule*

THE SCHEDULE reproduced here was followed in the Africa-Jamaica studies during private interviews with adults which lasted two to three hours. The items are numbered consecutively so that easy reference to them can be made in the ten tables (pp. 282–98) which summarize the research. Unless an item was used exclusively in Jamaica, the wording is exactly the one that served as the basis for translation into an African language. Omissions include:

1. Minor variations in wording that a particular culture or language demanded.

2. Explanations that established the investigator's role and sought to diminish an informant's hostility or anxiety and to encourage or thank him, as well as to clarify the rationale of certain procedures; as a reward and a respite, for example, many Africans were shown stereoscopic pictures two or three times during the interview.

3. Probing questions that were necessary when the original items did not elicit information.

4. Certain items that appeared only in the earliest version of the schedule in a society or that were used only among small groups.

Two additional guides may be helpful: (a) The name in parentheses preceding an item or part indicates the society or societies where the item was used; if the name "Africa" is there, it was used in the three African societies but not in Jamaica; if there is no name and if no alternative appears subsequently after the same number, it was used in all four societies. (b) The order in which the different parts were administered was substantially the same in the three African societies but not in Jamaica. In addition, the Jamaican sample was confronted with some tests

311

not tried in Africa. For these reasons, most of the parts are numbered differently for Jamaica, and also parts XIV–XXI refer only to Jamaica.

The text and the tables of this book do not refer to items of the schedule that were included for some purpose unrelated to acculturation, but all items are reproduced here in order to make known the precise content of the interview.

With amused but genuine embarrassment I must admit that I have forgotten the sources of many items which were used to measure beliefs and values and which, I am now inclined to think, I myself did not design. At the time the schedule was first organized in Uganda in 1954, items were desperately seized when they seemed to fit the problem at hand. Some came from lists I had prepared before leaving my files at Yale University. Others had to be pulled out of my memory since library facilities were either absent or inadequate. In a few instances printed sources in Africa could be consulted. At any rate, for interesting but unimportant reasons, my scattered notes on sources have not survived. Formal, scholarly research to locate the proper progenitors and owners has been difficult and boring, for I often deliberately altered the original form of some items in order to adapt them to Africans and Jamaicans. Retroactive inhibition has necessarily occurred during five years or more. And I lack patience and motivation. At this moment, the search does disclose that items 70, 76, and 79 have been derived, in whole or in part, from Adorno et al. (1950, pp. 255–6); items 27, 28, and 61 from Gillespie and Allport (1955, pp. 47–9); and items 53, 56, and 60 from Musgrove (1952, p. 238). To others whose contribution I cannot acknowledge, I would apologize and say: I confess, I am guilty, I really did plan to pay you in the usual academic currency of footnotes, and to atone for my crime I shall wear for twenty-four nights a scarlet letter in honor of your surname if you call the theft to my attention.

I. Direct Questions (Jamaica: Part II)

1. What is your occupation?
2. (Jamaica: omitted) When you are at work, what kinds of

people do you see most frequently: Europeans, Asians, or Africans?

3. (Jamaica: omitted) Do you own land? How much?

4. How old are you? (Africa: if necessary) Who was chief (or king) when you were born?

5. Have you gone to school? How far did you go in school?

6. What is your religion?

7. (Zulu) Where do most of your relatives live? (Jamaica) Are you married? How many children do you have?

8. (Africa) Do you own a bicycle, motorcycle, motor car, gramophone, wireless?

9. (Africa) When you were a child, who was kindest to you?

10. (Africa) When you were a child or before you went to school, who taught you the most?

11. (Africa) When you were a child, whom did you love the most?

12. (Africa) When you were a child, whom did you respect the most?

13. (Africa) As a young child, did you always live with your parents except for very short periods away from home?

14. (Africa) When you were a child, with which member of your family did you quarrel most?

15. (Ganda) What should be done with people who ride bicycles carelessly? (Jamaica) What sort of music do you like?

16. (Luo, Ganda) What should be done with people who do not cooperate with the government in checking soil erosion? (Zulu, Jamaica) What should make you decide which food to eat when you have a choice of food?

17. (Ganda) What should be done with young children who steal unimportant things? (Zulu) What makes you decide whether you like a musical selection?

II. TAT-Type Projective Drawings (Jamaica: Part III)

> *I have some pictures here that I am going to show you. After each picture I shall tell you who the people are supposed to be, and then you tell me what you think is happening. What are the people doing?*

18. A chief and his subject. (Jamaica) Two Jamaicans, one rich, the other poor.

19. A European and an African; between them are other people. (Jamaica) A group of Jamaicans, and this is a shopkeeper.

20. A father and his son.

21. This time you tell me what you see.

III. Open-Ended Questions (Jamaica: Part VII)

22. Do you often make plans for yourself or your family which cannot be completed for a year or so? What are they about?

23. What do you think you will be doing (in your occupation) five years from now?

24. You have just said what you think you will be doing five years from now; is this what you would like to be doing? What would you rather be doing?

25. (Jamaica) As time goes on, does everything in your life seem better or worse to you?

26. (Jamaica) As time goes on, do you think the world in general gets better or worse?

27. What would you like to do during your life that would make you happiest and most proud of yourself?

28. (Africa) Aside from being put in prison or acquiring a very bad disease, (Africa and Jamaica) what is the worst thing that could happen to you during your lifetime?

29. If a person says he would give you £5 now or £50 one year from now, which would you choose?

30. If you were given £500 and told to spend the money within a week, how would you spend it?

31. (Zulu) If you had things your own way, would you like to live in a city or in the country? (Jamaica) If you run into a lot of bad luck, who or what do you blame?

32. (Africa) What do you like and not like about (Luo, Location; Ganda, Saza; Zulu, tribal) chiefs?

33. (Africa) What do you like and not like about (Luo, Headman; Ganda, Gombolola; Zulu, village) chiefs?

34. (Africa) What do you like and not like about (Luo, Subheadman; Ganda, Miruka; Zulu, Advisory Board) chiefs?

35. What do you like and not like about your present occupation?

36. (Africa) What do you like and not like about the Europeans you know?

37. (Africa) What do you like and not like about the Indians (Asians) you know?

38. (Ganda, Zulu) What do you like and not like about (Ganda, the governor of Uganda; Zulu, the nationalist government)?

39. (Africa) What qualities should a good chief possess?

40. (Africa) Have you ever had a European for a close friend?

41. (Africa) Have you ever had an Indian for a close friend?

42. (Africa) What kinds of people do you admire most: Africans, Asians, Europeans (Zulu: colored people), or some other type of people? (Jamaica) What sort of person or man do you respect most?

43. (Africa) Whom do you want most to respect and admire you: Africans, Asians, Europeans (Zulu: colored people), or some other type of people? (Jamaica) What sort of person do you want most to respect you?

44. (Jamaica) Does time seem to you to go slower or faster once in a while? When slower? When faster?

45. (Jamaica) Does time in general seem to pass slower or faster for you as you grow older?

IV. *Presentation of the Communication (Jamaica: Part VI)*

> *Note:* The text below was used only among the Ganda; the same procedure was used among the Zulu and in Jamaica, but the text concerned nutrition; the communication was omitted for every sixth informant who thus served as a control.

46. Now I would like to read a brief statement which recently appeared in a Kampala newspaper. Just sit back and listen to it.

> Good soil is essential to man. It takes hundreds of years to make the minerals in the soil and many years to make humus or top soil, but man can lose that soil in a few seasons

unless he uses his brain and is prepared to work efficiently.

The danger of soil erosion exists everywhere in the world, but that danger is very great in Africa because of the hot sun and long dry seasons when the soil dries and cracks; because of the heavy rains at other times when the dry and dusty soil can be swept away; because of large treeless areas which expose land to hot sun and hard rain with no tree roots to hold up the soil; and because of ignorance among farmers of the danger.

Here in Uganda the soil is our principal source of wealth. Each year we obtain from it over 410,000 bales of cotton; 27,000 tons of coffee; 2,400,000 pounds of tobacco; and countless other crops. We must preserve this soil. To prevent soil erosion, therefore, all of our governmental services are engaged in programs which require the cooperation of everyone. Those people who do not cooperate must be severely punished. Otherwise our soil will disappear.

a. Do you think this article is written in an interesting manner?
b. Do you think the Ganda like to hear about such matters?

V. *Visual Retention Test* (*Jamaica: Part I*)

47. This is Form F of the test designed by Benton (1950): a geometrical design is exposed for 10 seconds and then removed; the informant is then shown four designs and is asked to "point to the one which you have just seen": 19 designs are thus exhibited.

VI. *Sorting Test* (*Jamaica: Part V*)

48. This is a simplified version, designed by the writer, of many previous tests, particularly that of Goldstein and Scheerer (1941). The materials consist of 16 pieces of cardboard which differ with respect to four primary colors, four shapes, and two sizes and to each of which a small silver or gold star or arrow has been affixed in the center. The basic instruction to the informant is to "sort these pieces into piles; put those in one pile which seem to

belong together, which have something in common; put as many in each pile as you wish and have as many piles as you wish." Africans were asked to repeat the assignment twice; Jamaicans once.

VII. Closed Questions (Jamaica: Part XIII)

> *Note:* Informants were told that "I want you to tell me whether on the whole you agree or disagree with each statement." The order of the statements in Jamaica was different, and some were phrased as open-ended questions.

49. (Africa) A person should not become too successful because people will be jealous of him.

50. It is usually a waste of time to plan for the future because too many unforeseen events can interfere with the plan.

51. (Luo, Ganda) People used to be happier in the past than they are at present. (Zulu) It is better for a man to have his wealth in money than in cattle.

52. (Africa) A man with more than one wife can be a good Christian.

53. (Luo, Ganda) Some people can change into real animals. (Zulu) A hereditary chief can intercede with his ancestors to make it rain.

54. (Africa) Brothers can never be friends.

55. The threat of punishment is usually more painful than the punishment itself.

56. (Luo, Ganda) Some animals (Ganda: stones) can talk. (Zulu) A young man who attempts to get a wife by abduction should be severely punished.

57. Luck is as important as ability in determining success. (Luo) A woman who marries by eloping brings permanent disgrace to her people and her home.

58. (Luo) Professional prophets can predict the future at all times. (Ganda) The eldest son should always be his father's heir. (Zulu) A native doctor can treat any disease.

59. Life in the next world (heaven) is better than life in this world.

60. (Africa) A cook can put something into his employer's food to get his wages raised. (Zulu) The groom's family should offer certain gifts in addition to a dowry; it is right and proper for cross-cousins to marry.

61. (Africa) The world is a dangerous place in which men are very evil and dangerous.

62. (Africa) A peasant ought always to obey his chief under all circumstances.

63. (Africa) A person should speak only well of his rival behind his back, even when that rival has been spreading false tales about him. (Zulu) A man who is sick may die if he is touched by the shadow of an unclean person (i.e., a menstruating woman).

64. (Africa) A person who does not cooperate with the government in preventing soil erosion should be put in prison for a year. (Zulu) Food which tastes good never fails to help people remain strong and healthy.

65. (Africa) Kinship is closer than friendship. (Luo) Sickness and other misfortunes can be produced by ghosts.

66. A wife who earns money should be allowed to spend it as she pleases without asking her husband's permission.

67. (Africa) Which person is more likely to be successful: (a) a person who carefully plans his existence and then makes every effort to carry out those plans or (b) a person who quickly changes whatever plans he has to take advantage of every new opportunity which is offered him?

68. (Africa) Which person is more likely to be a successful farmer: (a) a person with modern ideas about how to farm or (b) a person with a great deal of practical experience in farming?

69. (Africa) Who is more important in helping people improve their lives: (a) the people's leaders or (b) the people themselves?

70. What should a person do who has a problem or worry: (a) keep thinking about it or (b) keep busy with more cheerful things?

VIII. Rorschach Plates (*Jamaica: Part IV*)

71. (Africa) Plate II
72. (Africa) Plate III
73. Plate VI
74. Plate VIII

IX. Recall of Communication (*Jamaica: Part XVI*)

75. This part was omitted among the Luo and for those informants in the other societies who served as controls; the instructions were: "You recall that a few minutes ago I read you a statement which appeared in a newspaper. Now would you tell me as much of it as you can remember; what did it say?"

X. Test of Suggestibility

> *Note:* All informants were asked to indicate whether they agreed or disagreed with each statement. Those acting as controls heard the statements without attribution; one experimental group among the Ganda and Zulu heard them attributed to "most Europeans"; and another experimental group in the same societies and also among the Luo heard them attributed to "most" members of their own society. (The test itself was not used in Jamaica but some of the items appeared as open-ended questions in Part XIII.)

76. Everyone would be happier if people would talk less and work more.

77. People who tell lies in this world will be punished in the next world.

78. (Africa) The present laws of the government help rich people more than poor people.

79. We fail because of the difficulties other people secretly put in our way.

80. (Africa) A chief (Zulu: school inspector) is justified in taking local government (Zulu: school-meal) funds to pay his bus fare to visit his parents provided he repays them later.

81. (Africa) It is possible for an African to have a European as a close friend.

82. (Africa) A headman (Ganda: Gombolola chief; Zulu: tribal chief) should treat his own brother like any other person charged with crime if that brother is brought before him and charged with theft.

83. (Luo) Long-time security can be attained as easily by working in a city as by working on the land. (Ganda) The people of Uganda will benefit greatly when more industries come to this country. (Zulu) People working in factories lead happier lives than those working on farms.

XI. Embedded Figures Test

84. Eight figures which Witkin (1950) has adapted from Gottschaldt and which he kindly made available to the writer were used, but his procedure was altered. The instructions in part were: "I am going to show you sets of drawings. One is a simple one, the other is larger and more complicated. Your task is to find the simple figure in the larger one. It will always be there, the same size, the same shape, and in the same position."

XII. Time

85. (Ganda, Jamaica) How long do you think you and I have been talking here?

86. (Jamaica) I shall say "ready" and then "stop"—you tell me how much time has gone by. (Note: The interval was 15 seconds.)

87. (Jamaica) Now you say "ready" and then say "stop" when you think 10 seconds have gone by.

XIII. Preference for Forms (Zulu only)

88. I shall show you two drawings; you tell me which you like more. (Note: Three paired comparisons of circle, triangle, and square.)

XIV. Stereoscopic Pictures (Jamaica only: *Part VIII*)

89. (Jamaica) Now I am going to show you some pictures in this machine; look at each one and tell me what you see. (*Note:* The first four and the sixth were conventional scenes projected stereoscopically; the fifth and seventh offered a dark-skinned figure to one eye and a light-skinned figure to the other eye; the eight was like the seventh except—to test further for eye dominance—the position of the figures was reversed.)

XV. Sentence Completion (Jamaica only: *Part IX*)

> *Note:* Informants were instructed to say "what comes into your mind, say it quick."

90. Fathers frequently . . .
91. White people always . . .
92. Religion is . . .
93. Poor people never . . .
94. Mothers frequently . . .
95. Food should . . .
96. Rich people never . . .
97. Money is . . .

XVI. Open-Ended Questions (Jamaica only: *Part X*)

98. If you meet someone for the first time, what do you notice about him that makes you like or not like him?

99. What sort of person would you want to be like if you could change positions with him?

100. What else in life brings you joy or pleasure (besides your job)?

101. What sorts of people do you think are important here? What do you like and not like about them?

102. Do these people want men like you to better yourself, to improve your lot? Why?

103. Do you feel that you have a chance to get ahead here? Why?

104. Are you better or worse off than your mother was at your age?

105. Are you better off than your brothers and sisters?

106. When you were a boy, what did your family do for a living?

107. Was your family better off than your grandmother's when she was young?

108. When you were a little boy, did you know what your mother wanted you to be when you grew up?

109. What do you want your oldest boy to do when he grows up?

XVII. Reference Group (Jamaica only: Part XII)

Note: For one half of the informants, each of the following questions began with "What will happen . . ."; for the other half they began "What do some people say will happen . . ."

110. if a person makes a wish when a star falls?
111. if a person with child drinks a lot of milk?
112. if a mother cuts her baby's hair before the baby talks?
113. if a woman has no children?
114. if you eat food which tastes good and which you like?
115. if you see a shadow and no person is near?
116. if a child does not obey his mother and father?
117. if you cut a baby's nails?
118. if a person tells lies?
119. if you dream something is going to take place?

XVIII. Various Questions (Jamaica only: Part XIII)

Note: Other questions in this part have been noted elsewhere; for example, see Part X.

120. Do dreams sometimes have in them messages from the dead?

121. What does the moon do to our lives?

122. People in Jamaica are all friendly to one another, they don't worry at all about the color of a man's skin.

123. Some people are born to become good, others to become bad.

XIX. Photographs (Jamaica only: Part XIV)

124. After showing five small photographs of men of varying skin color and features: "Tell me which one you think is most intelligent, the smartest; which one is most successful; which one you like the most."

125. After showing two small photographs of women, the one quite Negroid and the other moderately Caucasoid: "Tell me which one is more beautiful; which is more intelligent; which one you like more."

XX. Memory of Blocks (Jamaica only: Part XV)

126. The informant was asked to look carefully at four piles of blocks (one was a single block, another consisted of two blocks glued together, another four, another six). The informant turned his eyes, all piles were moved about, and an additional pile of three blocks was placed among the newly arranged piles; the informant was then asked to "show me the one pile which was not there before."

XXI. Open-Ended Questions (Jamaica only: Part XVI)

127. Should people obey all the laws of Jamaica? Why?
128. What do you like and not like about rich people?
129. Do you think people should live decently? Why?
130. What sorts of people believe in duppies (ghosts)?
131. When you were a child did you believe in duppies?
132. Have you ever seen a duppy?
133. What do you think is going to happen to Jamaica in the future?
134. What would you like to see changed?
135. What would you like to see stay the same?
136. What do you like and not like about Americans?
137. Have you been to America? Would you like to go there?

APPENDIX C *Hypotheses*

AFTER EACH hypothesis appears in parentheses the number of the page in the text on which it is first presented.

1. In comparison with those who remain unchanged or who have changed, people changing from old to new ways are likely to be more discontent (p. 74).

2. In comparison with those who remain unchanged or who have changed, people changing from old to new ways are likely to feel more aggressive (p. 80).

3. People changing centrally from old to new ways are likely to become more tolerant of delay in the attainment of goals (p. 88)

4. People who are experiencing some discontent with a prevailing form of behavior are likely to accept rather than to reject an alternative form when that new form has one or more of the following attributes: (a) it is accessible; (b) it has advantages which are intelligibly demonstrable in the present and which can be anticipated to continue in the future; (c) it demands responses which people feel confident that they can learn (p. 94).

5. People are likely to accept rather than reject a new form of behavior which is displayed by an outsider: (a) when they recognize his general or specific competence as an instructor; (b) when they are favorably disposed toward him, and more especially when they identify themselves with him; (c) when, provided they are favorably disposed toward him, they can assume that he would have them change (p. 104).

6. People changing from old to new ways are likely to retain traditional attitudes toward family forms and practices until or even beyond the occurrence of central changes within them and their society (p. 112).

7. People changing centrally from old to new ways are likely to feel antagonistic toward traditional leaders who do not reveal similar changes (p. 117).

8. In comparison with those who remain unchanged or who have changed, people changing from old to new ways are likely to feel more ambivalent toward outsiders associated with those new ways (p. 121).

9. In comparison with those who have remained unchanged, people changing from old to new ways are likely to be members of newly established groups whose members demonstrate similar forms of behavior (p. 130).

10. In comparison with those who remain unchanged or who have changed, people changing from old to new ways are likely to be generally sensitive to other people (p. 135).

11. After people change centrally from old to new ways, they are likely to value in others and in themselves traits which indicate initiative, independence, and self-confidence (p. 141).

12. In comparison with those who remain unchanged, people changing from old to new ways are less likely to have readily verbalizable opinions on traditional issues and more likely to have such opinions on nontraditional issues and on issues involving self-awareness and awareness of society; those who have changed are likely to be similarly different from those in the process of changing (p. 148).

13. People who are confronted with alternative beliefs and values are likely to retain traditional ones which appear to serve a continuing need and to reject those which do not, but always to retain some of the traditional views (p. 150).

14. In a society having outside contacts, beliefs and values are likely to change at similar rates unless old ones are particularly satisfying or unsatisfying, or unless new ones are particularly attractive or unattractive (p. 165).

15. After people change centrally from old to new ways, they are a little less likely to be dogmatic concerning the validity of their own beliefs and the goodness of their own values (p. 169).

16. In comparison with those who remain unchanged, people who are changing or have changed centrally are likely to be more proficient in novel situations; the degree of their proficiency

will vary with the perceived similarity between those situations and ones in their past experience (p. 175).

17. After people change centrally from old to new ways, they are likely to develop facility in abstracting (p. 187).

18. After people change centrally from old to new ways, they are likely to be more proficient in making subjective judgments of objective time intervals (p. 191).

19. After changing people learn a new language, they are likely to perceive differently significant stimulus patterns (p. 195).

20. After people change centrally from old to new ways, they are likely to be more proficient in using language to describe and express their feelings and reactions to the external world (p. 200).

21. New forms of behavior are likely to be learned which are in accord with modal personality traits in the old society (p. 205).

22. A heavily reinforced form of behavior that remains satisfying is likely to change, and a new form of behavior that is difficult to learn is likely to be learned, only after some of its components have been, respectively, changed and learned (p. 214).

23. The proficiency with which people change from old to new ways is likely to be increased when they seek a central goal that transcends the specific form of behavior being changed (p. 221).

24. All new forms of behavior are modified while being learned; modification is likely to be relatively slight (a) when there are marked similarities or dissimilarities between the old and new societies especially with relation to the form in question and (b) when that form inherently possesses or is permitted to possess little flexibility (p. 233).

25. A change in one form of behavior within the old society is likely to be followed eventually by other changes, but a central change is likely to have more repercussions than a segmental one (p. 236).

26. All societies eventually become civilized in a distinctive manner or perish (p. 243).

27. Basic changes in personality are likely to occur as people become adequately civilized (p. 256).

INDEX

The pages on which an author is listed in
the References (pp. 268–80) are not indexed.